MW00757582

Batch 5228I5BVX0001ZB

5228I5BVX00019BA	9780973411522	That Month in Tuscany	5.50X8.50	338	MATTE	PERFECT (3
5228I5BVX0002IBA	9780253025357	Gender, Justice, and the Problem of Cult...	6.00X9.00	204	MATTE	PERFECT (2

522815BV00012B/17
ADF:BW
PERFECT **MATTE**

22815BVX00019BA - 522815BVX00021BA [2 : 5]

‖‖‖‖‖ * 5 2 2 8 1 5 B V 0 0 0 1 2 B *

BOOK
CREAM13_5
REWORK
Will Medero

Department	Operator's Name (Please print)
Printing	
Binding	
Cutting	
Shipping	

Batch Location

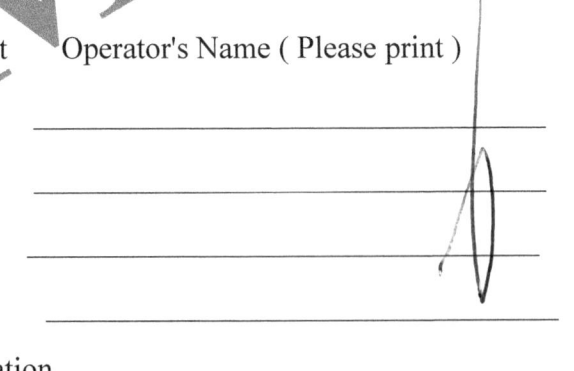

* 5 2 2 8 1 5 B V *

Promise Date: 28-JUL-18

Printed at: Fri Jul 27 12:01:50 2018 on device bvhp03-90

Gender, Justice,
and the Problem *of* Culture

Gender, Justice, *and*
the Problem *of*
Culture

*From Customary Law
to Human Rights in Tanzania*

Dorothy L. Hodgson

INDIANA UNIVERSITY PRESS
Bloomington & Indianapolis

This book is a publication of

Indiana University Press
Office of Scholarly Publishing
Herman B Wells Library 350
1320 East 10th Street
Bloomington, Indiana 47405 USA

iupress.indiana.edu

Manufactured in United States of America

Library of Congress Cataloging-in-Publication Data

Names: Hodgson, Dorothy Louise, author.
Title: Gender, justice, and the problem of culture : from customary law to human rights in Tanzania / Dorothy L. Hodgson.
Description: Bloomington : Indiana University Press, 2017. | Includes bibliographical references and index.
Identifiers: LCCN 2016039569 (print) | LCCN 2016039937 (ebook) | ISBN 9780253025203 (cloth : alk. paper) | ISBN 9780253025357 (pbk. : alk. paper) | ISBN 9780253025470 (e-book)
Subjects: LCSH: Customary law—Social aspects—Tanzania. | Women's rights—Tanzania. | Women, Maasai—Legal status, laws, etc.—Tanzania. | Maasai (African people)—Tanzania—Social conditions. | Women, Maasai—Tanzania—Social conditions. | Non-governmental organizations—Political aspects.
Classification: LCC KTT46.7 .H63 2017 (print) | LCC KTT46.7 (ebook) | DDC 342.67808/78—dc23
LC record available at https://lccn.loc.gov/2016039569

1 2 3 4 5   22 21 20 19 18 17

For Luke, with love

Contents

Acknowledgments

As ALWAYS, I AM MOST grateful to the many Tanzanians who have let me into their lives, if only for a short time, to listen and learn from their experiences, ideas, and perspectives. And since in many ways this book is a culmination of my more than thirty years of ethnographic and historical research with Maasai men and women (since the early days of my work with the Arusha Catholic Diocese's community development team in the mid-1980s to my last visit in January 2011), I have many, many people to thank. Some material is drawn from my years of comparative, longitudinal research with residents of Emairete, Embopong', and Mti Mmoja in the 1990s and 2000s, including return visits during my research stay in 2005–2006. I also use experiences and evidence from my studies of several Maasai NGOs. The leadership and staff of the Maasai Women's Development Organisation (MWEDO) and Pastoralist Women's Council (PWC) welcomed me into their meetings, workshops, programs, and debates. I thank Ndinini Kimesera Sikar (MWEDO) and Maanda Ngoitiko (PWC) for their leadership and vision. Other key interlocutors in Tanzania for this project include Marjorie Mbilinyi, Saning'o Milliary, Alais Morindat, Esupat Ngulupa, the late Moringe Parkipuny, and Edward Porokwa. I am indebted to the Tanzanian Commission on Science and Technology for permission to undertake this research, and to Professor Simeon Mesaki for serving as my local research contact. Morani Poyoni worked as my research assistant for much of that time, but Esupat Ngulupa accompanied me on my return survey of communities in Monduli and Longido districts in 2005 and 2006.

Many of the ideas I explore in this book were developed, challenged, and strengthened from an array of initiatives and opportunities. As director of the Institute for Research on Women (IRW), I facilitated a year-long weekly seminar on "The Culture of Rights/The Rights of Culture" for faculty members, advanced graduate students, postdoctoral fellows, and visiting scholars (2008–2009). With the assistance of Beth Hutchison (then associate director of the IRW) and Marlene Importico (officer manager), I led a three-day symposium on the topic in the spring of 2009. I subsequently edited a book, *Gender and Culture at the Limit of Rights* that collected the best papers from the seminar and symposium. A few years later, in 2012, I organized an interdisciplinary workshop at Rutgers on "Gender Justice in Africa: Historical and Contemporary Perspectives" that brought together senior and junior scholars and activists. That same year, I served as a research director (with Pamela Scully) of an SSRC Dissertation Proposal Development Fellowship Workshop on the topic of "Gender Justice in the Era of Human Rights."

Throughout this period as first director of IRW and then chair of the Department of Anthropology, I used every lecture and conference invitation to cultivate this project. I have presented aspects of this work at numerous conferences, workshops, and universities, including, among others, the University of Cambridge, the University of Cologne, the University of Copenhagen, the University of Dar es Salaam, Depauw University, Emory University, the University of Florida, Florida International University, Hamilton College, Harvard University, Michigan State University, the University of Minnesota, the National University of Mongolia, the College of New Jersey, Notre Dame University, Université Paris-1 Panthéon Sorbonne, Rice University, Rochester Institute of Technology, Smith College, the University of Texas-Austin, the University of Washington, and various annual meetings of the American Anthropological Association, African Studies Association, European Conference on African Studies, and Berkshire Conference on the History of Women, Genders and Sexualities. I am deeply grateful to colleagues and audiences at all of these venues for their questions, comments, and criticism.

I am indebted to numerous institutions for funding key phases of research and writing. Much of the book's evidence draws on a year of research that I conducted in Tanzania in 2005–2006, with the support of a John Simon Guggenheim Memorial Foundation Fellowship, a Fulbright-Hays Faculty Research Abroad Award, and an American Council of Learned Societies

Fellowship. During 2006–2007, a Faculty Fellowship from the National Endowment of the Humanities and Competitive Fellowship Leave award from Rutgers University enabled me to analyze my data, write a draft of my earlier book, *Being Maasai, Becoming Indigenous* (Hodgson 2011a), and prepare notes for this book. After almost five years of developing pieces of the book, including a return research trip to Tanzania in 2011 and three challenging years serving as chair of my department, I had the extraordinary luxury of spending a month at the Rockefeller Foundation's Bellagio Center in Italy during the summer of 2013. During this magical time in the Villa Serbelloni, in the midst of ancient tapestries, fabulous colleagues, delicious food, stunning vistas, and peaceful, uninterrupted work time, I wrote a rough outline of the book (based on numerous presentations and short papers), clarified the overall arguments, and drafted the introduction and two chapters. I am grateful to Andres Barba, Jacob Bertrand, Carmen Caceres, Daniel Esser, Elena Gabre-Madhin, Santosh Mehrotra, Mahdev Mohan, Vinita Ramani, and C. Dale Young for their intellectual fellowship and fun. With the support of a second Faculty Fellowship from the National Endowment for the Humanities, I spent the following academic year (2013–2014) conducting additional archival and documentary research and drafting the remaining chapters. My progress on this book was interrupted by two other major writing projects, but I finally completed the revisions and submitted the manuscript to the press in the summer of 2015.

Priya Lal and Brett Shadle provided thoughtful reader's reports that helped to clarify and strengthen the book's arguments, evidence, and accessibility. Many friends, students, and colleagues read portions of the manuscript or contributed ideas and insights to the overall argument and project. They include Lila Abu-Lughod, Ousseina Alidou, Srimati Basu, Mona Bhan, Abena Busia, Emily Burrill, Barbara Cooper, Clifton Crais, Elliot Fratkin, Ben Gardner, Daniel Goldstein, Carol Greenhouse, Marla Jaksch, Jessica Johnson, Omotayo Jolaosho, Temma Kaplan, Corinne Kratz, Benjamin Lawrance, Salma Maoulidi, Sally Engle Merry, Sheryl McCurdy, Marit Østebø, Richard Roberts, Zakia Salime, Pamela Scully, Aili Mari Tripp, Judith Van Allen, and Richard Waller.

Almost twenty years ago, I had the good fortune to meet Dee Mortensen, my now longtime editor at Indiana University Press. As we bring this fourth book to completion, I am grateful yet again for Dee's support, encouragement, and critical advice.

And finally, I am thankful for the love, laughter, and labor of my family. My husband, Rick Schroeder, is my partner in life in every meaning of that term. Through the challenges of leadership, surviving the whims of academia, raising a teenager, and the many other ups and downs we have encountered in our more than twenty years together, Rick has been my foundation, guide, mentor, ally, confidant, best friend, and more. As I complete this book, our son Luke readies himself to graduate from high school and leap into the excitement and awe of college and beyond. I am curious to see the pathways he chooses as he draws on his many talents, strengths, and accomplishments as a scholar, musician, athlete, and, most importantly for me, kind, empathetic, thoughtful, caring, feminist young man. I suspect he will work making this world a more just place for those on the margins, and so I dedicate this book about justice to him.

* * *

I am grateful to the following publishers for permission to draw on previously published material for this book.

Sections of chapter 2 are derived in part from an article, "'My Daughter . . . Belongs to the Government Now': Marriage, Maasai and the Tanzanian State," which was originally published in 1996 in *The Canadian Journal of African Studies* 30, no. 1: 106–23, copyright Taylor & Francis, available online: http://www.tandfonline.com/doi/abs/10.1080/00083968.1996.10804410.

Sections of chapter 3 are drawn from a chapter, "'These Are not Our Priorities': Maasai Women, Human Rights and the Problem and Culture," published in *Gender and Culture at the Limit of Rights*, a book I edited for the University of Pennsylvania Press in 2011. Small portions are also reproduced from "Women's Rights as Human Rights: Women in Law and Development in Africa (WILDAF)," *Africa Today* 49, no. 2 (Summer 2002).

Gender, Justice,
and the Problem *of* Culture

Introduction
Gender, Justice, and the Problem of Culture

In July 1985, I had the pleasure and privilege of attending the Non-Governmental Organization (NGO) Forum that accompanied the United Nations Decade Conference on Women in Nairobi, Kenya. Before that event, I had seriously considered becoming a lawyer, but two years of work as a paralegal convinced me to pursue other dreams. And so I quit my job, bought a three-month air ticket to East Africa, and started on a journey that would change my life forever and lead me, ultimately, to a career in anthropology. A key moment in that journey was my experience at the NGO Forum. I was a young white American woman who had long been a feminist activist in the United States. From personal circumstances, I was sensitive to class issues, and I had been deeply influenced by such notable black authors as Maya Angelou, Ntozake Shange, and Angela Davis. But I had never encountered the range of global activists and ideas as those I did at the NGO Forum. The discussions I shared in shook my world, challenging my comfortably held ideas about women, feminism, and the possibilities and perils of "global sisterhood."

One event in particular still resonates with me today. At a crowded workshop on "Custom, Law and Ethnicity," I listened to participants share reports from all over the Global South about the "evils" of various "customs," the implementation (or not) of national laws to eradicate them, and the effectiveness (or not) of these state-based legal initiatives. During the discussion, a group of older white American feminists started berating the African women present about why what they called "female genital mutilation" (FGM) could still exist in contemporary Africa. Their paternalism (a kind word) and self-righteousness shocked me. Several African women stood up to explain that FGM was a concern for them but not a priority. The American women interrupted, again lambasting them for not doing more. As a rapt member of the audience, I listened intently to the increasingly angry debate. Several African women felt so cornered and angered by the Americans that they defended the practice of female circumcision as a sign of African "culture." The discussion ended when a young Kenyan woman stood up, demanded that the Americans focus on their own problems, accused them of being racist and imperialist, and stomped out of the tent, followed by most of the other African members of the audience. Race, class, and power were no longer ideas to be contemplated in literary texts but were now pulsating veins of emotion and outrage.

In many ways, this book is the product of my efforts, after more than thirty years of research, teaching, and learning, to address the questions raised by that encounter: Why did the American feminists feel so empowered to berate their African "sisters"? How and why had FGM become the focus of their obsessions as a marker of the "oppression" of African women? If FGM was not a priority for these African women, what issues mattered instead? How did this moment speak to larger debates about gender, justice, and the politics of "culture"?

A few years later, building on discussions at the NGO Forum and other sites, Charlotte Bunch and others argued for the need to restructure "human rights" to recognize and support "women's rights." Since that time, "women's rights are human rights" has become a global mantra, bolstered by a vast network of feminist activists, organizations, and even certain states (Bunch 1990). As a result, women (and men) around the world have reframed their often long-standing demands and needs in the (seemingly) more powerful language of rights in order to expand the visibility and recognition of their issues in local, national, and global arenas and to demand accountability from states to ensure and enforce their legal rights (Merry 2006; Hodgson 2003). As the dominant model for making claims against individuals and collectivities (primarily states) in the contemporary world, rights-based frameworks have had significant success in advancing the claims of women and men for political representation and legal protections (Peters and Wolper 1995). Yet some scholars question whether "rights"—which presume an individual, secular, gendered subject; which overlook the structural contexts and causes of injustice; and which primarily rely on state-run legal mechanisms for implementation and enforcement—can ever be a truly emancipatory strategy, especially for women (Cornwall and Molyneux 2008; Hodgson 2011b). Their critiques raise broader questions about how the dynamics of gender, culture, and power inform the rhetoric and realities of how justice is envisioned and experienced (Mohanty 1991, 2003; Narayan 1997; Abu Lughod 2013; Shachar 2001). Moreover, the intense focus on rights-based approaches has obscured other gendered modes of seeking justice that have historically functioned and continue to function alongside rights-based approaches. In African countries, for example, many societies like Maasai have a long history of women invoking their power and authority as mothers to collectively denounce and challenge injustice, whether from incestuous men, meddling colonial officers, or corrupt state officials (Van Allen 1972; Steady 2006). Collective protest and other "extra-legal" justice regimes are predicated on distinct ideas of personhood, agency, morality, culture, and gendered power, and they employ different mechanisms for implementing and enforcing outcomes (Boddy 2008; Griffiths 1997).

The concerns with the narrow reach of rights and the existence of multiple, overlapping legal regimes and other approaches to justice raise important questions, including: How and why have legal institutions premised on the "rights" of individuals become the dominant mode for framing and seeking justice? What are the limitations and strengths of an approach that privileges the formal legal system over customary justice mechanisms in resolving, for example, claims within communities and against the state? Which claims get translated into rights, whose rights are protected, and which rights become the priorities for advocacy and funding? Are certain modes of justice better able to address the structural contexts and causes of injustice? How are ideas about gender, culture, and social inequality expressed and contested in these different legal regimes?

To address these questions, *Gender, Justice, and the Problem of Culture: From Customary Law to Human Rights in Tanzania* compares indigenous law, customary law, colonial legal institutions, national law, "women's human rights," collective protest, and other approaches to identifying and rectifying various forms of injustice through a case study of Maasai pastoralists in Tanzania. Drawing on historical and ethnographic evidence, this book analyzes the gendered assumptions, experiences, and consequences of these overlapping legal regimes for Maasai ideas and practices, in which women and the (primarily female-identified) Maasai divinity Eng'ai were historically significant. It examines relations between and among Maasai men and women and relations between Maasai communities, colonial and postcolonial state authorities, and, eventually, nongovernmental organizations (NGOs).

In contrast to broad histories of the origins of human rights, this book uses the Maasai case to examine the historical emergence and dominance of rights-based legal institutions and ideas in Tanzania—from the colonial period to the contemporary era—as a specific form of justice that reflects particular conceptions of gender, culture, power, and social change. The book documents how the legacies of certain colonial policies and practices informed national and international legal initiatives, which have in turn shaped contemporary Maasai expressions and experiences of justice and obscured alternative female modes of seeking justice, such as collective protest.

Specifically, the book analyzes three key aspects of the emergence and dominance of rights-based approaches to justice. First, the book traces assumptions and debates about the relationship between "law" and "culture," from early efforts to regulate social and cultural practices like marriage in "customary" law, to recent initiatives by transnational and Tanzanian feminists to criminalize cultural practices like FGM.[1] How and why has "culture" come to be viewed as not just a "problem," but as inherently oppressive to women? Why is "culture" invoked in debates about women's rights but not in other discourses of rights, such as the right to clean water? Why have some activists been obsessed with using law as a tool to regulate and sometimes criminalize certain cultural and social practices—especially those like marriage, "adultery," and FGM—that are central to the intimate lives of families and households? What are the cultural (and thus moral) assumptions of these supposedly "natural" and "universal" forms of justice and rights? Following Lila Abu-Lughod, I seek to analyze the "social life of rights," "track[ing] carefully, across multiple terrains, the way both practices and talk of rights organize social and political fields, producing organizations, projects, and forms of governing as much as being produced by them" (2011, 118).

Second, the study examines how ideas about gender, class, "race," and ethnicity have shaped these debates and related interventions. A recurring trope in both colonial and contemporary debates about law and rights is that of the inherent vulnerability and oppression of rural, illiterate African women (and thus the inherent repressive, patriarchal tendencies of rural African men) (e.g., Scully 2011). Such tropes have been used to justify interventions into the lives of these African men and women by outsiders—whether British officers, Euro-American feminists or Tanzanian feminists—in the name of "justice" and "rights." How does the creation and implementation of these laws and legal institutions affect these forms of social difference and inequality?

Finally, both of these issues speak to larger questions of power and politics: When, where, why, and by whom is law used to try to force desired social changes? How does this drive to legislate morality and social change deflect attention from the political-economic issues that may be of more concern to the everyday lives of the people being targeted? What are the consequences of efforts by first British colonial officers and now human rights activists to channel the resolution of disputes and political claims through formal, state-based legal systems, especially when state policies and practices are often the source of oppression and injustice? Who decides which rights are priorities for advocacy and protection?

To summarize, my purpose in this book is threefold: first, to complicate static ideas of "culture" and "custom" as they have been perpetuated through legal discourses that have tried to codify, demonize, and sometimes criminalize certain cultural practices like marriage and FGM; second, to challenge enduring paternalistic (and often racist and classist) portrayals of illiterate, rural women as somehow lacking the capacity to understand or act on their situation, a stereotype that has been intensified with the emergence and dominance of rights-based approaches; and, finally, to explore how certain legal ideas and practices are used as political tools to regulate (and at times forcibly change) some of the most intimate aspects of people's lives in the name of "justice."

A Brief History of Justice, Law, and Rights in Africa

By tracing the continuities and changes in the practices of law and justice from the late precolonial period to the present, grounded in the lived experiences of everyday people, I seek to complicate often abstract debates about the contours and content of "justice." As Amartya Sen (2009), among others, has recently argued, "justice" is a notoriously polyvalent term; legal theorists, political philosophers, and others have long debated its meanings. But, as I discuss in this book, these deliberations about the "idea" of justice tend to echo colonial invocations of "natural justice," projecting Euro-American ideas of due process, individual rights, and "impartial" legal principles as universal ideals with little attention to alternative paradigms, much less to how the realities of power, gender, and culture have historically produced those very ideals (Hodgson 2011b; Hunt 2007). However "natural" or "universal" they may seem, prevailing ideas about "law," "rights," and "justice" do not exist outside of history or culture, but are themselves historical and cultural products that reflect dominant cultural assumptions and ideals at specific times and in particular contexts (e.g., Clarke and Goodale 2010). In other words, "rights"—whether legal, human, women's, or indigenous— have become the dominant mode for thinking about justice in Africa and the rest of the contemporary world *because of* certain historical processes and events, including colonialism, nationalism, military conflicts such as World War I and World War II, humanitarian crises like the Holocaust, and liberal and now neoliberal economic policies and projects.

In this book I present some of this history, from the early colonial period to the present, through the prism of the Maasai case. To do so, I draw on the work of numerous scholars of Africa (and elsewhere) who have explored the relationships among law, culture, power, and gender in specific historical periods. I use the term "legal regime" to name and distinguish each of the key periods to help distill the constellation of factors that characterize and shape the dominant approaches to and experiences of "law" in that time. Embedding these discussions of law in the relevant historical period is intended to support and facilitate my analysis of continuities and changes through time and to emphasize the relevance of political-economic context and translocal connections to the production of legal norms and institutions. My intention is not, however, to reify these regimes as self-contained systems or to imply that they represent some linear, modernist narrative of "progress." To the contrary, I situate my analysis in the Maasai case to show how the regimes have developed, changed, coexisted, and mutually influenced and contradicted one another.

Anthropologists and others have tried to describe fundamental processes and principles of "African law" as practiced in *indigenous legal regimes*, including dispute-resolution practices, legal procedures, and ideas of justice and jurisprudence (Gluckman 1955, 1965; Bohannon 1957; Kuper and Kuper 1965). For some African societies, "law" (like "religion") was not a separate domain but was integrally connected with spiritual ideas and practices and social norms of respect and authority. As Jan Vansina (1965) argued many years ago, these were societies in which "social norms" were themselves "legal norms" and thus not distinguished or named as a separate realm of "law." Nonetheless, anthropologists used the terms "law" and "legal" as analytic categories to describe these aspects of social life. In other societies, especially in West Africa, "legal functions" were more distinct, with, for example, clearly designated bodies to hear and decide disputes (Forde 1965). Although some earlier scholars tried to use law as one factor in categorizing societies on social evolutionary scales that ranked them from "primitive" to "civilized" (e.g., Morgan 1877), anthropologists made important contributions to the study of indigenous legal regimes. They described alternative principles and procedures for resolving grievances (from ordeals to elders councils) (e.g., Schapera 1938), presented diverse concepts of justice (e.g., Bohannon 1957; Gluckman 1955, 1965), and recognized the centrality of expressions of power to the exercise of legal authority (e.g., Gulliver 1963). Few scholars, however, considered the gendered aspects of these ideas and practices or acknowledged that these regimes were not fixed, homogenous, ahistorical "primitive" or "traditional" "systems," but were dynamic, contested, historical products. In most cases these "indigenous" regimes had already been transformed in response to migration, conflict, conquest, and colonialism. In fact, many of these early studies, like Isaac Schapera's *Handbook on Tswana Law and Custom* (1938), were produced to assist colonial officials eager to learn about "indigenous" legal systems so as to better codify and regulate their use.

Historians and legal scholars have built on this work to thoughtfully analyze key aspects of colonial legal regimes, especially as they were imposed on and transformed pre-existing indigenous legal regimes in Africa. John Comaroff's evocative term "lawfare" captures the idea of colonial legal interventions as a "mode of warfare," that is, "the effort to conquer and control indigenous peoples by the coercive use of legal means" (2001, 306). But as Kristin Mann and Richard Roberts argued years ago, the power dynamics of colonial legal regimes were perhaps not as one-sided as the term "lawfare" might suggest: "During the colonial period, law formed an area in which Africans and Europeans engaged one another—a battleground as it were on which they contested access to resources and labor, relationships of power and authority, and interpretations of morality and culture" (Mann and Roberts 1991, 3). Scholars have explored many aspects of these complicated cultural and political engagements, including the gendered dynamics of the codification of customary law (e.g., Chanock 1985; Moore 1986) and the articulation of indigenous and colonial regimes (e.g., Hay and Wright 1982), African use of native courts and colonial judicial institutions (e.g., Mann 1982; Byfield 2001), and efforts by colonial officials and elder men to develop legal means to regulate the domestic affairs of women and junior men (e.g., Pederson 1991; Thomas 2003; Kanogo 2005; Shadle 2006; Boddy 2007). They provided important insights into the use of law by colonial administrators to extend their power and reach, the creative strategies of African people as they took advantage of new legal concepts and forums, and the gendered and generational repercussions of the reification of "custom" in customary law. But most historians ended their stories at or just before independence, leaving open the question of how the creation of these new legal ideas (like individual "rights") and judicial institutions shaped the expression and experience of law in newly founded nation-states like Tanganyika (as Tanzania was called before it merged with Zanzibar in 1964).

Among the African elites who led these fledgling states were growing numbers of lawyers, scholars, and politicians who dominated decisions about the content and form of postcolonial legal institutions. As Jean and John Comaroff have argued, most postcolonies became deeply obsessed with "the law" as a means to express and exert state authority, producing what they call "a fetishism of the law" (2007). A key concern of these *national legal regimes*, especially in former British colonies and protectorates like Tanzania, was how to balance the desire of national leaders to build a nation that transcended ethnic differences with the colonial legacy of recognizing distinct laws and legal institutions for different ethnic groups. Thus, as discussed in chapter 2, Tanzania, like many African countries, built on the colonial system of native courts and recognition of "customary law" to create formal, state-sanctioned systems of legal pluralism (as it is often called) as a way to accommodate cultural, political, and religious differences among its citizens.[2] Of course a major problem, as described in this book, was that the version of "customary law" enshrined in national laws was itself the historical product of colonial practices and racial and gendered assumptions, which rarely reflected the principles and procedures of indigenous legal regimes. Moreover, the "customary" laws that were codified focused on marriage, divorce, child custody, and other issues of "family law" and ignored customary modes of accessing and controlling property and resources that, at least in the Maasai case, provided women with crucial protections and rights.

More recently, *transnational legal regimes* in the form of international protocols and institutions promoting human rights have become dominant and have influenced national activists, national laws, and national priorities. International activists and ideas have shaped "local" forms of law since the early colonial period (see chapter 1), and human rights have, of course, a much longer history (see, for example, Hunt 2007). But, as discussed in chapter 3, the realization of human rights in the form of "women's human rights" only gained traction over the past few decades. Many, many scholars of Africa and elsewhere have probed the opportunities, contradictions, and challenges of adopting these self-proclaimed "universal" principles in diverse local situations and sites. Scholars have highlighted the cultural dimensions of these encounters (e.g., An-Na'im 2002), the gendered dilemmas produced by the reframing of certain practices as criminal violations (e.g., Benedek, Kisaayake, and Oberleitner 2002; Shell-Duncan 2008), and the complex politics produced by the pervasive involvement of intermediaries, especially NGOs, in the promotion of women's human rights (e.g., Merry 2006). Most of these studies, however, lack a historical perspective that would show, for example, how and why human rights have emerged as such a powerful discourse or that would demonstrate some of the parallels between colonial and contemporary interventions to "improve" and "protect" the "rights" of all, especially rural, illiterate women who are persistently represented as "victims" of their "cultures" because of the persistence of "traditional harmful practices."

Each of these legal regimes was (and is) distinct in certain ways, whether because of the dominant "scale" (Fraser 2009) of justice to which people had recourse (ethnic, national, international); the key principles of justice they expressed; or the political-economic contexts in which they were shaped and circulated. But they also, in time, shaped one another: colonial legal regimes provided the foundation for national legal regimes, which were in turn deeply influenced by transnational legal regimes. And while indigenous legal regimes were transformed and marginalized by these new state-based legal formations, certain practices, such as female forms of collective protest for Maasai, retained their vitality and moral force and adapted to changing social, political, and economic circumstances. Moreover, all these regimes, however "natural," "impartial," or "universal" their proponents might claim them to be, were historical products that reflected specific cultural and moral assumptions about gender, class, "culture," and the appropriate mechanisms for challenging injustice. And, as always, the story about whose assumptions and interests were reproduced in these legal regimes is a story of power and politics.

Maasai as Exemplars of "Culture"

The more than 300,000 people who identify themselves as "Maasai" these days, spread across northern Tanzania and southern Kenya in East Africa, are an ideal case through which to examine these questions. Since early European travelers coined the ethnonym "Maasai" in the late 1800s to name Africans who spoke Maa (a very different language from Swahili and other Bantu languages spoken by the majority of Africans in eastern Africa) and who herded cattle, goats, and sheep for their livelihoods, Maasai have been alternatively admired and disparaged by Europeans and other Africans for their distinct language, lifestyles, and livelihoods (Bernsten 1980; Hodgson 2001a, 2005, 2011a).[3] Images and accounts of Maasai in the past and present emphasized their "cultural" distinctiveness (often conveyed as a racial difference), focusing on the (supposedly) fierce warriors, proud patriarchs, and oppressed women who were no more than "beasts of burden." These images, in turn, shaped interventions into Maasai lives, such as British demands in the 1920s that all "Masai" move into the "Masai Reserve" so they could be more easily monitored and controlled, but also "protected" from outside influences and removed from valuable fertile land destined for more "productive" uses (such as settler farms).[4] The forced move into the reserve, decades of neglect followed by fierce demands in the late colonial period to "change" and "modernize," and other interventions reinforced Maasai claims to a distinct ethnic identity (Hodgson 2001a, 2011a). For many people, including tourists today, Maasai were viewed as embodiments of cultural difference, a people who somehow existed outside of history and social change. Take, for example, an article from 1956–1957: "The most picturesque people in East Africa are those of a tribe which has changed little of its ways since the advent of the White Man—the Masai. The tourist, when he spots a Masai herding his beloved cattle, or leaning gracefully on the haft of his long bladed spear, cannot but feel the spirit of Africa of yesterday" ("Kilusu" 1956–1957, 135). As the excerpt suggests, Maasai were in many ways icons of "primitive" Africans not only in East Africa, but in the African continent more generally.

Their enduring iconic status as exemplars of "the spirit of Africa" or, in less celebratory accounts, "primitive," "traditional," "culturally conservative," or even "savage," reflected these obsessions with their seemingly exotic "culture," a culture that served as a convenient foil to claims of "modernity" by Westerners and, eventually, by African elites (Hodgson 2001b). The fixation on Maasai as exotic "others" masked the fact that their "culture" was of course historical and dynamic: their increased impoverishment was the historical product of politics and economics, not "culture," and that relations between and among men and women of different ages were never fixed but fluid, complicated, and often contested. For all these reasons, as will become clear in the ensuing chapters, Maasai are thus a useful case through which to explore how "culture" became a central "problem" in debates about gender and justice in the shifting legal regimes.

Although I examine Maasai history and lives in great detail in my previous books (Hodgson 2001a, 2005, 2011a), I present some brief background here for readers who are not familiar with them. At least several hundred years ago, Maa-speaking peoples migrated into what is now known as Kenya and Tanzania from a homeland they call "Kerio," which some archaeological and linguistic evidence suggests might be in southern Sudan. They were originally agro-pastoralists until certain changes in climate (decades of high rainfall), technology (mastery of iron forging), and social organization (the emergence of male age grades) enabled a group of Maa speakers to specialize almost solely in livestock herding and develop a heightened sense of themselves as pastoralists (Sutton 1993; Galaty 1993). These pastoralist Maa speakers were eventually called "Maasai" by Europeans to distinguish them from Maa speakers who continued to farm, gather and hunt, and sometimes herd. By the late colonial period, people themselves came to fiercely identify themselves as "Maasai," an assertion of ethnic identity that continues today, despite (or because of) continued attacks on their land, livelihoods, appearances and practices.

Historically, Maasai lived dispersed across the rangelands in small homes (*enkaji*, pl. *inkajijik*) clustered into homesteads (*enkang'*, pl. *inkang'itie*) surrounded by thorn fences to protect the inhabitants and their livestock from predators like lions and leopards. They were seminomadic, which meant they maintained long-term homesteads for years, but moved livestock, as needed, to smaller encampments during the dry season in search of grass and water.

For homesteads and families to survive, every member had to fulfill his or her responsibilities, which, like the rights that accompanied them, were organized by gender and generation. Young girls assisted their mothers with child care, food processing and preparation, gathering wood and water, and other household chores. Once married, women eventually built their own house in their husband's homestead, in which they lived with their children. (Men had no separate house of their own, but moved between the houses of their wives.) Husbands and wives shared overlapping rights in their family herds, although women often had a few animals of their own that they had received as gifts. Women milked the cattle (and sometimes, when desperate, sheep and goats), processed the milk, and controlled the distribution (and eventually the sale) of milk, milk products, and hides. Many women traveled to towns and markets to trade these products for other household needs. Once their children were grown, older women often moved to the homesteads of their adult sons, where they could rely on the labor of their daughters-in-law and grandchildren for household work. Boys started herding as toddlers, shifting from young animals, to sheep and goats, to cattle as they aged. Once circumcised between the ages of about thirteen and twenty-one, they became *ilmurran* (sg. *olmurrani*), a term often translated as "warriors." These young men were responsible for protecting their homesteads from predators, cattle raids, and other dangers. They accompanied the cattle on long treks, often in the company of their young girlfriends. Eventually, they were allowed to marry, settle down, and focus on managing their herds and supporting their (hopefully) growing families. Maasai were polygamous, so some wealthy men could have three, four, even ten wives. And, like elder women, elder men depended on the labor of others as they managed their household, homestead, lineage, and clan affairs.

Of course, as I describe in this book and others, Maasai livelihoods and social relations have changed tremendously over the past decades as a result of migration, disease, colonial policies, state interventions, education, Christian (and now Islamic) evangelization, climate change, and more.

Moreover, even the generalized description of roles, responsibilities, and rights described above varied by individuals based on their characters, fortunes, wealth, and relations.

A Historical Anthropology of Law and Justice

To tell this story of how and why rights-based legal regimes have become dominant and how earlier gender, cultural, and political formations shaped later legal ideas, I draw on the theories and methods of historical anthropology (or what some prominent scholars have recently called "anthrohistory" [Murphy et al. 2011]). In contrast to legal scholars, who are concerned primarily with the analysis of texts, principles of case law, or philosophical discussions about the nature of justice, anthropologists use ethnography to illuminate the dynamic contexts in which laws and legal regimes are produced, lived, and sometimes challenged. Through conversations, interviews, surveys, participant observation, and other methods, ethnographers gather information about the lived realities of different legal regimes through attention to people and practices, sites and spaces, ideas and assumptions, contexts and conflicts. Ethnography, in other words, shows how power operates and is produced in the everyday life of the law. Anthropologists use the insights and findings distilled through ethnography to challenge many of the assumptions and categories that are too often taken for granted by legal scholars, providing a sense of the varieties of law and legal regimes and new ways of analyzing them.

Similarly, a historical perspective traces and makes visible process and contingency and reveals that categories (such as culture, rights, gender, ethnic identity) that might seem stable and fixed in the present are themselves historical products. Historians gather and analyze texts such as letters, newspaper articles, diaries, memos, and court transcripts, as well as oral histories and life histories. Like detectives, they track and follow leads (names, dates, places, concepts), then critically assess this always incomplete information (and its silences), asking such questions as Who? Why? Where? When? How?

Thus the combination of anthropology and history provides a powerful set of analytic tools to document and analyze continuities, changes, and contestations in meanings, relationships, and practices over time. Historical anthropology also illuminates interactions across scale, that is, the intertwining of local, national, and transnational ideas, practices, and processes.

Historical anthropology can trace, for example, how dominant normative ideas and practices (such as ideals about a "good wife," a "proper marriage," or a "repugnant practice") emerged through struggles from a field of alternatives. It can reveal how culture and power operate in the everyday lives of citizens and subjects to produce differences that are political, economic, and social, but are marked, at least by the powers that be, as "cultural." Since the way "culture" has been (and is still) used by reformers to demand (and often legislate) change is by erasing history and complexity, I seek to restore both to my analysis of gender and justice.

Research for this project has been conducted with Maasai over the past thirty years on an ad hoc basis as part of other book projects, a short research trip in 2011 to Tanzania, and numerous visits to review archival material in Tanzania (Tanzania National Archives in Dar es Salaam and Arusha, the Tanzania Gender Networking Programme Library), the United Kingdom (Rhodes House Library, Women's Archives at the London School of Economics, National Archives [formerly Public Records Office]), and the United States (Schomburg Library, Library of Congress, Cooperative Africana Microfilm Project). From these sources I gathered an array of primary and secondary materials, including extensive archival materials on colonial debates about customary law, forms of Maasai dispute resolution, and court cases; oral histories, life histories, and transcribed interviews with approximately two hundred men and women of different ages that discuss, among other topics, Maasai ideas and practices of morality, justice, and gender; participant observation of Maasai involvement with courts and other state legal institutions, the agendas and activities of two Maasai women's NGOs, recent collective protests by Maasai women, and customary forms of dispute resolution; interviews with the leaders of several major Tanzanian feminist organizations; and documents, pamphlets, websites, and other materials from these and other organizations that have worked with Maasai communities to promote legal awareness and human rights.

My work has been shaped by the depth and breadth of my relationships with hundreds of Maasai and other Tanzanians over the years, young and old, male and female, educated and illiterate, wealthy and poor, urban and rural. I have talked to them in mud and dung houses in dire need of repair, in cement block homes with electricity and running water, in their modest offices in Arusha, in the glossy lobbies of the United Nations in Geneva and New York, and in my home in New Jersey, among other places. These conversations have been in English, Swahili, and Maa, according to the preference of my interlocutor. Many interviews were recorded and transcribed, others were recounted in my field journals from detailed notes and jottings. Over the past thirty years, technological revolutions have also transformed my research and relationships; I now also communicate with friends in Tanzania by e-mail, cell phones, Facebook, and other media. Following anthropological conventions, I use pseudonyms throughout the book, except for public personalities like politicians and the leaders of NGOs (see Hodgson 2011c).

CHAPTER OUTLINE

Although the book is organized chronologically, it does not pretend to provide a thorough picture or detailed linear narrative of changing forms and ideas of justice from the precolonial period to the present among Maasai or in Tanzania. Instead, each chapter focuses on a key event, case, or issue that illuminates the dynamics of gender, culture, and power operating within that dominant legal regime and provides insight into the framing questions of the book. I describe the relevant political, economic, and historical factors in broad strokes; situate the case or issue in its context; and analyze the connections and contrasts with earlier chapters. I have thus only been able to hint at other arguments and ideas (such as the distinct concepts of personhood and agency expressed by different legal regimes) that could easily have been alternative major framings for the book. This project includes some material from my earlier books (Hodgson 2001a, 2005, 2011a), which provide substantial historical and ethnographic documentation of changing aspects of Maasai lives from the late 1880s to the present. Although I try to minimize the repetition of earlier arguments and evidence and note where readers can look for further information, some details are necessarily repeated. But the focus of this book—on continuities and changes in ideas and practices of justice—at once draws on and is distinct from those previous studies.

Chapter 1 explores and contrasts the complex system of justice that existed among Maasai in the late 1800s with British ideas of "natural" justice and "native" law. I examine some of the challenges confronted by colonial officials as they tried to reconcile their moral and cultural ideals with Maasai practices through the codification of "customary" law, especially in their efforts to regulate the myriad forms of Maasai domestic relations under the rubric of "marriage."

Chapter 2 examines Maasai experiences during the early postcolonial period, where they negotiated the contradictions between the legacies of colonial interventions that had enhanced the political-economic power of men and the forceful imposition of President Nyerere's socialist vision, which promoted, at least rhetorically, the political and economic equality of women. The 1971 Law of Marriage Act, for example, codified certain rights of women in marriage but also formally recognized the validity of "customary" and "religious" law and judicial institutions. I document some of the consequences of these multiple legal regimes through an extended analysis of a legal case in which a Maasai woman accused her father of forcing her to marry against her will.

Chapter 3 analyzes the political dynamics of the transnational women's human rights legal regime through a study of how and why some elite Tanzanians, especially leaders of prominent feminist organizations, drew on the language of women's human rights and gender-based violence to lobby their government to criminalize certain cultural practices like FGM and launch vigorous anti-FGM campaigns. The chapter examines the class dynamics of these efforts and their consequences for Maasai leaders, NGOs, and community members, all of whom have other, more urgent priorities—such as for adequate food, secure livelihoods, and quality education and health care—as a result of neoliberal policies that have taken their lands and undermined their livelihoods.

Chapter 4 explores a series of recent collective protests by Maasai women against government corruption, land alienation, and other economic and political concerns in order to examine customary forms of female collective protest. I compare the ideas of justice, morality, and personhood expressed by those protests with those entailed by human rights approaches. In the concluding chapter, I reflect on the continuities and transformations in ideas and practices of gender justice and collective action from the colonial period to the present and on the theoretical contributions of the book to the study of gender, law, and justice.

NOTES

1. Anthropologists have long been interested in analyzing the fraught relationship between "law," "culture," and "rights." See, for example, Cowan, Dembour, and Wilson 2001; Goodale and Merry 2003; and Wilson 1997.

2. See Merry 1988 for a useful overview of debates on legal pluralism.

3. For more detailed examinations of Maasai history, livelihoods, gender relations, and more, please see my previous books (Hodgson 2001a, 2005, 2011a).

4. Where possible, I use the preferred spelling "Maasai," although I have retained "Masai" when it is used by others in writings, letters, and other quotations, such as, in this case, the "Masai Reserve."

CHAPTER 1

Creating "Law"

Colonial Rule, Native Courts, and the
Codification of Customary Law

HISTORIANS, ANTHROPOLOGISTS, AND OTHER SCHOLARS of gender in Africa have long looked to the implementation and interaction of colonial and customary legal regimes as rich sites through which to explore colonial gender productions and contestations. Some scholars have examined how colonial efforts to codify customary laws caused previously fluid and dynamic considerations and decisions to become fixed, written legal principles that reinforced the power and privileges of elder men over women and junior men, especially in the realms of marriage, divorce, bridewealth and adultery (Chanock 1985; Mbilinyi 1988; Schmidt 1990; Kanogo 2005; cf. Shadle 1999, 2006). Others have documented how some African women took advantage of new colonial judicial bodies to circumvent customary mechanisms for dispute resolution (Byfield 2001; Lovett 2001). Few of these studies, however, take a step back to consider what the colonial insistence on creating and naming a discrete field of social relations as the realm of "law" meant for the complex ideas and practices of gendered justice and dispute resolution among Africans: How did the colonial codification of customary law and creation of legal institutions like native courts marginalize other understandings of justice, including those deployed by women? What were the gendered consequences of reinforcing androcentric forms and forums of "law," which are predicated on principles of individual rights, secularism, rationality, and neutrality, for alternative conceptions of justice premised on ideas of morality, respect, and social interdependence?

To explore these questions, this chapter examines the mechanisms of gendered justice and dispute resolution that existed among Maasai in the late 1800s. It examines the creation and implementation of customary law and colonial legal institutions and its consequences for not just relations between and among men and women, but for broader Maasai ideas and practices of justice, respect, and morality in which women and the (primarily female-identified) Maasai divinity Eng'ai were significant.

MAASAI IDIOMS OF GENDER JUSTICE

As Martin Chanock (1985) argued years ago, it is notoriously difficult for contemporary scholars or policymakers to describe ideas of justice, practices of dispute resolution, and other aspects of what we call "law" and "justice" for African societies prior to colonial conquest and control. For societies like Maasai who did not keep written records, there are two primary sources for this information. The first source, oral histories with African men and women, are rich but problematic, shaped as they are by memory, perspective, nostalgia, affect, and other influences (White, Miescher, and Cohen 2001). The second set of sources are the accounts and reports of European travelers, missionaries, and early colonial officials, all of which are partial, interested, and often contorted by racist and sexist assumptions about the lives of Africans. One of the most problematic assumptions was of course that all Africans lived in discrete, self-contained social groups called "tribes" led by "chiefs" in which their cultural ideas, social networks, political structure, religious beliefs, dominant modes of livelihood, and language were isomorphic. The other challenge was that by the time these Europeans wrote their reports, the ideas and practices they were writing about had already changed, sometimes quite dramatically, in response to colonial interventions—such as forced removal of Africans from their territories, violent "pacification," disease, and new commodities—and other historical events like slavery, the ivory trade, drought, disease, migration, and warfare.

All these problems complicate any effort to describe "Maasai idioms of justice" in the early colonial period. The ethnic term "Maasai" only emerged in the discourses of Europeans in the late 1800s to describe Maa speakers who relied primarily on pastoralism as their dominant mode of production, in contrast to Maa speakers who relied on farming (Il Lumbwa, Arusha) or gathering and hunting (Il Torobo) (Bernsten 1980; Hodgson 2001a, 25). Even as Maa-speaking herders began to adopt the name themselves and embrace a sense of belonging to a larger collective social body called "Maasai,"[1] their well-documented practices of intermarriage, adoption, and assimilation and their dispersed geographical presence and movements troubled any clear attribution of who was a "Maasai" and thus what was or was not considered a "Maasai" practice or idea. Moreover, when first the Germans then the British arrived in Tanganyika (as Tanzania was called at the time), Maasai were recovering from a series of devastating livestock and human disease outbreaks (a period they called *emutai*—"the disasters") that had killed much of their livestock, wiped out entire families, and produced dramatic social, economic, and political upheaval (Waller 1988; Hodgson 2001a, 36–39). Finally, as discussed in the introduction, early European accounts of "the Maasai" were full of images of them as either fierce, primitive savages at the bottom of the social evolutionary ladder or an obsessive fascination and admiration of them as proud, independent "warriors" (Hodgson 2001a). These images, some of which persist until the present, shaped ideas about and interventions into Maasai lives, including colonial efforts to understand customary law and develop judicial institutions, processes, and procedures.

Thus to describe "Maasai" idioms of justice as of the late 1800s and early 1900s is to presume a much more coherent, stable set of practices and ideas than probably existed. Nonetheless, in what follows, I draw on critical and contextualized readings of the available (if problematic) historical evidence to present an overview of ideas of "law" and "justice" among people who identified or were identified as Maasai during this particular historical moment, with the understanding that these practices and ideas were themselves dynamic historical products, not some idealized, never-changing, "precolonial" tradition. Whatever their origins and identifications, groups of people had to share certain common ideas, values, practices, and institutions in order to live, love, and labor together.

The evidence suggests that as of the late 1800s and early 1900s, Maasai, like many other African societies at the time, had no understanding of "law" as a discrete field of social relations, especially one that denied the centrality of the sacred to daily life.[2] As Moritz Merker, a German administrator, remarked in 1904, "Legal consciousness is very little developed among the

Masai" (1910 [1904], 212). In the Maa language, there was no term for "law" as a social field, just a word (*enkitanapata*, pl. *inkitanapat*) for distinct rules and commandments that people were supposed to follow in daily life to demonstrate and maintain relations of respect (*enkanyit*, see below) (Mol 1977, 94). A dispute or a case was called an *enkiguena* (pl. *inkiguenat*), a term that also meant a meeting of elders—the very forum used to resolve most public disagreements (Mol 1977, 94). The closest Maa word for "justice" was *esipat* (pl. *isipat*), which was derived from the verbs *asip* (to tell the truth) and *asipa* (to be true, to be evident) and thus actually meant "truth" or "true statement" (Mol 1996, 373; 1977, 94).

Instead, as I have discussed elsewhere (Hodgson 2005), most transgressions were interpreted by Maasai as disruptions of or challenges to the moral order, an order constituted through their relationship with their predominantly female divinity, Eng'ai. Since Eng'ai "was understood in feminine terms as the divine principle that created, supported, and nurtured life on earth" (Hodgson 2005, 22), Maasai women saw themselves, and were perceived by men, as closer to Eng'ai. Women's closeness to Eng'ai was expressed and experienced in many ways, including their shared power to produce and nurture human life. The closeness was not just metaphorical but material; Maasai men and women believed that Eng'ai was present in them through their *oltau*, their heart and spirit. *Oltau* was at once a unique, inner essence bequeathed to each person by Eng'ai, an agentive force, and the locus of moral value (Hodgson 2005, 213–15). A person's *oltau* could influence his or her actions, and people could improve or worsen their *iltauja* (the plural of *oltau*) through their practices, in part by "opening" or "closing" their *iltauja* to Eng'ai. Significantly, although both men and women embodied Eng'ai though their *oltau*, women's *oltau* was characterized as closer and more attuned to Engai's directives and moral sensibilities. Therefore women prayed throughout the day to Her, thanking and entreating Eng'ai for the continued protection, preservation, expansion, and prosperity of their family and herds. Since Maasai believed that She could also be harmful and vengeful if angered by their actions (Hodgson 2005, 23; Merker 1910 [1904], 205–6), women also prayed for forgiveness for any slights or transgressions.

Daily life for Maasai men and women was predicated on the values of mutual respect (*enkanyit*), reciprocity and social interdependence (*osotua*), and leading a good and holy (*sinyati*) life in the present so that Eng'ai would bless them with good health, children, and cattle: "The focus of their beliefs and practices was thus maintaining the complementarity between Eng'ai and humans, between the sky and the earth, and correcting—through daily prayers and ceremonies of reconciliation and forgiveness—any transgressions or disturbances that occurred to this relationship. These transgressions ranged from the relatively minor (lies or insults) to the fairly common (cattle theft from other Maasai) to the major (sexual intercourse between a man and a pregnant woman, or murder), and were dealt with accordingly" (Hodgson 2005, 62).

As a code of respect, *enkanyit* structured gender and age relations in terms of rights, responsibilities, and proper relationships through a set of shared and clearly understood expectations and prohibitions about proper greetings, practices, postures, diet, sexual partners, and more. Certain practices—like a father sleeping with his real or classificatory daughter—were harshly forbidden (*enturuj*) and very rare, while others were publicly condemned but fairly common (a "warrior" [*olmurran*] sleeping with a married woman). Following the rules and code of conduct central to *enkanyit*, especially in terms of realizing one's responsibilities to other people, particularly one's dependents, juniors, and less fortunate family and friends, was central to being seen as living a good and holy (*sinyati*) life. But these were, of course, ideals; the reality of individual reputations and relationships, challenges to dominant interpretations about how to properly express *enkanyit*, and so forth were far more messy and complicated.

As with most pastoralist groups, men and women relied on one another, their extended families, affinal relations, neighbors, age mates, lineage mates, and other social networks for information, access to resources (such as grazing land, water, and salt licks), political stability, and risk management in an environment marked by extreme microlocal differences in rainfall, disease, and vegetation. The exchange of bridewealth (and other gifts), marriage, polygyny, male age sets, ritual feasts and celebrations, and the birth of children were thus central to forging and maintaining bonds between families, homesteads, lineages, and clans (Hodgson 2001a, 2005). Individuals had relationships with one another, but these ties created and expressed larger social connections and obligations between their relevant social groups (kin, lineages, clans, age sets). These ties were, in turn, modulated by the values of *enkanyit*, *osotua*, and *sinyati*.

Conflicts, disputes, and transgressions were handled in a variety of ways depending on the age, gender, and relationship of the parties involved and the nature of the offense. In the case of inappropriate or disrespectful behavior by individuals, men and women expressed their contempt through symbolic actions like spitting on the ground in front of the offending person (which inverted the normative meaning of spitting as an act of blessing) (Hollis 1905, 315–16; Merker 1910 [1904], 122) or verbal curses such as "May Eng'ai trouble you!" (*Mikinjirie Eng'ai!*) or "May a wild animal devour you!" (*Tananga naisula!*) (Merker 1910 [1904], 109–10; Hollis 1905, 344). But people within certain close relationships—such as husbands and wives, parents and children—had to be careful about such curses, or even insults, as the consequences were powerful. If, for example, a husband insulted his wife by calling her a sexually explicit term (which men and boys and even young girls and boys often used to tease each other), she could move back to her natal home and return her bridewealth (Merker 1910 [1904], 110). Similarly, if a mother cursed her son by striking her stomach and saying, "You were born in this," he was said to sicken, and could only recover if his mother made a fiber rope to hang around his neck (Hollis 1910, 478; cf. Bianco 2000).

Transgressions that affected groups of people—such as cattle theft or bridewealth disputes—were usually heard by groups of elder male homestead and age-set leaders (*ilaigwenak*) from the relevant area, clan, or section. After lengthy prayers to Eng'ai, they would listen to all parties in the disputes (women were usually represented by male relatives but could directly address the male elders), each of whom invoked Eng'ai as a claim to be telling the truth. The elders then took turns sharing their perspectives on the case until they reached a consensus. They considered all aspects of the dispute: the relationship and responsibilities of the parties in terms of Maasai codes of *enkanyit*; their entanglement in wider social networks such as age sets, lineages, marriage, and patron-client relations; longer histories of relations between the parties and their relatives; and other facets of the social context and history that seemed relevant. If needed, they resorted to ordeals to force people to reveal the truth.[3] These lengthy meetings were then closed by another round of prayers to Eng'ai (Merker 1910 [1904], 218–20). Their goals were less to decide who was right and who was wrong than to seek compromises (usually involving some form of compensation through the transfer of cattle) that were satisfactory to all parties involved and would restore harmonious social relations between the disputing parties and with Eng'ai (what legal anthropologists call "restorative justice").[4]

For especially egregious moral transgressions such as the murder (*loikop*) of another Maasai, the penalties depended on whether the death was accidental or premeditated and on the gender, age, marital status, and parental status of the killer and victim.[5] They could include what colonial administrators called "blood revenge" if an adult man was murdered by another man, whereby the male members of the victim's family would try to kill the murderer, or the payment of "blood money" (*oloikapani*) by clan and section members of the murderer to the family of the deceased in the form of cattle (Merker 1910 [1904], 214–15; Hollis 1905, 311–12; cf. Maguire 1928).[6] But if a married man murdered a girl or woman, there was no blood revenge, only the payment of a fine in cattle (Merker 1910 [1904], 215).

Transgressions that were perceived as affronts to the fertility and procreative powers of women (and thus Eng'ai) were handled by several forms of collective attack and ritual protest by adult women. One form, *olkishoroto*, was deployed when, for example, a man slept with a pregnant woman or his real or classificatory daughters. According to Hollis (1910, 480), "In the event of a man having intercourse with a pregnant woman, and thereby causing her to abort, he must submit to a punishment which is called ol-kishuroto. All the women of the neighborhood collect together and, having stripped, seize the guilty person and flog him, after which they slaughter as many of his cattle as they can, strangling and suffocating the animals with their garments." Although Maguire does not name the practice, he also recounts that among Kisongo Maasai in the 1920s, women collectively beat any woman who caused herself to abort or her husband or another man if he was blamed for the abortion. As he explained, "They may beat the culprit, but the more usual procedure is for them to take an ox of the abortionist's to some quiet place and beat it to death with sticks. The women then eat this ox, but no men or pregnant women may be present while they are doing so" (Maguire 1928, 17).

Similarly, women would attack men who prevented their wives from participating in the regular collective fertility gatherings (*oloirishi*). Interviews with Maasai men and women have confirmed that the practice was much the same as recounted by Paul Spencer in 1988:

Those husbands who beat their wives at this particular time or prevent any of them from joining the gathering, are harried. If the women hear of such an elder, they will storm his village dealing tit for tat. If he has beaten his wife, they will want to beat him and seize some of his best cattle. If he has tried to detain any wife, they will snatch away all of his wives, and leave him to feed the children, milk the cows, and fetch wood and water. No other woman—and certainly no man—would help him. This is a severe degradation, and it is held to be dangerously unpropitious for elders to undertake such tasks. (201)

These forms of collective protest were recognized as legitimate and feared. Senior women also handled minor disputes that occurred among women and children within the homestead, such as accusations that a woman was mistreating a cowife's children. They would gather the relevant parties to discuss the matter and seek an amiable solution that would restore peaceful relations in the homestead (Hodgson 2001a, 32). Similarly, if an older woman had a grievance with her husband, she might brew beer and invite local elders to her house for a meeting to discuss the matter (Spencer 1988, 199).

To summarize, in the late 1800s and early 1900s, Maasai had a range of methods to address infractions and disputes, depending on the nature of the transgression and the relationship of the parties involved. Both men and women were involved in monitoring and restoring social order—which was contiguous with the moral order—but through different means. Women handled disagreements among women and children in the homestead through calm discussion, but they responded in collective, violent ways to actions perceived as gross violations of the moral order. Men recognized as leaders met together in councils to hear and decide cases involving people from different homesteads, age grade, clans, or sections. For all involved, the legitimacy of the men or women who tried to address transgressions and resolve disputes—whether through discussion or collective action— was predicated on their strong relationship to Eng'ai and the belief that maintaining the balance and strength of the social order was crucial to the continuity of the moral order.

Colonial Ideals of "Natural" Justice and "Native" Law

When the British took over Tanganyika from the Germans in the aftermath of World War I, they sought, as in their other African colonies, to impose order through creating power structures that relied on local people and leaders and developing rational, replicable processes and practices to guide their rule over and relationships with the "natives." The development of secular legal systems made up of judicial bodies (usually native courts or councils of elders), laws and statutes, and regularized processes for bringing and judging cases were central to their quest for order and control. As described below, however, these institutions and processes were predicated on British ideas of "natural justice" and "civilized standards," which privileged secular law over religious belief, valued "impartiality" over taking account of social relationships, sought to codify and apply "timeless" principles of customary law, and concentrated judicial power in the hands of a few men. Moreover, the creation of native courts and recognition of customary law were based on British understandings of "tribes" like Maasai as social units "possessing a common language, a single social system and an established customary law."[7] Together, these changes shaped and were shaped by the shifting dynamics of Maasai age and gender relations.

Although Tanganyika was a German protectorate from 1880 to the end of World War I, the Germans did little to try to develop a "native" legal system during their occupation; according to Donald Cameron, "under their Colonial system in German East Africa the Native had no law and no court of justice to which he could appeal for protection. He was outside the law" (Cameron 1937, 22; cf. Iliffe 1969). More accurately, the Germans left the adjudication of civil matters to local African leaders (Bierwagen and Peter 1989, 396). But once the British took over the rule of Tanganyika in 1916, they began to design and implement a system of native administration and native courts based on the principles of "indirect rule" developed in Nigeria.[8]

The writings of Cameron, who served as the governor of Tanganyika from 1925 to 1931 (and later as governor of Nigeria), and others provide insights into the logic and principles applied by the British during the early colonial period to create and implement a legal system for the "natives" as part of "indirect rule." Rather than apply a "ready-made scheme," Cameron insisted that native administration, including native courts, derive from native "law and custom" (Cameron 1937, see also Cameron 1930).[9] He demanded that lower-level officers learn about native law and custom by inquiring from "the bottom" up, "the family first, the extended family, and so on through the various age grades right up to the authority, whatever it may be, that they all acknowledge as the authority that has regulated the society of the unit according to their own law and custom" (Cameron 1937, 10). As a result, according to Margery Perham (1931, 303), "All through 1925 there poured into Dar-es-Salaam bulky reports bearing witness to the research that was going on in every district in the Territory." Based on conversations with key informants, discussions (through a translator) with elder men, and readings of prior ethnographic studies, these reports (supposedly) described customary institutions for resolving disputes and enforcing decisions as well as the principles ("customary laws") used to decide cases.

One issue that quickly arose was the difference between a "custom" and a "law," and how to determine whether a custom could be recognized as law. Julius Lewin, a recognized expert on African law at the time,[10] proposed that colonial courts adopt the procedure "normally followed" in English courts, whereby for a custom to be recognized as law, it had to satisfy the following tests: "(i) It must have continued without interruption for as long a period as living testimony can cover; (ii) it must be certain and definite in its incidence; (iii) it must be limited either to a locality or in respect of the class of persons affected or in its nature; and (iv) it must be reasonable" (Lewin 1938, 18). To ascertain the "facts" behind the first three tests, Lewin (1938, 18–19) argued that the court could be guided in three ways: (1) by the assistance of "native assessors" who, like "an expert witness," would advise it about the customs of any tribe, (2) the evidence of an "expert witness, of which the best type would be a competent anthropologist at work among the tribe concerned," or (3) following "a rigid code of native law established by statute."

Lewin's explanations for how to distinguish a "law" from a "custom" reflect key assumptions in British efforts to delineate a distinct domain of social interaction as "law" that was separate from other kinds of social, religious, and cultural practices and beliefs. In contrast to customs, laws were believed to be principles that were unchanging throughout living memory, clear and defined, limited in scope and application, and, of course, "reasonable" by British standards of morality. But, as discussed above, this very definition of law—as clear, unchanging principles—represented a starkly different way to address and resolve disputes and transgressions than that practiced historically by Maasai (and other African peoples) in which social relationships, context, and other circumstances were considered.

Moreover, as Lewin's claim that for a custom to be recognized as a law "it must be reasonable" suggests, respect for native customs and laws had its limits in terms of British ideas of "natural" and "ordinary" justice and morality. Colonial officers and courts developed the principle of "repugnancy" to assess whether or not to apply customary laws; "He [the 'chief'] can enforce Native law and custom—provided it is not repugnant to ordinary ideas of justice and morality or inconsistent with the laws of the territory" (Cameron 1937, 13; see also Lewin 1938, 16; Caplan 1964).[11] As Cameron argued:

We should not and need not interfere with Native law and custom in these early stages, I submit, unless the crime or misdemeanour is so flagrantly and dreadfully barbarous, so contrary to the accepted standards of modern civilisation or detrimental to the interests of others, that it is impossible to refrain from attempting to put a stop to it through the interventions of the Courts. Let the principle be applied in all cases; if the act is barbarous or injurious to the degree I have indicated, let us attempt to stop it; if, however, it is merely something which we should not do ourselves in our own society but is in accordance with Native law and custom without gravely offending the standards of modern civilisation, let it alone for the present. (1937, 23–24)

Some practices were quickly condemned by Cameron and others as "barbarous" and therefore unacceptable, including head hunting, twin murder, and trial by ordeal and slavery, "none of them offences against people's own codes, but which we cannot condone and have very nearly succeeded in stamping out through punishment in our Courts" (Cameron 1937, 24).

But the idea of "natural justice" applied not just to practices, but to processes and procedures as well. According to Lewin (1938, 21), "The meaning of natural justice can be conveniently considered under three aspects, namely, judicial procedure, content of substantive law and degree of punishment" (see also Caplan 1964). In terms of "judicial procedure," he cited the findings of a recent British commission of "eminent lawyers" that "summarized the law on the subject by stating the following three fundamental principles of natural justice":

(i) A man may not be a judge in his own cause. The mind of a judge ought to be free to decide on purely judicial grounds and should not be directly or indirectly influenced by, or exposed to the influence of, either motives of self-interest or opinions about policy or any other considerations not relevant to the issue.

(ii) The second principle is twofold. No party ought to be condemned unheard; and if his right to be heard is to be a reality, he must know in good time the case which he has to meet. But on neither branch of this principle can any particular procedure (a) by which the party is informed of the case which he has to meet, or (b) by which his evidence and argument are "heard," be regarded as fundamental. There is, for instance, no natural right to an oral hearing.

(iii) When further proceedings are open to a disappointed party, he is entitled to know the reason for or grounds of the decision. (Lewin 1938, 21)

Here, as elsewhere, a distinction was made between the "natural justice" of the British, presented as an ahistorical, uncontested set of shared values and principles, and the self-evidently (at least for the British) morally and procedurally compromised "customs and laws" of Africans and other "natives":

> On one side of an arbitrary line drawn by ourselves a court with a liberal constitution such as we should find in civilised life, where the person has the right to employ the services of an advocate to defend him or to urge his suit; the right, moreover, to seek a review of the case in a higher court. On the other side of the line a court where the unfortunate Native is not allowed the services of an advocate to assist him in proceedings in which owing to their novelty to him, he is at great disadvantage, and where he has no appeal whatsoever to a court of justice. He cannot compel a review of his case; in fine, he is at the mercy of the Executive, whom he can petition and no more. (Cameron 1937, 22)

In other reports, Cameron and his peers were far less subtle about their patronizing and racist views, calling for

> the need to educate the Native Authorities in their duties to their people according to civilised standards: let me repeat that: "according to civilised standards." To convince them that oppression of the people is not sound policy or to the eventful benefits of the rulers; to bring home to their intelligence, as far as may be possible, the evils attendant on a system which holds the lower classes in subjection, so destroying responsibility, ambition, and progress amongst them; and, last but not least, to inculcate the unspeakable benefit of justice free from bribery and open to all. (Cameron 1937, 15)

"The centuries which lie between ourselves and the Native in point of development," Cameron continued, "cannot be bridged in a generation or two" (Cameron 1937, 17).

Thus Cameron and other British leaders at the time presumed that Africans in colonial Tanganyika and elsewhere had a clearly defined field of social relations that could be called "law," which was separate, somehow, from "custom," religion, and other social interactions. Moreover, they believed that the differences between the British system of law and that of the "natives" were straightforward. In the more "civilized" British system, predicated on principles of "natural justice," courts were made up of impartial judges and, if needed, juries; the courts worked through standardized processes, procedures, and precedents; accused parties had the right to a lawyer and to appeal to a higher court of law; and certain practices were self-evidently barbaric and therefore illegal. In contrast, "native" systems of law were characterized as oppressive, unjust, and in dire need of reform to meet "civilized standards."

CREATING NATIVE COURTS AND
CUSTOMARY LAW IN "MAASAILAND"

To implement Cameron's directives, male British colonial officers met with male Maasai elders to learn and codify Maasai "customary" laws, created a council of Maasai male elders (called either the "Masai Council" or "Olki-ama") to debate and decide Maasai policy and legal matters, and instituted a system of "native courts" (staffed by men) to resolve civil disputes according to customary law (criminal matters were attended to by colonial officers). Their approach to native courts and customary law in "Maasailand," as in the rest of East Africa, was inconsistent, at times contradictory, and changed over time. From the early 1920s to the late 1940s, they struggled to understand who held political, judicial, and executive authority among Maasai and how to structure the native courts accordingly. They exercised minimal interference in Maasai "legal" affairs, except in those areas (raiding, trespass, killing) that challenged their efforts to assert their political and economic control. By the late 1940s, however, colonial officials were deluged with disputes about wayward wives, disobedient daughters, and other "family" matters. They met with elder men to discuss "customary law" and to develop a clear, fixed set of rules about marriage, bridewealth, divorce, child custody, and related matters in hopes of systematizing their approach and reducing the time they spent understanding the intricacies of the disputes. In the process, both British and Maasai men conveniently ignored the long-recognized political ability and moral authority of Maasai women to resolve certain domestic disputes and to punish select moral transgressions.

In the middle to late 1920s, colonial administrators had long debates among themselves about how to set up the native court system in "Masailand" (as they called it) to best reflect the "traditional" authority structure, tribal organization, and processes for deciding cases among Maasai.[12] "I should like to know," explained P. E. Mitchell, the secretary for native affairs in Tanganyika, "how their courts fit with tribal organisation."[13] According to Mitchell, who served as a district officer in Maasailand before his promotion, "I was only eight months among the Masai but I repeat, if I ever met a people who most completely managed their own affairs, it is the Masai. They very seldom bring a case to the Political Officer; they settle grazing and watering disputes for their thousands of head of cattle and small stock; they raise funds for their water conservation; they settle matrimonial and stock disputes among themselves (unless of course we assume none such occur!); what individuals or body of men is it who do this?"[14]

Drawing on their conversations with elder men, experiences in the field, and insights from early ethnographic accounts, administrators discussed the relative "judicial" and "executive" power of (male) elders and warriors, the role of the Laibon (a diviner and prophet), and the merits of specific Maasai men to head the native courts.[15] Eventually, in 1926 they created five native courts, two (one Second Class and one First Class for appeals) run by the current Laibon, Parit; a Second Class court run by a longtime government headman, Elder Kapurwa, and two other Second Class courts run by local Maasai leaders, all of whom could include other elder men in their deliberations, as necessary.[16]

The establishment of these courts, and especially the appointment of individual men to hear cases, was almost immediately disputed by H. C. Murrells, who became a district officer in Masai District in 1927. Of all the officers, Murrells seems to have had the clearest sense of the realities of Maasai political structure and dispute-resolution practices at the time. In a long memorandum on "Native Courts, Councils, and Authorities Organisation," he described, among other things, the role of "ingrained respect" rather than "fear of consequences, or of an executive authority" in regulating Maasai affairs; the "democratic," acephalous organization of political authority among Maasai through the selection of male age-set leaders (*olaigwenani*, pl. *ilaigwenak*); the various forums for resolving disputes (gatherings of village elders, meetings of *ilaigwenak*); and the role of social pressure and shame in ensuring that the decisions of these elders were followed. He wrote, "If a litigant refuses to accept the ruling or instructions given to him by his elders, he might be actually penalized by them, and effect would be given to the verdict by others present at the Council, in effect the public. A person dare not stand against such an assembly, and not obey, under fear of a form of social ostracism by the rest of the tribe." Maasai, he continued, are "respecters of age," and once any "difficulties" have been discussed and decided by a council of elders, "the decisions reached have been respected and the settlement has been arrived at in an amicable manner, 'out of court.'"[17]

But Mitchell, now the acting provincial commissioner, refused to be convinced that the power to decide and enforce decisions did not reside in a specific individual. As he wrote on the margins of the memorandum, "But how! Someone must have done it and so been the executive!"[18] "Clearly there must be a Superior Judicial Authority," which he mistakenly presumed must be the Laibon (who was instead a prophet and diviner).[19] Frustrated by both the complexities of Maasai social organization and thus his inability to design and implement an appropriate and effective Masai Native Authority, Mitchell ranted that Maasai "were more like a flock of sheep than an organized community of human beings."[20]

These debates about the appropriate structure of the Maasai Native Courts continued for years, and the organization of the courts and their mandates were revised numerous times.[21] All the proposed structures included a hierarchy of courts in order to adjudicate different kinds of offenses and to provide the possibility of appeal to a higher "authority." In general, as of 1929, litigants in the native courts could appeal a court decision to a native appeals court, then the district commissioner, the provincial commissioner, and, at the very top, the governor's appeal court.[22] District officers were required to review the decisions of cases in the native courts, and the provincial commissioner provided periodical inspections.[23] Moreover, like political authority (Hodgson 2001a), judicial authority was presumed to be the mandate of older men; women and junior men were never considered as arbiters of justice.[24] Instead of councils of elders, however, the British designated only certain men as court authorities, whether the Laibon, government headmen, or other senior men who they (the British) deemed to be suitable and "legitimate" representatives of their people. All these aspects of "law" as a distinct social field—the formation of the native courts, the processes and procedures for bringing and deciding a case, the right of "appeal" to "higher" authorities, etc.—were radically new ideas for Maasai that challenged their own understandings of and customary practices for ensuring and achieving "justice."

THE SCOPE OF "CUSTOMARY" LAW

In addition to protracted deliberations about the proper structure and procedures for native courts in Masai District, British officers also debated which kinds of customary practices and disputes were a matter of "law" and within the domain of the native courts. They demanded that Maasai refer transgressions that the British classified as "criminal," such as murder and "blood revenge," to the courts or risk large fines and other penalties. According to Murrells, "A case of this kind arose in 1926 and I instructed the whole tribe that this practice was to cease, and that 'Nyamu' [blood revenge] would be awarded by the Courts alone, and that failure to await a court decision would entail heavy penalties for the persons raiding."[25] Nonetheless, they tried to collect information about customary modes of classifying and resolving criminal offenses. In 1928, for example, R. A. J. Maguire published a short article on "The Masai Penal Code," which he described as "brief and unscientific" but designed to add "to our knowledge of Masai criminal offences in view of the recent formation of Native Courts throughout Tanganyika Territory" (1928, 12). He based his report on statements from certain male Maasai elders of the L'aimer age set, which he also discussed with Laibon Parit and compared with Hollis's ethnographic accounts (Hollis 1905).[26] Maguire reviewed the process and penalties for such "crimes" as murder (*loikop*), assault (*e'toosho*), theft (*'nyamin*), adultery (*en'giopo*), seduction (*engitaapare*), abortion (*e-taremu engioo*), and curses (*ildeketa*).

Transgressions that the British classified as civil offenses (which included some of the "crimes" like adultery that Maguire discussed in his 1928 article above), especially those involving marriage, divorce, child custody, and other areas we now call "family law," were more complicated. Prior to the 1950s, administrators made only modest efforts to understand Maasai family relations, focusing their meager efforts and resources instead on trying to decipher the structures and processes through which Maasai exercised political and judicial authority so as to design and implement appropriate structures for effective indirect rule (Hodgson 2001a). During this period, the few formal investigations into Maasai social practices were in response to pressure from various women's groups and other organizations in Britain who were concerned about aspects of "the status of African women," including polygyny, bridewealth, female circumcision, and forced marriage.

In 1930, for example, the House of Commons discussed "the status of African women and initiation rites" and considered proposals to create a law to ban female circumcision. They drew on reports requested by the secretary of state for the colonies from colonial governors in eastern and central Africa.[27] In his report about Tanganyika Territory, Governor Cameron made clear that he opposed any efforts to promulgate rules by the native administration "as to the form of the operation or as to the training of the woman who performs it, believing that if we persuaded the Native Authorities to make such rules, we should, in their minds and in those of the people, be giving a significance of permanency to observances which we desire to get rid of altogether." Drawing on a report he enclosed by P. E. Mitchell, who was secretary for native affairs at the time, he argued that only a small number of people practiced the "severe form," that "medical men" agreed that clitoridectomy caused "no mutilation" or any bad health effects, and that female circumcision, like male circumcision, was regarded with "the highest reverence and veneration, as an essential part of initiation ceremonies, and as the only avenue of admission to full membership in the tribe." Moreover, "not to have been circumcised is to be a complete outcast from the tribe. Such an outcast woman is ceremonially unclean, cannot marry a man of her own tribe, and must seek a detribalised, Europeanised husband, if she can find one, or, alternatively, live as a concubine of any tribesman who is bold enough to keep her." Thus to prohibit the practice would be "both undesirable and impracticable." They would "adhere to [the practice] even more strongly" and "the ceremony would be carried out in secrecy." Instead, he argued that "it is the policy of the Tanganyika Government to assist the tribes to foster and develop all that is good in native customs and gradually eradicate what is objectionable."[28]

More generally, he emphasized that women in Tanganyika were in "no way 'slaves,'" providing "examples of women's freedom and independence" from the records of native courts, including successful suits by women for divorce, enforcing women's rights to property, against husbands for failing to do their share of the work, and a widow's refusal to be inherited. Although none of these cases were from Masai District, the report emphasized that "a careful scrutiny of the Native Court records has failed to bring to light a single case in which the sex of the litigant would appear to have influenced the Native Court's decision."[29] Similarly, in 1936, the governor of Tanganyika, Sir Harold MacMichael, and other colonial governors had to respond to the inquiries of Eleanor Rathbone, a member of Parliament, about the "forced marriage of African girls." MacMichael conferred with colonial officers and missionaries and reported that there was no evidence of forced marriages in Tanganyika.[30] A few years later, Governor Mark Young responded to a similar request from the St. Joan's Social and Political Alliance about the prevalence of "forced marriage." He reported that "after a very full investigation, conducted with the assistance of missionary bodies, only six genuine cases of forced marriage were discovered."[31]

The St. Joan's Social and Political Alliance, an organization of Catholic women in Britain, was a visible and vigorous advocate for improving the status of "women of native races," especially "African women."[32] Moreover, as this excerpt from 1935 makes clear, they justified their calls for colonial legal interventions with an explicit link between "rights" and "Christianity":

> During the past year the [St. Joan's] Alliance has taken a leading part in working for raising the status of African women. We believe the time has come when it should be definitely laid down that a woman whatever her race, is not a chattel to be sold by her father or alleged proprietor to a polygamist or anyone else. Every woman must be a free agent to choose her own partner in life despite any contract entered into in her name by any other person. The inheritance of widows by their husband's heir, must be put a stop to. We base our claim on the Christian conception of the rights of every human being.[33]

In 1937, they presented a statement to the Assembly of the League of Nations calling for the adoption of an International Convention "granting to women equality of rights and responsibilities."[34] They attacked "native custom" and especially what they claimed were government efforts to protect the status quo; "we urge that one of the greatest benefits that white civilization can bestow on these races is to endeavor to raise the status of their women, which at present remains a blot on legislation which is often none other than 'native custom' stamped with Government authority." Based in part on input from missionaries working in the colonies, the "customs" they condemned included bridewealth, polygamy, arranged marriage, female circumcision, and the inheritance of widows (St. Joan's Alliance 1961, 15). Their characterizations of "native" culture as inherently oppressive to women, positioning of themselves as the protectors of colonial women (and thus the presumption that they lived more enlightened and less oppressed lives), and demands for international and state legislation and interventions to forcibly change these practices would be echoed in decades to come by Euro-American feminist groups and others seeking ways to, as Gayatri Spivak (1988) famously described it, ensure that "white men are saving brown women from brown men."[35]

The demands of the St. Joan's Alliance, Eleanor Rathbone, and others for direct government intervention rankled the administrators working in the colonies. Both Cameron's and Mitchell's 1930 reports to the secretary of state for the colonies were full of scathing assessments of the lack of knowledge and expertise of the British politicians and activists about "native life." For example, in response to claims that women in bridewealth exchanges (or "dowry" as they called it) were equivalent to slaves, Cameron replied:

"I am aware that it is alleged by *some persons, many of whom know nothing that is not superficial of the native populations of the Territory and have never touched the life of the people,* that 'women are slaves because a dowry is paid for them.' The dowry is in fact a pledge for the good conduct of the man and for the good conduct of the woman, it is not a vicious practice, and it is well suited to the conditions of the tribes" (my emphasis).[36] Mitchell echoed Cameron's assertions of authority and argued for the limits of legal interventions to change social practices: "Those of us who spend our lives in the administration of Africans would indeed be glad if the facile expedient of prohibition, which is so often urged upon us as the way to deal with objectionable aspects of primitive society, were in fact a weapon capable of effective use."[37] Instead, he, like Cameron, argued that these "objectionable aspects" would change through modernization, especially education: "If the African could be civilized by alien legislation, most of our difficulties would cease; but civilization is the cause, and not the effect, of improvements in the laws. Education in its best and widest sense must precede social legislation."[38] Members of the St. Joan's Alliance, in turn, found these responses "smug" and "cynical."[39]

The debates between feminist advocates and colonial officials reflected different interpretations of the status of African women and different ideas about how best to change them to conform to modern ideals. Eleanor Rathbone, the leaders of St. Joan's, and other British feminists saw African women as deeply oppressed by their husbands, fathers, and other men, "treated in many cases little better than slaves, chattels or beasts of burden" (St. Joan's Alliance 1961, 14). In support of their views, they claimed there was evidence of "forced" marriage and "child" marriage and argued that "brideprice" reflected the purchase and sale of women.[40] They demanded that the colonial government immediately pass legislation to criminalize and prohibit these and other cultural practices they believed were inherently oppressive to women. In contrast, most colonial officials at the time resisted calls to use law as a tool for social change. Instead, they argued for a more gradualist approach through the support (at least rhetorically) of education. Moreover, they accused the feminist advocates of misinterpreting the meaning of some practices (like bridewealth) and exaggerating the prevalence of others (like forced marriage). What both groups shared, however, was a sense that they knew what was best for African women, especially illiterate, rural women like Maasai. These women were the objects of much debate, but they were never positioned as subjects who might have their own opinions about their present and future.

Despite these inquiries, the Maasai native courts seem to have heard few marriage-related cases until the late 1940s.[41] Instead, troubled parties appealed to colonial administrators for assistance, usually about women who were accused of abandoning their husbands for other men. In 1942, for example, colonial officers reported the case of two men who were in search of a woman (one man was her brother, the other her husband) who had run away with her infant son from her home in Tanganyika to live with another man in Kenya. According to the officer, "The woman has not lived with her husband for some months and may not agree to return with him."[42] In another case that year, a Maasai woman complained to Page Jones, the district commissioner, that her daughter had run off to Moshi with a non-Maasai police constable who had been working in Monduli. Page Jones asked the district commissioner of Moshi to investigate whether the girl "had any intention of returning" and "what the man's views on the matter are." The district commissioner in Moshi responded that they were still together and now had a thirteen-month-old son. The girl promised, however, to see her mother soon "to settle the matter of dowry."[43]

As these examples suggest, while some Maasai sought the interventions of district commissioners and other colonial personnel, few of them brought these matters as formal cases in the native courts. As Webster, the acting provincial commissioner lamented in 1928, "owing to the Masai custom of settling their civil disputes among themselves by discussion, the established courts of both first and second class seldom have cases brought to them."[44] Instead, the colonial administration used the courts to charge Maasai with violating the new laws they had developed to regulate and control the movement of livestock and people (Hodgson 2001a). For example, of the few case records from the Monduli native court available in the Tanzanian National Archives, most were brought by colonial officers against Maasai for trespassing, disobeying livestock quarantine restrictions, stock thefts, or assaults and killings arising from cattle thefts or fighting among warriors. In 1931, for example, four Maasai men were accused of refusing to move their cattle to a quarantine area during a rinderpest outbreak. Even though they all claimed that they did not need to move their cattle because the animals were not sick, they were found guilty and charged with either paying a fine or doing one month of hard labor. They eventually paid the fine and moved their cattle into the quarantine area.[45] As Eric Rowe, a district officer, summarized in 1935:

> Of the native courts there is little to say. From time immemorial claims and disputes have been settled by arbitration among the elders, under a rigid compensation system. The Government's peculiar habit of writing such matters in a book and charging court fees is to then [sic] incomprehensible and unnecessary. Consequently the very few cases which appear in the Court Register even of a Subordinate Native Court are in effect, either appeals from the informal arbitrations described above or offences against the Native Authority Ordinance etc. referred to the Native Court by the Administrative Officer. Of the 45 cases enter during 1935 to date some 15 represent such appeals, and the remainder are offences under the Native Authority Ordinance.[46]

A few criminal cases were heard or considered as part of inquests into the circumstances of someone's death, but they all seem to have resulted in acquittal or were ruled death by accident or other means.[47] Moreover, even when certain cases were pursued through the colonial courts, Maasai often still followed their customary practices.[48]

REGULATING FAMILY LIFE

By 1950, however, matters had changed. Administrators were confronted both directly and to a lesser extent through the native courts with increasing numbers of appeals and disputes involving "runaway" wives, questions of child custody, and "adultery."[49] One reason for the increase was that the native courts and British efforts to codify customary law provided new resources and sites for asserting and contesting dominant ideas of proper marriage and challenging unwanted relationships in a time of significant social flux. As part of post–World War II efforts to modernize colonial economies to be more productive and profitable, the British intensified their interventions into the economic, political, and social lives of their subjects, producing both challenges and opportunities. In Masai District (which was formerly the Masai Reserve), the British launched the "Masai Development Project" (MDP), an ambitious five-year plan to increase Maasai livestock production through an array of technical interventions such as the construction of additional permanent water supplies (Hodgson 2000; 2001a, 100–26). The consequences of the MDP and related interventions (like taxation, alienation of land, and monetization programs) were to transfer the most fertile pasture lands and permanent water sources to more "productive" uses (such as settler farming and national parks), increase the need for cash and thus the commodification of cattle, decrease the size of livestock holdings, and thereby exacerbate the increasingly precarious political, economic, and ecological situation of pastoralists. Meanwhile, expanding urban areas like Nairobi and Dar es Salaam provided opportunities for Maasai and other rural women to escape the constrictions of unwanted relationships and find work in the informal economy providing food, alcohol, lodging, sexual services, and social support for the growing male labor force (Mbilinyi 1989; White 1990; Ivaska 2011). Junior Maasai men could earn money as wage laborers, traders, or livestock brokers or, if they were educated, as teachers, catechists, and government staff workers. Women and junior men thus had new possibilities for economic support, political power, and social mobility, while elder men struggled to retain and buttress their authority and control in a time of economic and political upheaval.

As part of the new willingness of the British to intervene in social, economic, and political matters in the name of modernization, they replaced their gradualist approaches to social change with more direct methods like law. They tried to understand and at times change certain customary practices through the offices of the "customary" institutions they had set up (the Olkiama and the Masai Council), as well as through consultations with select groups of elder men and reference to ethnographies and other reports.[50] In a speech to the Masai Olkiama in 1948, T. M. Revington, the provincial commissioner, "begged them to consider carefully the status of women and to allow them by law freedom of choice in their personal affairs and to amend their marriage and divorce customs to this end."[51] In 1949, the district officer asked that the Olkiama consider approving resolutions to legislate the period of moranhood, the age of male circumcision, and the age for men to "drink milk" (another step in their age-set rituals) in an effort to exert more control over junior men.[52] Much of the 1950 meeting of the Olkiama was devoted to clarifying and codifying Maasai "laws" with regard to marriage, divorce, and custody. According to J. C. Clarke, the Masai district commissioner:

> The annual meeting of the Masai Council achieved some useful work in regard to principles relating to the very thorny question of custody of children and legal ownership of women. Disputes over these question cause endless and often inconclusive arguments; eventually the Administrative Officer is called

in to adjudicate on an insoluble impasse which is often created from a failure in the first place to follow ancient custom. The exceptions made to rules derive doubtless from the independence which is such a feature of Masai life, and litigation is complicated as a result. An attempt to formulate certain agreed principles has accordingly been made, and appeal cases will be decided on the basis of those principles.[53]

As Clarke noted, the purpose of distilling the principles was to assist administrators who were being deluged by personal appeals of Maasai to resolve such disputes. As the district commissioner for Masai District complained in 1951, "there was an increase in the number of Appeals heard in the Mondul Division, being a total of 20 for the year. Although the number is small, the Masai Appeals in cases dealing with the custody of women and children are more time-consuming than any other of which the writer has experience."[54]

Another problem seemed to be the increasing number of Maasai women who were forging relationships with non-Maasai men and the resulting ambiguities about bridewealth, custody, and inheritance. For example, in preparation for the discussions about marriage at the 1950 Olkiama, a group of male elders sent a long letter in Swahili to the district commissioner insisting that these non-Maasai "strangers" (sw: *wageni*) must pay bridewealth of four cattle and four containers of honey. If the strangers did not comply, then they had to move out of Maasailand.[55] Of course, Maasai men were also "marrying" non-Maasai women. In 1955, a Maasai man sued an Arusha woman to return to him along with their three children (she already had three other children with another man). The court awarded him custody of the three children but did not require the woman to return to him. On appeal, the district commissioner decided that since they were not legally married, the woman could recover rights to her children.[56]

Nonetheless, Maasai still preferred to settle such matters out of court, regardless of whatever principles of customary law had been formalized by colonial authorities and male Maasai elders. According to Clarke:

> In practice, however, a number of decisions in Masai cases result from a preponderance of majority opinion, with a bias in favour of compromise, rather than from the strict application of principles of law. The practice of settling disputes out of Court by arbitration is ingrained in Masai life, and is not discouraged. Where customary law tends to lag behind current social practice, as in Masai marriage matters, the Administration encourages the Masai Council to set forth the agreed principles on which the Masai should act and on which their disputes will be decided.[57]

Thus, even by 1951, there were only 200 cases heard in the Native Court in Monduli Division and 125 in Loliondo Division, of which 110 were civil and 215 criminal.[58]

The Complexities of Maasai "Marriage"

As became quickly clear to administrators, one problem they faced in codifying these principles was setting aside their own assumptions about the form and content of "marriage" and the appropriate roles and responsibilities of husbands, wives, fathers, and mothers in order to grasp the complexities of Maasai sexual and social relations. The variety of relationships they encountered reflected historical precedents, competing claims of authority and freedom, new economic opportunities and challenges, alternative ideas of monogamy and fidelity introduced by Christianity and formal education, and changing relations of gender and generational authority. The increased concern of administrators to understand, codify, and regulate "marriage," and the eagerness of male elders to assist them, made sense in this time of social upheaval, since a recognized union between a man and a woman was the fulcrum of Maasai social, political, and economic relations in the present and for the future; it ensured the reproduction of patrilineages through the birth of children, provision of labor for domestic duties and livestock care, social networks for risk management and livestock mobility, and other enactments of *enkanyit* (respect), *osotua* (social interdependence), and *sinyati* (a good life).

Historically Maasai girls had sexual relations at a very young age with their "warrior" (*olmurrani*, pl. *ilmurran*) boyfriends, moving from digital manipulation to full penal penetration as they matured (Leakey 1930, 192–93; see also Talle 2007). Maasai believed that girls needed semen in order to mature into fertile women, and they developed several practices (such as *esoto* and the *orpul*) to ensure that girls and young men had many opportunities for sexual intimacy (Talle 2007; Coast 2007). Girls chose their lovers (*olsanjan*) through semipublic ceremonies (*inkipot*) in their mother's house, where they presented them with gourds of milk in front of other girls and *ilmurran*.[59] Despite these intimate relationships, most girls subsequently married much older men as part of polygynous families. Once they became wives, they often maintained sexual relationships with one or more men of the "warrior" age set that they "sang for," despite explicit prohibitions by their husbands and other elders (but with the implicit support of other women, including, at times, their mothers-in-law). Sexual relationships with their husband's age-mates were, however, encouraged, but only with the woman's consent (Storrs-Fox 1930, 455), and historical evidence suggests that married women had significant social and sexual mobility and autonomy (Thomson 1968 [1885]; Hodgson 2001a, 34–35).

Many scholars, including myself, have described the normative or "customary" marriage process that conferred specific jural rights over children to the husband's family. This kind of marriage, which is documented as early as 1899, often began with gifts of honey by a male suitor or his family to a prospective mother-in-law when her daughter was still quite young, followed by discussions between the two families as to the appropriateness of the union (which, as I have described elsewhere, entailed careful examination of the man's "seed," or patriline [Hodgson 2001a, 252]), intensified gift exchange and sometimes "loans," an extended initiation ceremony that transformed a girl into a marriageable woman, and finally a formal ceremony where the bride was escorted to the man's homestead and more gifts were exchanged and promises made. In this ideal form of marriage, with the proper exchange of bridewealth, the *pater* retained full rights to the children of his wife, regardless of the *genitor*; the social obligations between the families of the bride and groom were strong; a woman was under the authority of her husband; a woman had shared rights over livestock; and the primary purpose of sex was for procreation (although, of course, there could be pleasure as well) (e.g., Macdonald 1899; Merker 1910 [1904], 43–50; Hollis 1905, 302–3; Storrs-Fox 1931; Hodgson 2001a, 43; Hodgson 2005, 60–61; Talle 1988, 124–55; Spencer 1988, 25–28). Most early sources agree that young women would not be married without their consent (e.g., Merker 1910 [1904]; Jacobs 1970; Talle 1988; Spencer 1988), although clearly there was social pressure to marry in the dominant mode.[60]

Historically, however, there is significant evidence that despite the prevalence of the dominant "ideal" form, there were an array of other kinds of conjugal relationships with distinct kinds of rights, expectations, obligations, and connections. According to Merker, elopement was common in the late 1890s and early 1900s: "It is not uncommon for a girl, as soon as she becomes of marriageable age, to run away from her mother's hut and go to the man of her choice" (Merker 1910 [1904], 46).[61] Sometimes the relationship was eventually formalized by bridewealth exchange and the woman became an *esainoti* (the name for a woman married in the dominant form with bridewealth exchange); at other times no bridewealth was exchanged but the union was still recognized as legitimate. Other women "ran away" to join their lovers even after they were married (Storrs-Fox 1930, 455). Unhappy wives could leave their husbands permanently through an institution called *kirtala*, although the custody of their children depended on the exchange of bridewealth and type of union (Hollis 1905, 304). Another kind of relationship that has been documented from the early 1900s to the present was that of *Entito e enkang'*, or "daughter of the homestead." These women were often either a favorite daughter of their father or a daughter in a family with no sons to inherit the household's livestock wealth. They built a house in their father's homestead, received some livestock from their mother's herd to support themselves, and chose their lovers—but their sons belonged to the father's lineage and inherited accordingly (Talle 1988, 147–48; 2007, 355).

As of the 1950s, therefore, Maasai recognized a range of domestic and sexual relationships between men and women, only some of which were similar to British ideas of "marriage." These older forms and emergent ones, such as "selling the girl" (*amir entito*),[62] were reflected in a fascinating document from 1952.[63] Titled "Masai Marriage Law," the two-page report was based on a meeting between a British colonial administrator and "the elders of Simanjiro" as part of the British effort to codify Maasai "customary law," especially "family law." The document describes four kinds of adult women based on their relationships to men. I reproduce it in detail here because of the complicated portrait it presents of Maasai gender relations and thus the challenges to distilling and codifying fixed legal principles to reflect and regulate these relations.

The first category of woman was called an *esainoti*. She was described as "the wife in a proper marriage":

> Having proposed, the man paid the bride-price "mahari" and was married. Whether there are subsequently children or not is irrelevant. The bride-price is invariably four cows and four debes [twenty-gallon containers] of honey and is called "engapute".
>
> If there is trouble in the marriage there is a possibility that the offender will be punished according to Masai custom. If the woman is at fault and lives with another man any children she may have had or has by the other man are the property of the legal husband who has paid the bride-price. If the man is at fault he must pay to the wife's father or, if none, the elders of the wife's family's "mlango" [gate], one female calf and a debe of honey. If he continues to be at fault he will pay the same again.

If the marriage breaks up and there are no children to the union, the wife returns to her family and the bride-price is returned to the husband. If there are children they remain with the father and the wife returns home. No bride-price is then returned.

Having divorced a woman cannot again be "Esainoti" to another man, but if the husband dies, then, she can be married again in the same way.

The exchange of bridewealth was central to a "proper marriage" and key to patrilineal claims over children, according to these male elders (or, at least, as interpreted by the British administrator).[64] But they also acknowledged the existence of divorce and the possibility that even these "proper wives" might choose to leave their husbands, live with other men, and even have children with them. Moreover, the next paragraph described alternate routes to becoming a "proper" wife: "If a man and a woman live together for some time, even to having children, they can at any time by giving the correct bride-price get married in this way and legalise their position, provided that the woman is not barred by a previous divorce or other reason from becoming an 'Esainoti.'"

The second category of woman was called *engapiani*. According to the British official, "this is the wife in a marriage which though perfectly legal in Masai eyes is not the best form of marriage. It might be compared to a marriage in a registry office whereas 'Esainoti' is marriage in a church." It is unclear whether this kind of marriage was not "the best form" in his opinion or that of the elders. The difference seems to be in the kind, quantity, and manner in which the bridewealth was transferred, although the details are unclear. "The man pays a bride-price to the bride's father which is called 'mahongo,' not proper 'mahari.' There is no fixed amount and it may be more or less than the 'mahari.'" Since *mahongo* is the Swahili word for "bribes," and the transfer is made from the man to the woman's father in contrast to the usual distribution of bridewealth gifts from the relatives of the groom to a range of the bride's relatives, including her mother, I would argue that we are beginning to see in the 1950s what contemporary Maasai refer to disparagingly as the "selling" of a girl by a greedy (or needy) father to a wealthy man (see chapter 2). This form of marriage contrasts markedly with the first kind described above, in which a marriage was arranged between two families from different clans who exchanged bridewealth to strengthen their social connections, ensure the care of the woman, and determine the custody and lineage of her children.

My interpretation is supported by the ensuing description of what happens if the man and woman separated:

> On separation if there are no children the bride-price is returned, and the woman is free to be married again. If there is one child it stays with the mother and the bride-price is returned. If there is more than one child no bride price is returned and the children are divided as follows: First, third, fifth etc. to the mother. Second, fourth, sixth etc. to the father.
>
> Anything given to the woman during marriage, e.g., clothes, food, etc. cannot be claimed afterwards. They are her property. Similarly, the woman cannot claim anything from the husband.

The alternating allocation of children to the mother and father alone, regardless of their gender, suggests that the transfer of goods between the prospective husband and the woman's father was not considered bridewealth, but a payment, much like the "bribe" that it was called in Swahili.

The third category of woman described in the report was *engolioi*, or a widow. According to the elders, a widow should live in the homestead of the man "who inherits her," regardless of whether or not she had children. Any children she bore after the death of her husband "bear the name of the deceased husband." As the official added, "For a woman to bear children in this way is honourable in Masai eyes." A childless widow who "does not wish to live with her late husband's heir . . . may return to her father to be married again, but the bride-price must first be returned."

And finally, the most interesting category of woman for this analysis is the *esindani*:

> This is a prostitute or unmarried free lover, who either lives with her father or wanders about living with any man.
>
> It may happen that she sticks to one man—his tribe is irrelevant—and they get on well together without any agreement with her father and without any payment to him of any kind. She may even have children. These children are her property and the father has no claim to them, but he is paid a female calf by [the typescript ends, but someone has penned in "???? father or woman herself"].
>
> It is possible for a woman of this sort to have her own property, cattle, goats or cash, begged from her relatives or obtained in other ways, and even a hut. Her lover has no claim to any of this property. Similarly the woman can make no claim on the man for any of his property.
>
> If the man is in a position to make their connection legal by the payment of "mahari" or "mahongo" he may do so and she then becomes "Esainoti" or "Engapiana" depending on the circumstances.

The very existence of this category of woman, a "free lover" who could have relations with a series of men, bear and keep her own children, and own livestock and other property, suggests that, at least at this time, Maasai women had significant agency and autonomy in deciding whether to consent to an arranged marriage or pursue a partnership of their own choosing. Moreover, the fact that a group of elder men describes these women as a category indicates that there were more than a few of these female "free lovers."

The document thus described at least three kinds of adult women, in addition to widows. They ranged from *esainoti*, a "proper" wife married through the exchange of bridewealth and with the consent of her parents, to *esindani*, an "unmarried free lover" who chose her partners, retained custody of her children, and controlled her own property.[65] *Engapiani* (sometimes written as *enkapiana*) was located in the middle of the spectrum of relationships. Alan Jacobs reported that in the 1960s, such unions (which he called "concubinage") were "frequent in occurrence and often permanent in duration" (Jacobs 1970, 29). For him, these unions did "not constitute marriage" since bridewealth was not "handed over by the man nor accepted by the woman's father or guardian," thus "any children born of the union are the legal property of the women's father or guardian" (Jacobs 1970, 29).[66] While the elders in 1952 described *engapiani* as a different kind of union based on how and by whom bridewealth was transferred (as a "bribe" rather than exchange), other sources described *engapiani* as a woman who was living with the man of her choice rather than the choice of her parents. Writing about *engapiani* in a slightly later period, Paul Spencer, for example, called her "a trial wife who is really not in her husband's possession,"[67] but he acknowledged that "more strictly it refers to a woman who has run away to live with her lover" (Spencer 1988, 32). Similarly, S. S. ole Sankan explained that "in some cases a woman goes to live with a man without following the customs stated above [for *esainoti*]. She is relegated one stage below a properly-married wife and is known as 'Enkapiani' as opposed to 'Esainoti.' Should the 'marriage' break down due to disagreements or other factors, she is allowed to return to her parents' home with the children who might have resulted from the 'marriage'" (1971, 47). Others described *enkapiani* as "come we stay" marriage (Khamasi and Maina-Chinkuyu 2005, 102, 128).

Some Maasai men, both young and old, argued that the presence of these "free lovers" was itself a recent historical product, blaming the "exposure" of Maasai women to the unruly ways of women from other "tribes." In a

1950 letter in Swahili to the district officer from a group of "young Christian Maasai men," they contrasted marriage "laws" (*sheria za ndoa*) from the past (*zamani*) with the present (*sasa*), claiming that while most of the laws from the past were still followed, others had become "useless" (*ovyo ovyo*) "because women are seeing the practices of other tribes who follow the practices of prostitutes (*umalaya*) such as living freely without husbands. Moreover, these days many women are refusing to marry men who are very old, instead they are chasing young men (Ilmoran). Also, these days increasing numbers of men are selling (*huuza*—'habitually selling') their daughters to any man in order to buy property."[68]

These young Christian men, however, were not happy with either the practices of the past or the present. Instead, they argued that the practice of marrying young girls to old men should be stopped and that women should be able to marry the men they loved.

Similarly, some elder men were also clearly not happy either with what they perceived as the increased challenges to their authority from unruly wives and disobedient daughters. One agenda item for the 1955 annual meeting of the Olkiama, for example, was "modification of existing customary law re wife beating and custody of children."[69] The district officer in Ngorongoro explained that "the elders are concerned at the protection which the law would extend to undutiful wives who may be severely beaten, to the point of maiming. While nothing should be done to losen [*sic*] the ties of traditional marriage some legislation may be necessary at this point, and also to cut down the interminable legislation as to custody of children."[70]

Although the 1952 "Masai Marriage Law" document and related material suggest many interesting questions (such as why the kind of woman was named rather than the relationship), the purpose of reproducing it here is to demonstrate the challenges that colonial administrators faced in trying to understand and codify fixed rules about marriage, bridewealth, child custody, and other family matters. The kinds of unions that were recognized (if not always preferred, at least by male elders), and thus the meanings and practices of "marriage," were multiple, dynamic, and, at times, contested. Elders seemed as concerned with the process of forming a union (was bridewealth exchanged?) as with the result. Some kinds of relationships, like elopement, had a long history, while others, like selling a girl, were perhaps more recent, the product of changing economic and social horizons. Polygyny shaped the constraints and opportunities for men and women in markedly different ways. Christian missionaries introduced new forms such as companionate marriage, buttressed by the ideals of monogamy, fidelity, and permanence.

Moreover, the motivations behind different kinds of relationships, and the resulting disputes, were not always clear. Parents may have objected to their daughter's elopement less because she disobeyed their decisions about whom she should marry and more because they worried about her prospective mate's ability to provide for her social and economic well-being and that of her children.[71] Despite these questions and concerns, however, women and men exercised different kinds of rights, responsibilities, and autonomy in these relationships as they pursued the complex and sometimes contradictory goals and values of love, respect, procreation, pleasure, security, and more.

THE LEGACIES OF COLONIAL LEGAL REGIMES

British efforts to create a distinct domain of law based on their ideas of "natural justice"—through the implementation of "impartial" judicial procedures, creation of native courts with higher-level courts for appeals, appointment of certain elder Maasai men as native authorities, and, eventually, the codification of customary law with a focus on aspects of "family law"—had numerous consequences. The very definition of law—as a distinct field of social relations shaped by clear, unchanging principles—represented a starkly different way of addressing and resolving disputes and transgressions than that practiced historically by Maasai (and other African peoples) in which social relationships, moral authority, context, and other circumstances were considered. Although the sparse evidence suggests that in comparison to other groups and areas, Maasai seldom brought cases to the native courts, the effects of the implementation of the colonial legal regime were still profound, especially for Maasai gender relations. Moreover, as we shall see in subsequent chapters, the legacies of this regime, including its assumptions about gender, culture, and the lives of illiterate rural women, shaped the form and content of legal interventions after independence in 1961 and continue to inform legal regimes and advocacy today in the frame of women's human rights.

First, the creation of the courts and reliance on the "wisdom" of elder men as legal authorities strengthened the political and legal authority of elder men at the expense of the power and involvement of junior men and women.

The locus of power and authority, which was dispersed among respected men and women, became concentrated in one older male person (the Laibon) or just a few older men (the native courts). The creation of a territorial system of legal courts rather than reliance on established social networks of power and relationships (age sets, clans, sections) made it possible for one person to exert tremendous power by deciding cases for many sections and clans. And from the beginning, the British overlooked the power of Maasai women to render justice in minor domestic disputes and, more visibly, for gross violations of the moral order, like incest.

Moreover, since decisions were now made by the verdicts of one or several elder men, few of whom were perceived as respected leaders by Maasai, instead of by the collective consensus of a group of elders, the possibilities for self-interest, corruption, and biased decisions actually increased rather than decreased. For example, a man named Barnoti was appointed by the British in 1930 as a "headman" with the legal authority to settle disputes. He was soon accused of corruption by the British for accepting a bribe from an elder who wanted to raid the cattle of a neighbor as part of a long-standing "blood revenge" that "very nearly resulted in a pitched battle between two large parties of warriors of opposing clans." The district officer complained that Barnoti (and another elder) were "ineffectual"; they were "elected in the usual Maasai way, for their lack of personal force and inability to compel Masai obedience. The Masai are afraid of electing persons who will make them do things they do not want to do."[72] However ineffectual Barnoti may have been, it was the British insistence on creating the post of headman and providing men like Barnoti with juridical authority that produced the possibility for the kind of corruption of which Barnoti was accused.

The authority of elder men was further strengthened in the late colonial period when British administrators began to more systematically codify customary laws, especially regarding marriage, divorce, bridewealth, and child custody. Colonial versions of customary law reflected an interested perspective. As they sought to learn about customary law, they queried senior men, who, in a time of numerous challenges to their authority, reported strict rules that tightened their control over women and junior men, including limitations on junior men's rights and practices as warriors, power over women and children through bridewealth, and strict enforcement of arranged marriage. Evidence from the few available case summaries and from colonial reports suggest that, as elsewhere, these efforts to create and impose fixed, interested versions of customary law rather than resolve marital disputes through customary practices only heightened the struggles between men and women that were already amplified by shifting political, economic, and social power in other domains (Hodgson 2001a). Moreover, once written and codified, these "customary" laws lost their flexibility: their ability to probe the content and context of various charges, assess the relationships among people involved, and otherwise attend to the specifics of each case. And, as we shall see in the following chapter, these fixed, interested versions of "customary" law had consequences for the future. Although they differed from the precolonial practices and ideas, they were the versions referred to and enforced with the formal implementation of legal pluralism in the postcolonial period.

Second, even if Maasai men and women still relied primarily on customary modes of handling transgressions and resolving disputes, the colonial legal regime introduced not only new forms of authority, but new categories, languages, and ideas for understanding justice and injustice. Most fundamentally, of course, was the very idea of "law" as a distinct domain with separate legal institutions and authorities premised on British principles and procedures of "natural justice" as adapted to "native" courts. Related concepts that would have a lasting legacy were the language of individual rights, the reframing of certain transgressions from collectively enforced violations of the moral order to civil or criminal wrongs, and the creation of new transgressions like adultery and trespassing. Individual rights were distinct and sometimes in conflict with communal entanglements, emphasizing autonomy over social affiliation.[73] The focus was on the actions of individuals, the accused and accuser, with little attention to their relationships, context and histories of interaction, or ideals of *enkanyit, osotua*, or *sinyati*. Transgressions were now framed as secular crimes, not as moral violations against Eng'ai's will. Of course, despite being avowedly secular, colonial legal regimes were predicated on Christian ideals of morality that privileged monogamy, fidelity, female virginity, and more. Finally, by shifting responsibility for the enforcement of decisions to the authority of colonial officials, the colonial legal regime worked to undermine customary mechanisms for ensuring compliance (such as social pressure, shame, cursing, and *enkanyit*), *osotua* (social interdependence), and recognition of Eng'ai's authority to monitor and regulate human affairs.

Moreover, the British asserted their moral and cultural superiority by claiming that their legal system was premised on "natural justice" and by invoking the "repugnancy clause" to critique and criminalize certain African practices and beliefs as inherently "barbaric." The new ideas, procedures, and institutions they introduced were not alternatives to indigenous legal regimes but morally superior replacements. In the early colonial period during the height of the ideology of indirect rule, most administrators took a gradualist approach to social change, assuming that African peoples like Maasai would improve their "backward" ways through education and exposure to "civilised standards." To some extent their approach was deeply pragmatic and political; they recognized the limitations of their control over a vast terrain and complicated peoples, the need to cultivate the complicity of elder men to ensure political calm and compliance, and the priority of other tasks, such as finding sources of revenue to support the colonial enterprise. The economic demands and resulting social upheavals of the aftermath of World War II, however, produced more forceful interventions. The British could no longer wait for "culture" to evolve. They had to accelerate "modernization" and "progress" by legislating proper behavior.

Finally, the repeated efforts of Eleanor Rathbone, the St. Joan's Alliance, and other British individuals and organizations with no direct involvement in "native affairs" to advocate on behalf of "their African sisters" were the precursor, as we shall see in chapter 3, to the contemporary global, racial, and class dynamics of some women's human rights initiatives. The colonial and contemporary campaigns shared a presumption that rural African women were inherently oppressed, more vulnerable to violence, and incapable of asserting their own agendas and priorities. Both movements blamed culture as the source of women's oppression, rather than the colonial and postcolonial economic and political processes that undermined women's economic security and political power. They characterized culture as fixed, unchanging, and patriarchal, and thus in need of state-sponsored legal interventions to force change. The debates between British administrators (who positioned themselves as the defenders of women's status) and early feminist advocates (who challenged colonial administrators to "improve" women's status) presaged contemporary debates between advocates and activists, especially in the founding presumption that they knew, without asking, the realities and priorities of the very women they are claiming to support.

NOTES

1. Ethnicity and other forms of collective self-identification are dynamic, relational, and situational. The primary collective bonds during this period (and for many Maasai still today) were to one's lineage, clan, moiety, and section. Over time, numerous Maa-speaking sections like Kisongo, the largest section in Tanzania, came to see themselves as part of a supra-ethnic group called "Maasai," which shared certain social practices (like clans, male age sets, key life-stage rituals) in common while maintaining some differences in dress, ritual leadership, and other domains (Spear and Waller 1993).

2. These sources include oral histories that I have collected in my research; critical readings of early colonial ethnographies, especially by Moritz Merker (1910 [1904]), a German officer resident in northern Tanzania in the early 1900s, and Alfred C. Hollis (1905), a British officer who worked in Kenya in the early 1900s and later served as secretary then chief secretary in Tanganyika; and early archival evidence from colonial memoirs, letters, correspondence, reports, and more available in the Tanzania National Archives [TNA], Arusha Branch of the TNA [ATNA], Rhodes House Library [RHL], and other sites.

3. For a description of various ordeals, see Merker 1910 [1904], 219–20; Hollis 1905, 345; Maguire 1928, 17–18; Hodgson 2005, 63–64.

4. One of the most well-known examples of restorative justice is the Zapotec idea of "making things balance out" studied by Laura Nader (1991).

5. According to Merker (1910 [1904], 221), killing a non-Maasai was not understood as a transgression and therefore did not require compensation.

6. The amount of cattle paid seems to have varied. Merker reports that at times the payments were up to two to three hundred cattle, although he noted that it was often less (Merker 1910 [1904], 214). H. R. McClure, a British assistant district officer in Kenya at the time, claimed that by 1911 there was a fixed payment of nine head of cattle or forty-nine sheep. He notes, however, that "in pre-British times, the compensation paid seems to have varied very much. The relations of the dead man appear to have assessed the amount at what they pleased or rather at what they could deprive the offender by force. Forty nine head of cattle is said to have been the penalty some years ago. The Maasai themselves seem to be rather hazy on this point" (McClure, in Southern Masai Reserve District Political Book from the Commencement to the 31 December 1911, 38, copy from Oscar Watkins deposit, Mss Afr s 1409, RHL).

7. Tanganyika, 1930. "Native Administration Memorandum No II: Native Courts," 2nd edition, Dar es Salaam, p. 1. Cited in Iliffe 1979, 323.

8. The British established courts of common law for whites and other "non-natives," including a district magistrate court, a resident magistrate court, and the High Court (Bierwagen and Peter 1989, 398–390).

9. The support of Cameron (and other administrators) for the implementation of native courts, reliance on customary law, and involvement of colonial officers as legal authorities prompted continued and often fierce opposition from many British lawyers and magistrates, who felt that justice would only be achieved by a total imposition of British laws and procedures (Morris and Read 1972; cf. Chanock 1985, 48–67). One controversial issue was Cameron's demand that lawyers not be allowed to represent clients or argue cases in native courts, a principle that was codified by the 1929 Native Courts Ordinance.

10. Lewin graduated in law at the University of Cape Town, where he was called to the bar in 1930. In 1933, he moved to London, where he served as assistant secretary to the Royal African Society, became a barrister in London, a tutor and research assistant to the Colonial Department of the University of London Institute of Education, and then lecturer in colonial administration at the London School of Economics and Political Science. In 1939, he returned to South Africa to work and teach at the University of Witwatersrand, where he eventually became head of the Department of Social Anthropology and African Government. He was recognized as a key influence in developing the study of African government and law as both a scholar and journalist (Blacking and Pines 1968; Pines 1985).

11. Lewin (1938, 16) cites the relevant statutes and case law, beginning with section 19 of the Nigeria and the Gold Coast Supreme Court Ordinance of 1876. The 1920 Tanganyika Order in Council, which formalized British control of Tanganyika, introduced the general body of laws for the territory. Among other things, the order codified the repugnancy clause by requiring all courts in which "natives" were parties to "be guided by native law so far as it is applicable and not *repugnant* to justice and morality" (article 24, my italics). Similar versions of the repugnancy clause were repeated in subsequent laws, including the 1951 Local Courts Ordinance, which advised local courts that they could administer the local "customary law" where "it is not *repugnant* to natural justice or morality or is not, in principle, in conflict with the provisions of any law in force in the Territory" (article 15[a], my italics).

12. See, for example, correspondence between E. D. Browne, the senior commissioner at the time, and P. E. Mitchell, then the secretary for native affairs in Tanganyika in TNA Secretariat 2860/35.

13. P. E. Mitchell, 20 August 1925, handwritten comments. TNA Secretariat 2860/35.

14. P. E. Mitchell, typed comments about letter from E. D. Browne, Senior Commissioner, to Chief Secretary, 12 Oct 1925, TNA Secr 2860/35.

15. For example, in a 1925 letter to E. D. Browne, Mitchell attached some "translated extracts from Merker's work 'Die Masai.'" Chief Secretary to Senior Commissioner, 4 November 1925, TNA Secr 2860/35. See Merker 1910 [1904].

16. Masai District Native Courts Order, 1926. TNA 69/55/MS.

17. District Officer, Masai (Longido) (H. C. Murrells) to Provincial Commissioner, Arusha, 28 Feb 1927, "Native Courts, Councils, and Authorities Organisation," TNA 69/55/MS.

18. Handwriting on District Officer, Masai (Longido) (H. C. Murrells) to Provincial Commissioner, Arusha, 28 Feb 1927, "Native Courts, Councils, and Authorities Organisation" TNA 69/55/MS.

19. G. S. Kitching, for Acting Provincial Commissioner, Northern Province, to District Officer Masai, 16 March 1927, "Masai" TNA 69/55/MS.

20. P. E. Mitchell, Acting Provincial Commissioner, Northern Province, to Chief Secretary, 16 March 1927, TNA 17/43.

21. See, for example, P. E. Mitchell, Acting Provincial Commissioner, Northern Province, to Chief Secretary, 16 March 1927, TNA 17/43; Baxter, Acting District Officer, Masai, to Provincial Commissioner, Northern Province, 5 August 1933, "Native Authorities – Masai," TNA 69/54/MS/II; District Commissioner, Masai, to Provincial Commissioner, Northern Province, 17 April 1948, TNA 17/54.

22. While the Native Courts Ordinance of 1920 made the native courts subordinate to the High Court, the Native Courts Amendment Ordinance of 1929 shifted control of the native courts to the provincial commissioner and created a separate system of appeals (Bierwagen and Peter 1989, 397–98). Up to the late 1930s, the appeals were heard directly by the district officer or provincial commissioner, but by the mid-1940s they had established their own "appeal courts" to hear such cases (see also Gulliver 1963, 167–68). The Tanganyika Local Courts Ordinance of 1951 renamed the native courts "local courts." In the Northern Province, the number of appeals to these higher levels rose steadily through the years as a result of the increasing numbers of cases being heard by the "native" and "local" courts and the expanded awareness by litigants of their right to appeal. In 1939, for example, there were 66 appeals to the district officers and 6 to the provincial commissioner (Northern Province Annual Report [AR] 1939, 48). By 1944, these had increased to 113 to the district officers, 29 to the provincial commissioner, and 5 to the governor (Northern Province AR 1944, 57). In 1955, a total of 642 cases were appealed to the local courts, 262 to the district officers and 63 to the provincial commissioner (Northern Province AR 1955, 77; Northern Province AR 1956, 89).

23. See, for example, Northern Province Annual Report 138, 49.

24. See, for example, District Officer, Masai (Longido) (H. C. Murrells) to Provincial Commissioner, Arusha, 28 Feb 1927, "Native Courts, Councils, and Authorities Organisation" TNA 69/55/MS; G. S. Kitching, for Acting Provincial Commissioner, Northern Province, to District Officer, Masai, 16 March 1927, "Masai" TNA 69/55/MS; P. E. Mitchell, Acting Provincial Commissioner, Northern Province, to Chief Secretary, 16 March 1927, TNA 17/43.

25. H. C. Murrells, District Officer, Masai, to Provincial Commissioner, Northern Province, 1 May 1930, "Masai Native Authorities," TNA 69/47/MS.

26. According to Maguire, Laibon Parit demurred in his support; "[he] asked me to say that he cannot be responsible for the authenticity of what follows, though he has no doubt that it is correct, but being a comparatively young man of the Seure age set, he has not the knowledge of these things that the Elders have" (Maguire 1928, 12).

27. The secretary of state's request (dated March 8, 1930) and the responses and selected enclosures are reprinted in Colonial No. 65, "Papers Relating to the Health and Progress of Native Populations in Certain Parts of the Empire" (London: HMSO, 1931). These include Governor Cameron's response (May 22, 1930) enclosing a long report from P. E. Mitchell, then secretary for native affairs, on "Female Circumcision and the Status of Women in Tanganyika Territory" (April 26, 1930).

28. Donald Cameron to Secretary of State for the Colonies, 22 May 1930. Reprinted in Colonial No. 65, "Papers Relating to the Health and Progress of Native Populations in Certain Parts of the Empire" (London: HMSO, 1931), 41–52. See also D. J. J., "Notes made [indecipherable] discussion in House of Commons Committee Room on status of African women and initiation rites in Tanganyika, 22 July 1930, Mss Perham 501(2), RHL.

29. Cameron, 22 May 1930; D. J. J., "Notes made [indecipherable] discussion in House of Commons Committee Room on status of African women and initiation rites in Tanganyika, 22 July 1930, Mss Perham 501(2), RHL.

30. Harold MacMichael to Secretary of State for the Colonies, 6 February 1937. Reprinted in Cmd. 5784, "Correspondence Relating to the Welfare of Women in Tropical Africa 1935–37" (London: HMSO, 1938), 27–30. See letter from Ormsby Gore, Colonial

Office to MacMichael, Governor, 17 August 1936, and other correspondence generally in file TNA Secretariat/24450/I titled "Forced Marriage of African Girls."

31. Letter from Mogue to Young, 6 March 1941, TNA Secretariat 24450/II.

32. Once limited suffrage for women was achieved in 1918, the St. Joan's Social and Political Alliance (which was originally called "The Catholic Women's Suffrage Society) broadened its mission to include other women's issues in Britain (such as the age of marriage) and, increasingly, practices they believed were responsible for the "appalling conditions under which so many millions of women spend their lives" in the colonies (St. Joan's Alliance 1961, 14).

33. The St. Joan's Alliance, "Status of African Women." *The Catholic Citizen* 21, no. 3, 15 March 1935, 20.

34. "Statement from St. Joan's Social and Political Alliance on the Status of the Women of Native Races," presented to the XVIII Assembly of the League of Nations. Copy in TNA Secr 124450/II.

35. Antoinette Burton (1994) explored the imperial context and racialized assumptions of similar feminist organizations in Britain. These groups claimed "global sisterhood" with Indian women during the preceding historical period.

36. Cameron, 22 May 1930, 50.

37. Mitchell, 26 April 1930, 58.

38. Mitchell, 26 April 1930, 58.

39. Christine Spender, "Forced Marriages in Africa," *The Catholic Citizen* 24, no. 9, 15 September 1938.

40. See generally articles in St. Joan's publication, *The Catholic Citizen*.

41. Northern Province, Annual Provincial Reports, 1935–1948.

42. Page-Jones, District Commissioner, Masai, to District Officer, Kajiado, Kenya Colony, 15 June 1942, TNA 17/38.

43. Page Jones, District Commissioner, Masai to District Commissioner, Moshi, 25 August 1942, TNA 17/38.

44. Webster, Acting Provincial Commissioner, Northern Province to Chief Secretary, 4 May 1928, TNA 69/47/MS/2.

45. Criminal case 10 of 1931. ATNA/Monduli Criminal Cases.

46. Eric Rowe, District Officer, Loliondo, to Provincial Commissioner, Northern Province, 19 Dec 1935, "Memorandum on Native Administration among the Masai west of the Rift," TNA 17/43.

47. The cases included a Maasai woman who was accused of murdering her husband (she was eventually acquitted by the High Court), a young man who "accidently" killed a man with his sword at night, and a young man who died from an infected wound after a fight. Metau d/o Lengusho, murder. 17 November 1932. Case 333 of 1932, ATNA Court Records/Criminal Cases; Inquest 1 of 1932, Monduli Criminal Cases, ATNA; Inquest 2 of 1932, Monduli Criminal cases, ATNA.

48. In 1955, for example, Oldus Elshira, a Maasai *olmurran*, was acquitted by the High Court in Moshi for the alleged murder of Harold M. Stuchbery, a European farmer. Through his lawyer, Elshira admitted to the court that he killed Stuchbery, but he explained that he had done so in "self-defense" after Stuchbery threatened him and his friends with his gun for "trespassing" on his land at night with their cattle. Despite the acquittal, Maasai elders from his clan collected cattle as "blood money" to compensate Stuchbery's widow for her loss (Mbogoni 2013).

49. The phenomenon of "runaway wives" was widespread in Tanganyika and other parts of sub-Saharan Africa throughout the colonial period, but especially at this time. For Tanganyika, see Mbilinyi (1988) and Lovett (2001). For other parts of Africa see Byfield (2001), Allman (1996), and Schmidt (1990).

50. See, for example, "Sheria la Mahari za Kimaasai" [Maasai Bridewealth Laws], undated; "Sheria za Ndoa ya Maasai [Maasai Marriage Laws]," 20 July 1950; "Masai Marriage Law," 15 May 1952; and "Maasai Custom to be Followed in the Hearing of Cases," undated—all in TNA 17/250/1. Colonial officers consulted Merker (1910 [1904]), Hollis (1905), Krapf (1968 [1860]), and Thomson (1968 [1885]), among others. Chief Secretary to Senior Commissioner, 4 November 1925, TNA Secr 2860/35; R. A. J. Maguire to Page Jones, District Officer, Masai, 12 March 1937, TNA 69/54/MS/II.

51. "Memorandum on a Speech Made to the Ol'Kiama of 13th August 1948," ATNA 284/II.

52. District Officer, Loliondo, to District Commissioner, Masai, "Olkiama Ol'Masai—September, 1949," 19 August 1949, ATNA 284/II.

53. J. C. Clarke, "Notes for Provincial Annual Report, 1950, Masai District." TNA 69/63/20.

54. "Annual Report, 1951, Masai District." TNA 69/63/20.

55. Letter from Masai Leaders to District Commissioner, Masai District, 16 September 1950, ATNA 284/II.

56. "Khati ya Shauri ya Kunakili," 1955, TNA 17/38.

57. J. C. Clarke, "Notes for Provincial Annual Report, 1950, Masai District." TNA 69/63/20. According to Gulliver's study in the late 1950s, Arusha Maasai also preferred to try to resolve their disputes among themselves rather than through the local courts (Gulliver 1963, 167).

58. "Annual Report, 1951, Masai District." TNA 69/63/20.

59. I witnessed an *inkipot* ceremony in 1992 in Embopong'.

60. According to Merker (1910 [1904], 44), "The father first of all sues for the girl from her mother, after which the bridegroom assures himself of the girl's consent." Similarly, Jacobs (1970, 33) reports that "though formal consent of the girl is not required, in practice a suitor normally will not force himself upon such a girl who openly shuns his intentions."

61. According to Merker, her parents did not simply accept the situation, but there were ways to have the "marriage" recognized as official:

> Then it happens that the girl's father sends a crowd of boys armed with sticks, in pursuit of her, to beat her until she consents to return. As the boys are acting on the instructions of the parents, neither the bridegroom not anyone else may hinder them. Only one course remains open for the bridegroom in order to protect his bride from such deeds of violence—to leave the homestead with her at once and repair to the woods for a few days. By this action he indicates that anyone who dares to take his bride from him will be met by armed opposition. He also thereby deprives the girl's father of any further right to vote in the marriage. Directly the pair have eaten a beast in the forest, they return to the homestead, where they are recognized as married without any further ceremonies. (Merker 1910 [1904], 46)

62. Accusations that men had "sold" their daughters became more prevalent in both Kenya and Tanzania, and they continue today (Talle 1988, 135–36).

63. "Masai Marriage Law," 15 May 1952. TNA 17/250/1.

64. Although colonial officials, early scholars, and others often referred to "bride-price" and "dowry" to name the exchange of gifts between the families of a man and a woman, "bridewealth" is the preferred term.

65. Aud Talle reports in 1995 that *esindani* was used by Maasai men and women in Tanzania to describe their three or four "permanent lovers" in addition to their spouses (who are distinct from their temporary or occasional love relationships [*engare engeene*]) (Talle 1995, 76).

66. Other kinds of relationships have been reported as well, including women who are exchanged without the transfer of bridewealth, and the exchange of sisters (*enkibelekenyuta oo ntoyie*) between close friends and age mates (Talle 1988, 146).

67. According to Spencer (1988, 32), the early relationship is treated as a "trial marriage" because bridewealth was not fully transferred, the woman has not borne any children, and thus the marriage is not considered fully "stable."

68. "Sheria za ndoa ya Masai" [Maasai marriage laws], July 20, 1950. TNA 17/250/1/5. My translation from the Swahili original.

69. "Olkiama 1955 Agenda." Undated, ATNA 284/II.

70. District Officer, Ngorongoro, to District Commissioner, Masai District, 1 March 1955, "Ol-Kiama Agenda 1955," ATNA 284/II.

71. Carolyn Archambault (2011) provides a brilliant analysis of these trade-offs and concerns in contemporary debates about early marriage and arranged marriage among Maasai in Kenya.

72. H. C. Murrells, District Officer, Masai, to Provincial Commissioner, Northern Province, 1 May 1930, "Masai Native Authorities," TNA 69/47/MS.

73. I draw these terms and ideas from Naila Kabeer (2011).

CHAPTER 2

Debating Marriage

National Law and the Culture of Postcolonial Rule

BY THE TIME TANZANIA ACHIEVED independence from colonial rule in 1961, the idea of "law" as a distinct domain was well established, as were the procedures, laws, and institutions created by the British. As in many post-colonial states, law became a key form of power wielded by elites to impose their moral visions and extend state power even into the most intimate spaces of families and households. To this end, state officials retained many laws from the colonial regime. But they also developed and implemented new laws, including some that formally recognized "customary" law and Islamic law as legitimate legal authorities for the resolution of most civil cases, especially those pertaining to "family law," as long as they did not conflict with national laws. Of course, as described in chapter 1, the version of customary law that was codified toward the end of the colonial period, and the male-dominated judicial structures in which customary resolutions were adjudicated (the "native courts" were eventually replaced with "local courts" then "magistrates courts"), were designed to support the interests of senior men and had little resonance with indigenous legal regimes.

While these laws were being passed, Maasai confronted and negotiated the ambiguities between the legacies of colonial interventions, which had enhanced the power of men as legal authorities, household "heads," political leaders, and property owners; President Nyerere's socialist vision, which promoted, at least rhetorically, the political and economic equality of women; and the flourishing of the state feminist organization, Umoja wa Wanawake wa Tanzania (UWT) and other groups of Tanzanian feminists among political and intellectual elites. Many of the heated debates among these educated Tanzanians about gender politics, nationalism, socialism, productivity, modernity, and "progress" demonized Maasai people as "primitive" and "backward," echoing the images and language of the St. Joan's Alliance and other European feminist activists during the colonial period. But now the racialized superiority of the British over African "natives" was reproduced in class terms, with elite, urban Tanzanians presuming that their education, literacy, and economic privilege empowered them to speak for rural, uneducated farmers and herders.[1] Of course, British racial ideologies were also class ideologies, and many elite Tanzanians justified their class position in racialized terms vis-à-vis Maasai. Indeed, even though, as described below, President Nyerere and his government tried to overcome "ethnic" differences in the interest of building a nation, Maasai were almost always marked by their ethnic/racialized differences, including, of course, by the continued recognition of customary law for civil disputes.

As in the late colonial period, the contours and content of "marriage" became a key site of concern and debate between state officials and women's activists, culminating in the passage of the Law of Marriage Act (LMA) of 1971. The LMA was the first national law in Tanzania to regulate aspects of marriage such as age, consent, and custody. But the LMA also formally recognized (colonial versions of) customary law, which produced dilemmas for groups like Maasai who were at once citizens protected by national law and ethnic subjects under the jurisdiction of customary law. This chapter explores the class, gender, and ethnic dynamics of the national legal regime in the context of early postcolonial Tanzania through the lens of marriage, comparing elite assumptions about "proper" marriage as reflected in the LMA with the changing dynamics of Maasai practices and ideas about marriage. To illustrate the consequences for Maasai gender and generational relations of the formal recognition of customary law and implementation of national laws, I analyze one of the first court cases in which a Maasai woman used the LMA to accuse her father of trying to marry her against her will. The case demonstrates that although the practices of rural, politically marginal peoples like Maasai were ignored in the design and passage of the

LMA, a few Maasai were able to overcome the barriers of language, access, and knowledge to take advantage of the law to argue for their "rights."

GENDER, CULTURE, AND LAW IN SOCIALIST TANZANIA

The decades after independence were a turbulent time in Tanzania, especially for gender relations, as numerous social, political, and economic projects and processes converged and often clashed. Central to all of these interventions was the forceful imposition of President Julius Nyerere's socialist vision of *Ujamaa* (Swahili for "familyhood"). As Nyerere declared in his famous "Arusha Declaration" of 1967, the goals of Ujamaa were to prevent exploitation (especially class exploitation) and promote self-reliant development in Tanzania through state ownership and management of resources and industries, increased agricultural productivity, economic self-reliance, the pursuit of collective welfare rather than individual greed, and "good leadership" by the government and the sole political party, Tanganyika African National Union (TANU) (Nyerere 1968). Under Nyerere's leadership, the Tanzanian government implemented a series of policies and laws in the 1960s and 1970s to try to produce a "nation" that at once built on and overcame the legacies of colonial rule. They made Swahili the national language and thus the mandatory language for politics, education, and law; instituted universal free primary education in 1977 with a required civics curriculum that extolled the virtues of Ujamaa and socialism; forcibly relocated farmers and herders (including Maasai) into Ujamaa villages; and prohibited references to ethnicity, insisting instead that all "citizens" call each other *ndugu* (comrade). These and other initiatives greatly expanded the power of the state and the one political party (renamed Chama Cha Mapinduzi [CCM, "Revolutionary Party"] in 1977) to control daily life and the media, suppress dissent, and demand certain social changes in the name of socialist "progress" (Hyden 1980, 1999; von Freyhold 1979; Yeager 1989; Jennings 2008; Hodgson 2001a; Ibhawoh and Dibua 2003).

The gendered politics and consequences of nationalist projects like Ujamaa during this period were complicated. In the Arusha Declaration, Nyerere vowed to "safeguard the inherent dignity of the individual in accordance with the Universal Declaration of Human Rights" and promised "to see that the Government gives equal opportunity to all men and women irrespective of race, religion, or status" (Nyerere 1968, 14–15). He praised the "hard work" of "village women" and chastised the laziness of village men (Nyerere 1968, 30). Despite these and other invocations of the rights of women and value of gender equality, Ujamaa was predicated on a deeply romanticized, paternalistic idea of gender, family, and the virtues of "traditional African society" in which male elders managed political and economic affairs, women as mothers were responsible for the social and spiritual welfare of their families, and younger men worked to support their families and protect them from harm (Nyerere 1968, 4–5; Hodgson 2001a, 151–54; Lal 2010, 2015). As Priya Lal has argued, this state paternalism, with its implicit and sometimes explicit gender and generational coding, was replicated at every level of society, from the management of national resources by the male-dominated state and political party "for the good of the people" to the efforts of the official women's wing of TANU, Umoja wa Wanawake wa Tanzania (UWT)[2] to teach "modern" methods of child care, food preparation, and hygiene in addition to literacy (Lal 2010, 7). Even women's appearance and comportment were the subject of state-sponsored sanctions, such as a series of public campaign beginning in 1968 against miniskirts, makeup, hair straighteners, and other so-called "bourgeois," "inauthentic," "Western" cultural practices (Ivaska 2002, 2011). For instance, a 1972 meeting of TANU (male) elders and Sofia Kawawa, the national chair of UWT, resolved that "bar owners who allowed girls with dresses on their premises, such as miniskirts, hot pants and wigs, should not be granted trading licences. . . . The meeting discussed at length the disgraceful dresses put on by the youth of Dar es Salaam. The meeting agreed that UWT and TANU elders should jointly educate the youth on the need of safe guarding the nation's culture and on proper dresses."[3] These resolutions by elite male and female party members about the proper appearance of women were enforced by young men who roamed the streets harassing and sometimes beating "indecent" women (Ivaska 2002, 2011; Lal 2010). As in other nationalist projects where women were perceived as the embodiment of national culture and ideals, elite anxieties about women's dress reflected their broader concerns about the "proper" behavior, sexuality, autonomy, and mobility of young urban women.

The involvement of UWT in the dress campaign reveals some of the class and urban biases of Ujamaa and the nationalist effort. UWT was created as a self-standing national women's organization in 1962 from, among other organizations, the "Women's Section" of TANU that had been started in 1955 by the fearless female nationalist leader Bibi Titi Mohamed (Madabida

1974; Geiger 1982, 1987, 1997; Mulligan-Hansel 1999; Tenga and Peter 1996). UWT represented the institutionalization of state feminism; its policies and missions were designed to promote women's interests but always in alignment with state and party policies. The association between UWT and male government and party leaders was not just political but personal; many UWT leaders, like Sofia Kawawa, were the wives of these bureaucrats and politicians.[4] Because of this, some women workers accused UWT of being an organization of "big wives" more interested in protecting and promoting their elite class interests than in working toward radical change or the broad-based political empowerment of women (Mascarenhas and Mbilinyi 1983, 21–22; see also Tenga and Peter 1996). UWT did pressure the male-dominated government and party structure to achieve a few political victories, such as campaigning for the passage of the 1971 Law of Marriage Act (see below) and the 1975 Employment Ordinance (which provided maternity benefits to women workers) (Tenga and Peter 1996). But its dominant approach through the years was to organize urban, peri-urban, and to a far lesser extent rural woman into self-help groups to promote "gender-appropriate" income-generating activities (like food production, beer brewing, and managing small stores), adult literacy, and other "women-in-development" (WID)-type projects rather than to challenge gendered structures of power in their communities or the state (Geiger 1987; Mulligan-Hansel 1999). Women's political participation was channeled almost entirely through UWT structures, and only a few elite women who rose through the UWT leadership hierarchy achieved formal regional and national political positions (Mulligan-Hansel 1999).

Elite women were of course not a homogeneous group. At the same time that female leaders of UWT were promoting state interests, other elite women discussed gender issues, formed study groups, and eventually created organizations like the Women's Research and Documentation Project (WRDP) at the University of Dar es Salaam that called for more radical political projects and were, at times, critical of government policies and of UWT. The broad aims of the WRDP, for example, were:

> to promote the critical study and research of the women's question and gender issues in Tanzania in relation to problems and strategies of development at the local, national, and international levels; to focus on analysis of women in Africa in the context of issues of decolonization, national liberation, and socialist transformation; to use research, documentation, writing and publications,

and seminars to develop broad-based communications about gender issues and the women's question among Tanzanian women in particular; to develop a supportive context and collective framework for members and others who are concerned about women's issues; and to promote and encourage a participatory approach in research. (Meena and Mbilinyi 1991, 852)

Members of WRDP applied a "problem-oriented approach" that sought to clarify the causes of problems and influence policy through conducting and reporting research (Meena and Mbilinyi 1991, 855). They also tried to develop an organizational framework that would "sustain democratic and collective principles of decision-making" (Meena and Mbilinyi 1991, 857). In contrast to UWT's concerns with critiquing the proper dress of young women in towns or improving the child-care skills of rural women, WRDP focused on such issues as women's education, income-generating projects, schoolgirls' pregnancies, and women and the law (Meena and Mbilinyi 1991).

Whatever their differences of opinion and political agendas, none of these urban women's groups had much success involving or reaching out to rural or, as they were and still are often called, "grassroots" women. UWT's official organizational structure mirrored that of CCM: a tiered hierarchy of offices at each political-administrative level, from the local village branch through the district and region to the national office. In reality, however, they had little presence in rural areas far from Dar and other urban centers like Moshi and Arusha (Madabida 1974; Geiger 1982; Kuhanga and Kalokola 1990; Mulligan-Hansel 1999). Similarly, the WRDP and other university-based groups had limited access to grassroots women as well, despite occasional initiatives like the Jipemoyo participatory research projects.[5] Although it is difficult to assess how interested (or not) these women were in working with their rural counterparts, and all these organizations changed in terms of their membership, agendas, and perspectives over time, several other dimensions of the relationship are clear. First, UWT, WRDP, and other organizations faced numerous difficulties working in rural areas, especially given the poor roads, communication systems, and lack of infrastructure at the time (Geiger 1982; Mulligan-Hansel 1999; Meena and Mbilinyi 1991). Language was often a problem as well, as many rural Tanzanians who lived inland did not speak or understand Swahili with any fluency. Second, the leaders of these organizations generally shared a common perspective that illiterate, poor, rural women needed to be educated and assisted to over-

come the presumed desperation, drudgery, and ignorance that characterized their lives, and that the key obstacles preventing the "liberation" of
these women were their culture, customs, and traditions. When UWT revised its constitution in 1978 to include "the liberation of women" as one of
its objectives, it declared that it was "an organ of liberation for all Tanzanian
women from exploitation and all customs and traditions which are hamper-
ing their progress and that of the Nation as a whole" (UWT Constitution
1978, cited in Geiger 1982, 50). Finally, regardless of their political differences, most of these urban elites believed strongly in the power of law to
shape and "improve" troubling social practices and create modern, socialist
citizens. The postcolonial political structure of the one-party socialist state,
limited political autonomy of the judiciary, charismatic leadership of President Nyerere, and minimal channels for political debate and dissent made
designing and passing such laws relatively straightforward.

Legislating Marriage and Legal Pluralism

For Maasai, like other rural Tanzanians, several laws had more resonance
than others. First and foremost, "customary law" was formally recognized
as a source of law in 1961 by the Judicature and Application of Laws Act
(JALA).[6] Courts were advised to apply customary law in their deliberations
over civil matters "between members of a community in which rules of customary law relevant to the matter are established and accepted," unless the
law conflicted with "any written law." District councils (which eventually
replaced the native councils as the local form of government representation)
were empowered to record decisions and, if desired, request modifications
to local customary law. Moreover, the institutions for applying customary
(and Islamic law) were changed in the early 1960s through the creation of
a unitary three-tier court system (primary courts, district courts, High
Court) in mainland Tanzania that replaced all separate ethnic or religious
legal institutions such as native courts.[7] The lowest levels of courts (primary
courts, district courts, and resident magistrates courts) had jurisdiction
over minor civil debts, matrimonial proceedings, and cases involving customary law or Islamic law (Bierwagen and Peter 1989, 400). Each of these
lower-level courts was led by a magistrate and two assessors who advised the
magistrate (especially over cases where customary law or Islamic law was
applicable) and participated in the decision. Decisions could be appealed
by petition to the district courts. If the case involved issues of customary

or Islamic law, the district magistrate could sit with assessors for the case. District court decisions could also be appealed to the High Court by petition. The High Court could refer questions of customary law to a "panel of experts," but the court was not bound by their opinion (Bierwagen and Peter 1989, 401).

As discussed in chapter 1, the primary issues for which customary law was codified and applied were marriage, divorce, child custody, succession, inheritance, and certain property disputes. The form and content of what was considered customary law in 1961, however, was very different from the customary modes of resolving disputes and managing family relations that was practiced before colonial rule. Although JALA established the coverage of and procedures for customary laws, it did not specify the content of these (supposedly) diverse laws. In 1963, however, the Customary Law (Declaration) Order specifically mandated the support of patrilineal principles for disputes over guardianship, inheritance, and wills involving customary laws in patrilineal societies. Among other things, the law held that men were presumed to serve as guardians, husbands traveling on long journeys could appoint guardians to supervise their wives during their absences, and women could use but not inherit land. As is clear from this 1963 law, rural men, including Maasai, had taken advantage of the formalization and strengthening of their judicial and political powers through the formation of native authorities and native courts and colonial efforts to codify elder male versions of customary law. Their interested versions of customary law were then supported by the early expressions of state paternalism that at once idealized rural village life, reinforced the power of elder men as political and legal authorities, and pitied rural women for their seeming life of passive, powerless drudgery. The class bias was clear here: while elite women were increasingly provided some leadership opportunities by the state and party, rural or "grassroots" women were presumed to be too ignorant, constricted by their "culture," and in need of guidance to participate or lead.

State and party officials, however, under President Nyerere's leadership, had to navigate a delicate path in forging laws that would balance recognition and accommodation of cultural, ethnic, religious, and political differences among their constituents with their political ambition to transcend these same differences to build a sense of national unity and identity. These compromises were clearly evident in the formulation and passage of the LMA, which included key provisions on marital property, divorce, minimum age of marriage, and other "family law" matters. The LMA replaced what some commentators have called the "legal stew" (Rakstad, Kaiser, and Pribadi 2000, 92) of customary, religious, and common laws governing family relations with a common set of laws that superseded customary and Islamic law if there was a conflict in their provisions.[8] In an effort to accommodate customary and Islamic laws and practices, the LMA recognized the legitimacy of both monogamous and polygamous marriages (Article 10), set a younger minimum age of marriage for women (fifteen) than for men (eighteen) (Article 13), and recognized common law marriage (Article 160). But the LMA also strengthened the rights of women by requiring that no marriage could take place without "the consent, freely and voluntarily given" of all parties to the union (Article 16), requiring the consent of the first wife before a husband could marry a second wife (Article 20), granting married women the same rights as men to acquire, hold, and dispose of property (Article 56), providing women equal rights to petition for divorce (Article 107), and creating a right for women to demand maintenance from their husbands under certain conditions (Article 120).

Perhaps more than any other laws promulgated in Tanzania at the time (given the one-party state), the LMA was the product of much debate and compromise. After some initial concerns with certain proposed provisions, UWT leaders pushed hard for passage of the law, mobilizing both political and personal networks (especially the marriage between Sofia Kawawa, the president of UWT, and her husband Rashidi Kawawa, then vice president of Tanzania and the politician who led the debate and vote in Parliament) to pressure party members, politicians, members of Parliament (almost all of whom were male at this time), and the public (Tenga and Peter 1996).[9] Indeed, although the government initially planned for four weeks of public discussion of the proposed reforms (which were outlined in a white paper), President Nyerere twice extended the discussion period for several months because of the intensity of public discussion (Ivaska 2011, 175).

Certain provisions of the law were extensively discussed among urban elites in letters to the English and Swahili press, political cartoons, parliamentary sessions, and other forums, such as debates between educated husbands and wives over polygamy and marital property, between young men and senior men over bridewealth, and over other gender, generational, and class concerns (Mbilinyi 1972; Ivaska 2011). Different factions invoked "African tradition" to support or challenge their positions, whether as a value to be protected in the name of cultural heritage or an anachronism to be demolished on the road toward progress and modernity. According to Marjorie Mbilinyi (1972, 67), "One of the most debated sections [in the male-dominated Parliament] was that ensuring rights of inheritance for a widow at the time of her husband's death. Many M.P.s were outspoken in their opposition to this, on the grounds that women did not own property and therefore could not be entitled to inherit." Another controversial provision required the consent of the first wife before a husband could legally marry a second wife. One M.P. publicly complained that "if a man has to get his wife's consent to a second marriage, the African tradition where man has always been superior to a woman will be endangered. Unless the Law of Marriage Bill intends to change men into women this clause should be removed."[10] His invocation of "African tradition," which was echoed by other elite, senior men to defend polygamy and challenge the need for the first wife's consent, contrasted with the fervent accusations by elite women that polygamy (and the possibility to convert monogamous marriages into polygamous ones) was an "African tradition" that was outdated, primitive, and incompatible with a "modern," progressive nation like Tanzania premised on ideals of socialist equality (Ivaska 2011, 177–78). As one woman quipped, "This is 1969, gentlemen, not the Pleistocene era."[11] Similarly, young urban men denounced the increasingly large demands for bridewealth as an "African tradition" that should be stopped in the name of modernity and progress, but their demands received little support from senior men or women (Ivaska 2011, 191–200).

Marginal Citizens

For most Maasai men and women, the debates about customary law, culture, and "African tradition" by urban elites in discussions of the LMA and other laws and policies were not only inaccessible (since they took place in Swahili and English) but were far removed from their ongoing struggles for recognition, rights, and resources in a nation within which they were increasingly marginalized. At the same time that some urban elites celebrated a romanticized notion of "African tradition" (as male superiority or female modesty), most elite men and women scorned Maasai as "primitive" and "savage" because of their continued adherence to pastoralism as a primary livelihood and their marked cultural and linguistic differences from the dominant majority (Swahili-speaking farmers or urban workers).

While TANU and UWT leaders decried the miniskirts, straightened hair, and makeup of young women in the cities as inappropriate, state and TANU officials also waged intense media campaigns to force Maasai to "modernize" their dress and appearance. In 1968 and again in 1970, government officials launched "Operation Dress-Up," which banned old men from wearing blankets in the daytime, women from wearing leather dresses, anyone from wearing cloth treated with ochre, and *ilmurran* from treating their hair with ochre and growing it in pigtails. To ensure compliance, schoolchildren were "encouraged to ridicule Masai who were tribal dress,"[12] bus drivers were directed to reject passengers who did not comply with the regulations, and "no man or woman was allowed to use a public facility—shop, bus, dispensary, government office, etc.—unless he or she were wearing contemporary attire: shorts, trousers, dresses" (Ndagala 1990, 47; Hatfield 1977, 16; Schneider 2006). According to one report, "many Masai have been forcibly bathed and scrubbed to remove their paint, and their tribal costumes have been publicly burnt."[13] As Colby Hatfield, an American sociologist working in Maasai communities at the time, remarked, the government would "make the Masai modern by making them appear modern" (Hatfield 1977, 16).

In the name of socialist progress and "modernization," state and party officials waged other interventions to forcibly modernize Maasai and integrate them into the state.[14] As part of the national villagization campaign, many Maasai were relocated against their will during Operation Imparnati from their dispersed homesteads into concentrated "villages." These sometimes violent moves disrupted long-standing customary arrangements for access to grazing land, water, and other range resources based on clan and kin relations; concentrated the exploitation of resources for household use (wood, grass, and domestic water); and produced increased economic stratification and insecurity. In response, Maasai men and women sought to diversify their livelihoods through farming, wage labor, trade, and other productive strategies.[15] To "improve" the production and offtake of Maasai livestock for national benefit, the state partnered with the US Agency for International Development (USAID) to launch a ten-year (1969–1979), twenty-million-dollar project called the "Masai Range Project." Like earlier colonial interventions, the Masai Range Project focused on Maasai men as the presumed owners of livestock, household heads, and agents for economic development. Rather than address the political causes of the low productivity of Maasai livestock husbandry practices, increased overgrazing on remaining rangelands, and lack of access to permanent water supplies produced by the ongoing alienation of Maasai lands by the state for more productive pursuits, the project proposed technocratic solutions to solve these problems. These projects included constructing permanent water supplies, clearing brush to eradicate tsetse infestation, providing veterinary services and medicines, forming ranching associations, and providing training in "modern" livestock methods (Hodgson 2001a, 202–40). Although neither the state nor USAID had much interest in improving the social and economic conditions of Maasai people, and the Masai Range Project failed to meet its own technical goals, the project did exacerbate gender, generational, and class tensions among Maasai and reinforce their increasing distrust and dislike of the postcolonial state (Hodgson 2001a, 202–40).

The economic marginalization of Maasai reflected their exclusion from national politics and debates. Neither the state, TANU, or even UWT were visibly present in rural areas like Maasailand. Since so few Maasai men (much less women) were educated or fluent in Swahili, few were able to run for political office or participate in politics beyond the village level. As Hatfield commented in 1977, "Two general factors have influenced Masai participation. First, both modern governmental and political structures have only recently been implemented in Masailand. In many areas they are barely present. Thus the opportunity for participation and for political education is hardly there. Second, skilled manpower to enter into public office and administration is still in very short supply and will remain so until a cadre of better educated men and women is established. Thus the question of participation of Masai is less related to lack of desire for entry into public life than in a relatively negative opportunity structure" (19). Although he tried to encourage Maasai to join TANU in order to influence national decisions such as the dress code, he was told that "neither women nor morani [*ilmurran*] would join." "Of course," he added, "the Umoja wa Wanawake and TANU Youth League could hardly be said to be functioning in most of the rural areas of Maasailand" (Hatfield 1977, 16).

As Hatfield suggests, part of the problem was the almost complete absence of educational opportunities for Maasai girls or boys. Until the 1950s, colonial efforts to "preserve" Maasai culture and the reluctance of missionaries to work with them meant few primary schools. Once the Catholic and Lutheran churches finally built a couple of primary schools, they were designated for boys.[16] The lack of schools in Maasai areas continued after independence, despite a national policy for universal free primary education for all citizens. In 1977, for example, there were still no secondary schools in Maasai areas (Hatfield 1977, 2). A few boys attended secondary schools with the support of the missions, but girls only trickled into the schools in the 1990s. Maasai also lacked access to functioning health care facilities. In 1977, Hatfield characterized Maasailand as "woefully lacking adequate health care" (Hatfield 1977, 13), including both an absence of sufficient facilities and marked decline in the "quality of medical care" because of a lack of recurrent funds to operate government facilities.

To summarize, during this period, Maasai men and women experienced substantial economic dislocation, especially through the increased alienation of their lands, forceful efforts to change their livelihoods, and political disenfranchisement from the new national institutions of power. The various political and economic efforts by the state and others to "modernize" Maasai livestock production reified economic stratification among Maasai; a few herders were able to expand their herds, while most became increasingly impoverished.

They also sustained heightened attacks on their appearance and social and cultural practices. These interventions and changes were justified, in part, by dominant images of them as backward, primitive, and the antithesis of the self-proclaimed modernity of the national elites. According to one Tanzanian commentator, "We are trying to take the Masai from the Stone Age to the Atomic Age."[17]

Gender and Generation through the Prism of Marriage

These political, social, and economic changes provided new obstacles and opportunities to Maasai gender and generational relations, as seen most clearly through struggles over marriage and other forms of domestic union. As in the colonial period, marriage (and associated practices like polygyny, bridewealth transactions, child custody, divorce, sexual relations) was still a complicated process with multiple forms that reflected shifting gender and generational relations and, increasingly, educational, class, and religious differences. The ideal form of union continued to be a marriage arranged between the bride's and groom's parents (for the first wife) and recognized through the presentation of bridewealth gifts from the groom's family to the bride's over a period of time. This form provided the husband custodial rights over any children and confirmed the woman's status as an *esainoti*. A man was expected to follow these steps to marry additional wives, although often his first wife helped him select her new cowives. The other kinds of unions mentioned in the 1952 document discussed in the previous chapter also continued to exist: a woman (*engapiani*) who lived with a man of her choice without the exchange of bridewealth and a woman (*esindani*) who had lovers but retained custody of her children and property. Elopements increased, as did the number of educated men (and eventually women) seeking companionate forms of marriage. With the slow and uneven spread of Christianity, some couples preferred monogamy to polygyny. Married women now faced increased labor burdens, as they had to walk farther for wood and water, cultivate small fields, and sell hides and milk at local markets to support their households (Hatfield 1977, 36). For many rural women, polygyny became more desirable as they yearned for cowives with whom to share the additional work. I recall a poignant conversation in 1985 with Namunyak, a middle-aged Maasai woman struggling to keep her household of four children afloat as her husband managed their dwindling herd of cattle. "I am so lonely," she complained. "All I want is another wife so that I can have someone to work with me in the homestead (*enkang'*)." Elder men who demanded exorbitant amounts of bridewealth for their daughters in order to replenish their diminished herds faced accusations of "selling" their girls. Poor young men sought opportunities to marry by performing bride service for wealthier families. Other young men found work in towns and cities as wage laborers, guards, and even teachers and government workers. They used their independent wealth to make bridewealth gifts and marry at younger ages, sometimes without parental approval (May and McCabe 2004; May and Ole Ikayo 2007). And, as in the colonial period, some women, both young and old, also moved to urban areas in search of economic security and social autonomy.[18]

In my work with Maasai men and women in the mid-1980s and interviews and research with them in the 1990s, I witnessed a range of such unions. Older women and men I interviewed tended to describe their marriages according to the normative ideal, at least in terms of the exchange of bridewealth. Although the amounts and kinds of gifts that were exchanged varied, they all claimed that bridewealth was received or provided. What was lost (or consciously not mentioned) was the timing of those exchanges: did the initial gifts precede or follow sex, pregnancy, or cohabitation between the man and the woman? As Maing'o, a middle-aged Maasai man explained to me: "My [first] marriage was very traditional. My mother gave gifts to a pregnant woman to arrange an engagement. If her child was a boy, we would have waited for the next child, but it was a girl. She eventually became my wife."[19] Like Maing'o, all the middle-aged and older people claimed that their marriage was approved and often arranged by their parents, but for some it was unclear if approval was sought through the exchange of bride-wealth after a couple had come together. Certainly these questions were relevant for the unions of many younger men and women I observed or learned about in the 1990s, especially as new ideas and forms of marriage based on monogamy and companionate unions emerged, in part through the spread of Christian ideals. The following three stories suggest some of the complex contestations and consequences of the older and emergent kinds of relationships claimed as "marriage."

Case 1: Steven and Elena

Steven, a former Catholic seminarian, lived and worked in the large town of Arusha. He soon met and fell in love with Elena, the daughter of a Maasai man who had moved years ago from Kenya to Tanzania and insisted on educating all his daughters. She was smart, Maasai, and conversant with life in the town and the homestead. When Steven and Elena decided to marry one another, they notified their parents. Elena's parents were pleased, as they believed Steven would be a good match for their daughter. But Steven's parents were upset. They had grown close to a neighboring family. The other family wanted to recognize and strengthen the friendship by arranging a marriage between Steven and one of their daughters. After some thought, Steven's family proposed a compromise: Steven could marry both women. Steven refused, arguing that because he was a Christian, he wanted to marry only one wife. His parents said fine, we are your parents, and you should marry the woman of our choice. Caught between his respect for his parents, love of Elena, and desire for a companionate, monogamous marriage, Steven was unable to resolve his dilemma. Eventually, Elena and her parents accused Steven of being an "mtapele" (Swahili: con man), claiming he had misled them and was not fulfilling his promise of marriage. Elena finally married another educated Maasai man, and Steven married the daughter of his family's neighbors.[20]

Steven's dilemma reveals that arranged marriage was not just a concern for young women, but for young men as well. Both women and men were sometimes caught between obeying their parents' decisions as a sign of respect (*enkanyit*) and their desire to forge unions with partners of their own choosing. Fortunately for Elena, her parents supported her choice of Steven, given the compatibility of their education and class aspirations for urban work and life. Steven's parents, however, viewed marriage as a way to strengthen the social networks of interdependence necessary for their rural livelihoods as herders. Their proposed solution—that Steven marry both women—was untenable for Steven or Elena, since as educated Christians they both believed strongly in monogamy.

Case 2: Songoi and Nashipai

In 1992, Songoi and his lover Nashipai ran away. One night he went to her home, accompanied by two of his closest friends, to convince her of his seriousness and the goodness of his intentions. Finally she agreed. She quietly packed her bag so as not to wake her sleeping mother, told her siblings that she would return soon, then walked to Songoi's house, where he lived with his mother (she left his father many years earlier). The next morning, Songoi's two friends returned to her house. They brought *pombe* (an alcoholic beverage made from fermented grain) to her parents, told them where Nashipai was, and explained that Songoi wanted to marry their daughter. The parents drank the *pombe* and agreed, but later in the day they changed their minds and went to Songoi's home to try to retrieve Nashipai. They changed their mind, in part, because of pressure from Nashipai's brother, who had paid for her secondary school education. He demanded that Songoi refund him all the money he had spent on her education before he could marry his sister. After a lot of talking, they agreed that Songoi could marry Nashipai if he gave them a female calf that day. Songoi had no cattle of his own, nor access to any animals owned by his father. A friend offered to lend him an animal, but his livestock were being kept about twenty kilometers away. Nashipai's father returned to Songoi's home the next day to try to bring her home. He called to her and she came out, but he refused to accept her greeting. He argued with her to come home, but she ran back inside. He told Songoi to produce the calf in two days, or else he would involve the elders.

A week later, Songoi told me that the marriage was going well. He had provided his father-in-law several cattle, a blanket, and more *pombe* and had given his mother-in-law some goats. Songoi explained that his father-in-law was much happier now that he had his cattle; it was part of "the custom" for him to have been upset since Songoi and Nashipai had not "followed custom" in the way they got married. He had also built a small separate house to live in with Nashipai. But the next day when I spoke to Songoi before services started in the local Catholic church, I asked if his wife was present. No, he replied, she would not come to church until he had cleared up the "marriage problems" with her parents. Once the *kimila* (Swahili for "customary") marriage was straightened out, they would have a church marriage, and then she would come again. It was hard, he told me, to balance the *kimila* and Christian marriage since her parents only understood the *kimila* marriage.

Three years later, Nashipai left Songoi for another man, taking their daughter with her. Songoi had struggled to support them through the meager earnings from his small store. But they still had no animals of their own, no proper home, and dismal prospects. Distraught, he begged her to return, but to no avail. A few years later, he joined the Pentecostal church, married again, and was somewhat more successful.[21]

Songoi and Nashipai's story suggests some of the economic risks of elopement. Nashipai's parents and brother were rightfully concerned about Songoi's ability to support a household. Like many parents, their concern in arranging a marriage for their daughter was to ensure that her husband was economically secure and from a family and lineage with a good reputation (see also Archambault 2011). Poor men like Songoi with no capital and no family support could earn the right to marry through performing several years of bride service, caring for the cattle of their prospective father-in-law in exchange for marriage to one of his daughters. But Songoi was young, uninterested in livestock, and eager to marry his lover. Thus even though he tried to retroactively seek the approval of Nashipai's parents through the provision of livestock and other gifts, his marriage to Nashipai was never formally recognized by either her parents or the Catholic church. And, eventually, she tired of their poverty and moved on, with her child, to live with another man. Since Songoi had never fully provided the necessary bridewealth gifts to her parents and other relatives, he had little recourse to seek her return or to assert custody over their daughter.

Case 3: Nalari and Lesika

Nalari ran away one night with her lover Lesika and their newborn child in a vehicle that Lesika and his friends had borrowed. They drove to a town about a hundred kilometers away, where Lesika was trying to set up a business selling sugar, flour, and other dry goods. Her parents were furious that she had eloped; they demanded that she return home to marry the man they had chosen for her. Her brother, Simon, was more supportive. He told me that he didn't believe in arranged marriages, that there was no point in making people unhappy for life. But he did demand that Lesika sign a "letter of intent" to marry his sister, to make sure that he did not just stay with her then abandon her. Simon's father was convinced that Simon was involved; he told Simon that he was now Nalari's father should Lesika ever bring the *pombe*. But unlike Songoi, Lesika never brought any bridewealth gifts to Nalari's parents.

Two months after they eloped, Lesika died of cholera during a local outbreak. Many people in his home village interpreted his death as retribution for not providing bridewealth to legitimize the marriage. Nalari and her child returned home. Six weeks later, her parents married her to an older neighbor of their choosing. She would become his fourth wife. One morning I heard a group of women ululating in Nalari's parents' homestead. As I watched, Nalari walked slowly out of her homestead toward that of her new husband. She was dressed in new cloth, carrying her baby on her back. Two men walked in front, and a group of about ten women accompanied her part way. I met her brother, Simon, later that day. He explained that he had slept late on purpose because he did not want to be involved in the wedding. "I told my sister to make the best of it," he said. "I was no longer getting involved."[22]

Although Lesika was slightly more prosperous than Songoi, his refusal to provide bridewealth or seek reconciliation with Nalari's parents was a direct affront to their authority and dominant expectations. For her parents and many community members, Lesika's death shortly after their elopement was not tragic but deserved. Moreover, like Nashipai's brother, Nalari's brother Simon was involved in the deliberations and decisions. In his case, however, his support for Nalari and Lesika, and his novel demand that Lesika sign a "letter of intent," upset his father, who accused him of assisting in the elopement. And Nalari, who tried to assert her independence by "running away" to live with the man she loved, ended up forced to marry a man of her parents' choosing.

Together, these accounts demonstrate that the array of forms of union, kinds of women, and fluidity of relationships described in 1952 persisted into the 1990s, now complicated by new ideas and ideals of monogamy and companionate marriage and the changing economic, political, and social context of postcolonial, socialist Tanzania. Young men had new options for income and economic support, enabling them to seek unions of their own choosing. Young women thus had more opportunities to marry their lovers, often (but not always) in defiance of their parents. The generational differences between parents and their children were further exacerbated by emerging class differences of education, work experience, and urban life that produced very different ideas and aspirations among some young adults. Finally, all these cases are striking in that none of the young men and women sought to challenge the authority of their parents to arrange their marriages by invoking their "rights" under the 1971 LMA in local courts. Instead, most couples sought to establish customary recognition of their unions through the exchange of bridewealth and possibly Christian recognition with a "church" marriage *after* customary recognition and parental approval had been achieved.

There were also, as before, numerous women who were not part of any long-term union. Historically, because of the common age difference of ten to even twenty or thirty years between a husband and his wives (especially his more recent wives), most women became widows at some point in their lives. Some, especially those with young children, were incorporated into the households of their husband's brothers. If bridewealth had been exchanged, they could have lovers but not marry again, and any children they bore would belong to their husband's lineage. Older widows with adult sons usually lived with one of their sons, supervising their daughters-in-law and homestead affairs.

Other women were permanently separated or divorced from their husbands (what Maasai call *kirtala*). Some women fled their marriages claiming abuse, neglect, ill treatment, or impoverishment at the hands of their husbands. Usually, if bridewealth had been transferred and especially if children had been borne, her family or relevant elders would try to resolve the dispute, often by demanding that the husband compensate his wife with cattle for his infraction. But sometimes these mediations failed or the women just refused to return. Other women were kicked out or abandoned by their husbands. Depending on their financial circumstances, age and gender of their children, and other factors, some lived independently while others moved into the homesteads of their fathers or brothers. Most had lovers, and some developed long-term relationships with other men. And some women were never part of a long-term union. The "daughters of the homestead" (*entito e enkang'*) documented in the colonial period and described in chapter 1 also continued to exist in the 1990s. Two such women lived in my primary research community; they had their own homes in their father's homestead, had their own livestock, and chose their lovers.[23]

In sum, as a result of the deep "paternalist state modernization" that characterized socialist Tanzania, and the numerous political, economic, and social interventions into their lives, Maasai men and women faced new gender and generational tensions that were reflected and expressed, in part, through disputes over the form, function, and meaning of marriage. During this period, Maasai women experienced increased workloads on behalf of their families and households, political and economic marginalization, and, for a few, opportunities to forge new kinds of marriages and relationships. In general, their lives were shaped more by political economic interventions like land alienation, education, development projects, villagization, and modernization campaigns than by the demands and priorities of elite women in urban centers for legal rights, employment opportunities, and political voice.

The Case of the Disobedient Daughter

To better understand the changes in Maasai gender and generational relations in the wake of socialism, and the experience of Maasai as individuals and collectively with customary law and civil law, I would like to explore a court case I witnessed in 1992 where a young, educated Maasai woman took her father to court rather than marry a man of his choosing against her will. A close analysis of the context, testimony, and outcome of the case—in which the judges queried Maasai "customary law" in terms of the 1971 Law of Marriage Act—reveals some of the legacies, contradictions, and consequences of colonial efforts to codify customary law and develop legal procedures and institutions; the possibilities and limits of national laws like the LMA; and glimpses of challenges to dominant ideas of "daughter," "father," "wife," and "marriage." Although technically socialism was being dismantled by this time, the legacies of early nationalist interventions like the LMA, forced villagization, education, and "development" were still evident in 1992. Indeed, the LMA is still valid law in 2016.

The facts of the case are complicated. In the early 1970s, a man named Aladala kicked one of his wives, Nayieu, out of his homestead after her first three children died in infancy. She moved to her brother Ronda's homestead, where she eventually gave birth to four healthy children, two boys and two girls. Ronda cared for her and her children as a husband should have. He helped Nayieu to feed and clothe her children, financed the children's primary education, and contributed livestock for slaughter on the required ritual occasions.

Aloya, one of her daughters, started a relationship with Masierr, a young, educated, successful Maasai farmer and livestock trader who lived nearby. They soon had a son, and Masierr presented several bridewealth gifts to Aloya's mother and uncles. Simultaneously, however, Aladala arranged a marriage for Aloya with another man named Shongon, then negotiated a settlement with a group of male clan elders to re-establish his rights over

Aloya. He provided Ronda five cattle and bridewealth rights over another daughter, then took Aloya, her son, and Nayieu to his homestead to prepare for Aloya's marriage to Shongon.

On the same day that Aladala moved Aloya to his home, Masierr made plans with his brothers to recover her. That evening they walked to Aladala's homestead, quietly woke Aloya, and escorted her and her baby to Masierr's homestead. The next morning, they hired a car, and Masierr, Aloya, and the baby drove away to hide with a relative of Masierr's.

When Aladala woke up that morning and realized what had happened, he was furious. He sent a man to the police to report that Masierr had "stolen" his daughter, then quickly called a meeting of the elders of his Lukumai clan. That same afternoon, the clan elders walked together to a neighboring homestead where a woman from their clan was married to one of Ronda's brothers. They forced the woman and all her children to pack immediately and come with them; even though she and her husband were completely uninvolved in the elopement, she was now the Lukumai clan's "hostage" until Ronda helped return Masierr and Aloya. The elders were pleased by her calm submission to their demands and promised her a sheep as a reward for her good behavior as a clan daughter.

While the hostage woman and her children lived at Aladala's homestead, the search for Masierr and Aloya continued. In about two weeks they were found and forced to return to their village. Masierr spent the night in police custody on charges of "stealing" Aloya, but was released the next morning. A few days later, Aloya and her son returned to Aladala's homestead. Preparations were renewed for her impending marriage to Shongon. That evening Masierr and his brothers returned for Aloya. But this time they took her directly to the police station in Monduli. At the station, Aloya swore out a statement in fluent Swahili accusing Aladala of forcing her to marry against her will and threatening to kill herself by drinking cattle dip if he persevered. And so began the court case of Aloya versus Aladala, daughter versus father, the law of the Tanzanian state versus current renditions of Maasai customary law.[24]

News of Aloya's accusations against her father and her threat of suicide quickly reached the village. Most people I spoke to were shocked, astonished that a young woman would have the audacity to take her father to court. They claimed it was the first such case they had heard of. Village elders, especially those of Aladala's close-knit Lukumai clan, were furious, recognizing in Aloya's actions a direct challenge to their authority: if, as fathers, they could not control their daughters, then who could they control? A somber mood infused the villagers as they observed the elders' frequent meetings. Almost immediately, the Lukumai elders threatened to curse Aloya if she pursued the court case against her father. Their prompt threat revealed their anxiety over her refusal to respect their authority. As their ultimate weapon, the curse would both stigmatize and ostracize Aloya in one act.

Elder men from all the clans moved quickly to reassert their control over their other daughters. After a flurry of meetings, they nominated an elder man to serve as the *laigwenani lo mila* ("chairman of tradition/customs") for the three villages in the area. His mandate was to settle debates within Maasai customary law—such as Aloya's case—before they went to the government court. The novelty of the office, and its intermediary position between Maasai and state authorities, was clearly marked by the merging of the local and national language in its title: *laigwenani* means chairperson or leader in Maa, while *mila* is a Swahili word meaning culture or tradition. And state administrators were complicit in this effort to strengthen male Maasai authority: local CCM officials and area elders attended the improvised blessing ceremony, and a document detailing the ceremony and the new chairman's duties was quickly carried to the district officer for endorsement. With the agreement of the state, the male elders had swiftly regained their authority to decide their own "customary" affairs, such as the marriages of their daughters, outside the purview of the LMA. They were too late, however, to regain jurisdiction over Aloya's case.

Other reactions were diverse. Humiliated by his daughter's actions, Aladala assured the elders that no matter what the court decided, Aloya would marry Shongon as promised. As the bereft suitor, Shongon was outraged. I met him a few days later at a ceremony, and he coldly told me that if Aloya had been his daughter, he would personally have handed her the cattle dip to drink rather than suffer such insolence. Only two extended families, that of Masierr and that of Aloya's maternal uncles, overtly supported her. A few educated men and women with whom I spoke privately told me that they admired Aloya and disapproved of the institution of arranged marriages. But they were all reluctant to voice such opinions in public, as they were afraid the elders would accuse them of having assisted Aloya. Like most villagers, they too feared the anger and curses of the elders.

Despite the lack of public support and the looming threat of the elders' curse, Aloya pursued her case.[25] On the first day of the trial, she stood quietly in her witness box, across from her father standing in his, both boxes a symbolic equal distance from the elevated platform where the male magistrate sat between his two elder male advisors. Both her witnesses and Aladala's witnesses would be men; no women would speak for or against her. The magistrate did ask Aladala if Nayieu, Aloya's mother, would testify, but Aladala replied that she would not come and that he was satisfied with the two witnesses he had, both elder male members of his clan. Despite her disadvantage as the lone woman in an intensely male space, Aloya had one advantage: unlike Aladala, she had attended a government primary school and spoke fluent Swahili. She could therefore address and understand the court directly, while Aladala had to use an interpreter throughout the proceedings.

First the magistrate read, in Swahili, the charge against Aladala—that, contrary to the 1971 LMA, which forbids forced marriages, he had tried to force Aloya to marry against her will. Then Aloya, in fluent Swahili, quietly but firmly told her story to the court:

> It was on May 5th, 1992, that the accused tried to force me to marry another man when I was already married. He tried to force me to marry [Shongon]. I am already married to [Masierr]. But [Aladala] told me that I had to marry the man he wanted, not [Masierr]. But Masierr and I were married in 1985 in Monduli Juu. The accused knows that I am married to [Masierr]. [Aladala] is my father, my parent, but since I was born I have grown up at my uncle's homestead. When I was married, my mother received my bridewealth. During all of my life I never knew that the accused was my father since I was not born and was not raised by his hand. I only ever knew my uncle. . . . I was told that my father had banished my mother a long time before I was born. . . . That is all. I just don't want to be forced to marry someone I don't want. (Official Court Transcript [OCT], 2–3)

In response to questioning from her father, she replied, "I told you that I didn't want you to force me. One day you came to my uncle's homestead. You didn't hit me, but you told me that you didn't want me to marry [Masierr] because he was snot (Swahili: *kamasi*). You tried to force me to marry that other man. My uncle had already married me to [Masierr]. My uncles drank the bridewealth beer. I didn't know that you were my father" (OCT, 3). Under further questioning from the magistrate's two advisors, she added:

[Aladala] never came to my uncles before I was married. My mother told me my father was around but I didn't know he was the accused. My uncles were always there as well as other elders who were neighbors. . . . My father never came to slaughter for my mother, and when I was circumcised I didn't see him. My uncles slaughtered for my mother. I have given birth to one child with my husband [Masierr]. [Aladala] tried to force me to marry after I had given birth. I asked him what would happen to my child and he told me my child would be taken by my new husband. It is not good to give the blood of one person to another person. If I had given birth outside of marriage, the child would have been paid for, but I gave birth while I was married. (OCT, 3)

Masierr testified next, repeating and confirming much of Aloya's testimony. He explained that Aloya was his wife, that he had begun courting her in 1985 after she had finished school and had provided bridewealth gifts to her mother and uncles for her, marrying her in the "traditional" Maasai way. Although he could have taken Aloya to his homestead after she was circumcised, usually a man waited until his new wife had given birth to her first child at her parents' home. So when Aloya gave birth, he began to arrange her move, which was when Aladala appeared. Masierr did add some new information, however: Aladala had threatened to whip Aloya if she refused to marry Shongon. During questioning, Aladala and the advisors to the magistrate all asked Masierr if he had known at the time who Aloya's father was. He repeatedly denied that he knew about Aladala, explaining that that was why he had given the engagement beer to Aloya's uncles.

In questioning the remaining witnesses, the court concentrated on three main issues: eliciting the details of "traditional" Maasai marriage; clarifying the rights and obligations of a "father"; and determining whether Ronda or Aladala should be properly regarded as Aloya's father. In order to understand traditional Maasai marriage and bridewealth practices, the magistrate and his advisors, like their colonial predecessors, deferred to the authority of the male elders. They asked Aladala's two witnesses, elder male members of his Lukumai clan, to describe how Maasai marriages were arranged, focusing on the issue of consent. "According to the traditional customs of the Maasai," asked one advisor, "does a girl have the freedom to be able to search for a man that she likes?" "She is not able," answered the first witness. The advisor continued, "So you are saying that the accused used that traditional power to tell [Aloya] you WILL be married by that man?" The witness replied, "She wasn't forced." But the magistrate badgered him until he admitted that Aladala had the ability to use his "traditional" power to force Aloya to marry. "So," the magistrate said, "we can say that this girl had no choice?" "A long time ago yes," the witness replied, "but these days . . ." "I am asking about a long time ago," interjected the advisor. "In the past," continued the witness, "she couldn't have chosen the person, . . . [but these days] she is told that a certain person is her fiancé, but if she doesn't want him she should say something before his wealth is sent." "So when," continued the magistrate, "did [Aladala] receive the [bridewealth] cattle? . . . He didn't tell her, did he, that he had accepted the wealth of a person?" "No, he didn't tell her." Similar questions were asked of Aladala's second witness: "If a father has decided to give his daughter to someone, does his daughter have a voice [in the decision]?" "According to Maasai custom," the witness replied, "she has none" (Transcribed Transcript [TT], 50–53, 71).

In his testimony, Aladala asserted his traditional right to arrange Aloya's marriage without her knowledge in accordance with the version of Maasai customary law described by his witnesses. He claimed that both he and Aloya's mother Nayieu had known that Shongon was Aloya's fiancé, but that "with us, a child does not ask who she is engaged to." As to Aloya's accusation that he tried to force her to marry, he claimed that she had never said that she did not want to marry Shongon: "If she had told me at home that she didn't want him, I would have let it go. But she never said anything at home, she came straight to this courtroom" (TT, 26, 29).

Several themes emerged from this discussion. One was the ambiguous role of consent in determining the difference between a voluntary marriage, an arranged marriage, and a forced marriage. Aladala's witnesses and Aladala himself argued that Aloya's marriage to Shongon was merely arranged, and that unlike in the past, she had the right to consent or not to consent to the arrangement. But Aloya's and Masierr's testimonies, and even part of Aladala's, disproved such claims: First, Aladala admitted to receiving a substantial amount of bridewealth before Aloya was ever aware of or "consented" to her proposed spouse. Second, Aloya claimed several times that even after she told her father that she did not want to marry Shongon, he insisted that he would force her to. She was not going to marry Masierr, as she wished, but Shongon, as he wished. And finally, Masierr mentioned that Aladala had threatened to whip Aloya if she did not comply; surely the threat of physical violence implied that consent was not "freely and voluntarily" given.

A second theme was the legitimacy of her marriage arrangements with Masierr. For Aloya, Masierr, and Ronda, the marriage was legitimate; the proper permissions were requested and granted, gifts were offered and accepted, and now a child was born of the union. But in Aladala's eyes, it was not a legal marriage because he, as Aloya's father, had not made the arrangements or received the bridewealth: "If there is someone who has deceived [Aloya] into believing that he would take her, then he has deceived me because I am her father, and that girl does not have two fathers, only me" (TT, 4). Aladala claimed that he first saw Masierr, "the one who deceived Aloya," on the day that he brought the five cattle to Ronda, and that very night Masierr stole Aloya. So, since in his opinion Aloya's relationship with Masierr was not a legitimate marriage, he felt free in arranging a "real" marriage for Aloya.

The payment and receipt of bridewealth was crucial to both parties in determining the legitimacy of the marriage. Masierr had given Ronda several cattle in bridewealth for Aloya. But Aladala had received thirty-five head of cattle from Shongon for Aloya. And according to all accounts in the village, Aladala, a once wealthy man turned poor, had already "eaten" them, used them all up. So he offered the court a deal: he would let Aloya marry Masierr if Masierr agreed to reimburse the thirty-five cattle that Shongon had paid Aladala. And if Masierr refused, then Aloya could return "home" with Aladala and stay with him until she found a man she liked who was willing to pay the full number of cattle (TT, 3–4). The magistrate, shocked at the number of cattle ("Thirty-five!"), registered Aladala's offer but continued the interrogation. When the court probed Aladala later about "traditional" Maasai bridewealth, he claimed that thirty-five cattle was the customary amount of bridewealth, the amount he had provided for his wife and that Shongon had promised to give for his daughter (TT, 22).

But these definitions of "traditional" Maasai marriage and bridewealth now raised another issue before the court: If Maasai "tradition" allowed a father to arrange his daughter's marriage, as Aladala and his witnesses testified, then who was the father in this case, Aladala or Ronda? If bridewealth was crucial to both parties in determining the legitimacy of the marriage, who, as Aloya's father, should have been the recipient?

The court's probing exposed at least two competing definitions of fatherhood: a jural definition based on rights established through marriage and bridewealth, and a more social definition based on the duties and responsibilities of a father. For Aladala, it was enough that Nayieu, despite more than twenty years of separation, was still his wife, making Aloya, as her child, his daughter. The elders had affirmed his rights (and thus their own power) when they decided that he could take Nayieu and Aloya to his homestead if he compensated Ronda. And, by current renditions of Maasai customary law, he was right; since the bridewealth he had paid for Nayieu had never been returned by her parents or her brothers, she was still legally his wife. And any children she conceived, whoever their biological father, would therefore be recognized legally as the children of Aladala. For these Maasai elders, their authority as husbands and fathers was constituted and expressed through the exchange of bridewealth.

The court, however, found Aladala's definition of "husband" and "father," and by implication the constitution of male Maasai authority, unconvincing. Their disbelief was evident in a question they asked Aladala's second witness: "According to Maasai custom, once you have married, even if your wife stays apart at her family for forty years and you never go there, she is still your wife? Because your name is there? Even if you never took care of her and you just left her?" (TT, 63). "Yes," replied the witness, "she is mine" (TT, 63).

The court was less interested in such jural definitions. For the magistrate and his advisors, the authority and rights of a father were established through the fulfillment of certain obligations and duties; such authority was not bought but earned. During cross-examination of Ronda, Aladala, and Aladala's two witnesses, the court probed for the answers to the following questions:

- Where did Nayieu and her children, including Aloya, live during the past years?
- Who helped to feed and clothe Nayieu and her children?
- Who sponsored and paid for Aloya's schooling?
- Who provided animals at ritual occasions such as the name-giving ceremony (*orokiteng' le ntomonon*) and Aloya's circumcision?
- Had Aladala ever visited Nayieu and her children before the meeting with the elders?
- Had Aloya ever seen Aladala before the meeting?
- Who did Aloya consider to be her father?

Ronda testified that he fulfilled most of the above duties: he provided Nayieu and her children with a place to live and helped them meet all their food, clothing, schooling, and ritual needs. As a student, Aloya had used his name, "Ronda," as her family name. He claimed that Aladala had never visited, coming only when Aloya reached marrying age. Furthermore, Aladala had never contributed anything to the family's maintenance, "not even tea leaves, much less a goat" (OCT, 6). Finally, neither Aladala nor Ronda had provided the animals for Aloya's circumcision ceremony; Masierr, as her fiancé, had.

Sensing the importance of these matters to the court, Aladala disputed Ronda's testimony. Awkwardly, he tried to characterize himself as fulfilling the court's definition of a father. He claimed that he had visited and slept with Nayieu while she lived at Ronda's and that Aloya and the other children had known for many years that he was their father. He admitted that he knew that Aloya had used "Ronda" as her second name at school but said it had not bothered him. The court remained unconvinced: "So here you are confirming for us that you had nothing to do with your child, but now when she is 'sweet' you remember her?" Aladala disagreed: "That's a lie.... I have fed her since she was little until now" (TT, 19–20).

In rendering his judgment, the magistrate first discussed the conflict evident between the marriage laws of the Tanzanian state and the customary marriage laws of the Maasai. According to the magistrate, the LMA clearly states that "anyone involved in any way with a marriage who knows that the permission of one of the parties to the marriage was not given, or was given only under force or by coercion; that person is guilty, and deserves a sentence of three years in prison" (Decision [D], 3). The magistrate continued: "But this law contradicts the customs and beliefs of the Maasai that give the power to decide about marriage to the parents of both parties. Even if the party to the marriage is male or female, he or she has no choice about the marriage other than to obey the decision of his or her parents. Since these customs directly conflict with Marriage Law 5/71, we will follow the Marriage Law in our decision" (D, 3).

The magistrate then asked each of his two advisors to present their views. Both advisors agreed that Aladala was guilty, as accused, of trying to force Aloya to marry against her will. The first advisor said he believed Aloya's testimony, and he understood how Aladala's actions had forced her to run away to her fiancé and finally bring this case. He thought Aladala should return Shongon's bridewealth himself, not Masierr. The second advisor agreed, adding that he found the evidence that Aloya had already borne a child with Masierr compelling. Her suicide threat was also strong evidence that she was being forced to do something against her will; he worried that "the accused could lose her life from taking poison." He agreed that Aladala should return Shongon's payments, and he thought Aloya should marry the man she wanted, following the customary marriage process.

The magistrate agreed with the recommendations of both advisors. Then he lectured the courtroom about the "evils" of forced marriages:

> The accused knows the results of forcing his daughter to marry another man, but still, disdainfully, he does it. The harm done won't affect him but his daughter; she who is to be married will carry the burden of the house, even though she won't like it. She won't be patient, and a marriage of this kind will only be a marriage of misery, with the following likely results: 1) hate; 2) suffering; 3) death.
>
> A person who has been forced to marry another person she doesn't like because of the greed of her parent over bridewealth must confront such misery, such hate in the marriage house, and finally she will take poison to remove herself from such a life. So that this affair is able to be understood in the community, I must openly pronounce that it is a very bad offense to force a person to marry another person she or he doesn't like. I find [Aladala] guilty as charged. (D, 4–5)

Aladala was outraged. From his box, he yelled at the magistrate in Maa: "Take my daughter then, she is yours, she belongs to the government now. You take care of her, you marry her off, you receive her bridewealth. I disown her here and now." Then he sat down, bitter with anger, humiliation, and confusion. How could a magistrate deny him his rights as a father over his daughter, rights recognized by the Maasai elders themselves? How could the court support the accusations of a daughter against a father? What kind of legal system and government was this that could say that certain Maasai laws and customs were wrong?

The magistrate did consider the conflicts between the LMA and Maasai customary laws when he sentenced Aladala ten days later. First Aladala stood, pleading for leniency: "I am an old, sick man. My family depends on me. My children have no food" (D, 5). Then, after listening to the punishments suggested by his advisors, the magistrate explained that since this was Aladala's first such offense, and since he recognized that Aladala had been acting according to Maasai custom, he would reduce the punishment recommended by the LMA: "[Aladala], as a first time offender, will pay a fine of 5,000 shillings or go to jail for six months. . . . He will pay all the court costs. Furthermore, he will not continue to force [Aloya] to marry another man. As to the bridewealth of thirty-five cattle that he received from another man, Aladala is responsible for returning that bridewealth himself.

That bridewealth will not be part of the marriage of [Aloya] and [Masierr]" (D, 5). The sentence sounded lenient to Aladala's accusers and severe to his supporters, but all were happy that the case was over. Many villagers were surprised at the outcome and worried that the case set a bad precedent for the authority of parents to arrange the marriages of their children.

As of 2011, the last time I saw Aloya, she was still living with Masierr and their children in his father's homestead. Nayieu, her mother, had moved back to Ronda's homestead. Shongon, disgusted with Aloya's actions and the outcome of the case, told Aladala that he did not want Aloya or any daughter of Aladala's seed, so Aladala had promised to give him another young woman instead, the daughter of a fellow clan member. And the "hostage" Lukumai woman, after living at Aladala's *enkang'* with her children for several months, finally returned to her husband and home, without the permission or blessing of the elders and without her promised sheep.

CUSTOM, CONFLICT, AND CHANGE

The case of Aloya versus Aladala illustrates, yet again, the complexities of Maasai "marriage" (including that of Aladala and Nayieu) and some of the dilemmas produced by efforts to categorize and regulate these relationships through legal means that both recognized customary legal regimes created during the colonial era and tried to introduce national, "modern" norms of marriage that buttressed the rights of individuals. Although the 1971 LMA was clearly the product of elite, educated visions of the ideals of marriage and the rights of women, these ideals and discourses of individual rights resonated with some young men and women like Masierr and Aloya. The LMA and its supporting structures of police, courts, and magistrates became a key resource for them in seeking their idea of justice: confirming the legitimacy of their own marriage and challenging Aladala's efforts to force Aloya to marry another man against her will.

But, as Aloya's case also demonstrates, the LMA had considerable limitations. As citizens, Maasai men and women confronted barriers of language (fluency in Swahili) and cultural assumptions in the law and the process of adjudication about Maasai life and practices. Aloya's limited education enabled her to understand the law, access its benefits, and represent herself directly in court. But few Maasai women at this time shared this advantage, and even her father, Aladala, was hampered by his lack of proficiency in Swahili and thus his reliance on translators and other intermediaries.

Moreover, as evidenced in the three marriage cases discussed earlier in the chapter, most other young men and women who had some education and fluency in Swahili were reluctant to seek justice through the courts, preferring to negotiate with their elders and parents to have their unions recognized as legitimate. Given the anger, threats, and curses the male elders directed at Aloya, and the possibility of permanent ostracism, their reluctance was understandable.

The political and economic context of the case matters as well. The numerous social, economic, and political interventions by Nyerere's socialist government had, as described above, exacerbated gender, class, and, for some groups like Maasai, ethnic inequalities. The loss of grazing land, forced relocations under villagization, heightened attention to men as development actors, inequities in access to quality education and health care, and attacks on Maasai appearance and livelihoods had empowered a few wealthy, educated Maasai but had impoverished many others. Elder men like Aladala who had no education and spoke no Swahili had few options when they lost their cattle but to try to restock their herds and provide for their families by "selling" their daughters in marriage. Other parents, concerned about ensuring the future of their daughters, preferred to arrange marriages with older, more established and prosperous men rather than the young men favored by their daughters. Arranging suitable first marriages for their sons, as in the case of Steven (Case 1), mattered as well as a way to establish and reinforce social networks (and thus access to grazing, livestock, and other resources) important for their own increasingly precarious survival. Aloya and Masierr were thus empowered not only by their (minimal) education but also by Masierr's economic security and financial autonomy from his father. Unlike Songoi (Case 2), Masierr had sufficient livestock (from herding and his success as a farmer) to provide bridewealth to Aloya's family and to support her and their son.

Aladala and his fellow male Maasai elders, however, pursued a different idea of justice: state recognition of their legitimate customary authority to arrange the marriages of their sons and daughters. The male elders, whose authority had been buttressed by colonial practices, clearly sided with Aladala when they agreed that he could re-establish his paternal rights over Aloya by the transfer of five cattle to Ronda. Aladala and his fellow elders used several strategies to defend their customary authority against Aloya's attack: outside of the courtroom, they threatened to curse her; inside, they appealed to tradition and custom, argued that being a father was established through bridewealth payments, and articulated the rights of fathers and deference of daughters as natural and immutable. To speak of these duties, rights, and obligations as culturally determined, as based on tradition, and therefore as normative and natural, served their interests by obscuring the possibility for challenge or change.

In Aloya's case, the elders failed to convince the magistrate. Although the court dwelled on the issue of whether Aladala or Ronda should be considered Aloya's father, their main concern was the matter of consent. Aladala and his witnesses argued for the version of Maasai custom and tradition that had been developed and strengthened during the colonial period, which centralized legal and political authority of male elders over women and junior men and thus, they claimed, allowed fathers to force their daughters to marry without their consent. The magistrate and his advisors, however, reacted with astonishment and even disdain at some of these claims of custom (such as the size of bridewealth transfers) and male authority. And in the end, the court overruled these claims of tradition and custom, following the LMA to rule that fathers could not force their daughters to marry against their will and condemning the "evils" of forced marriage.

Infuriated by the denial of his rights, Aladala, as the representative of the elders, wielded their ultimate weapon: he cursed Aloya in the courtroom, both stigmatizing and ostracizing her in one verbal act. If Aloya could not be a proper Maasai daughter, then she could live outside of Maasai society as the daughter of the government. By morally and physically marginalizing Aloya as a disobedient daughter unwanted by her family, Aladala's curse warned other daughters tempted to follow her example about the dire consequences of such actions for their social relations. Moreover, to prevent similar cases from being heard in the Tanzanian court, the elders, with the sanction of local state officials, cleverly created a new customary institution, the "chairman of tradition/customs," to handle future marriage disputes. Thus at the same time the state undermined the power of the elders in the court case, it reinforced their power by endorsing the creation of this new intermediary legal institution.

In conclusion, the chapter has shown some of the complexities produced by the legacies of colonial practices, especially the legal codification and recognition of customary laws and elite efforts to control, regulate, and "improve" social relations through the development of laws such as the LMA.

The introduction and enforcement of ideas of individual rights that would be enforced by the power of the state contrasted in marked ways with the Maasai ideas of mutual respect (*enkanyit*), social interdependence (*osotua*), and leading a good and holy life (*sinyati*) that had shaped and regulated social relations and disputes in the precolonial period. These values still existed in the 1980s and 1990s, but their meanings and manifestations had changed as a result of colonial interventions that consolidated the power of elder men; new ideas about appropriate social relations, especially of marriage, introduced by education, Christianity, and other influences; and the political-economic dislocations created by President Nyerere's socialist policies. While urban elites disparaged Maasai dress, culture, and "primitive" ways and turned to national law as a means of "modernizing" Maasai and other marginalized peoples, Maasai themselves were trying to survive as second-class citizens in an increasingly hostile nation. The resulting gender, generational, and class struggles shaped and were reflected in the changing dynamics of domestic unions that were categorized, and now legally codified, as marriage.

Notes

1. In 1967, 86.71 percent of rural women were illiterate as compared to 69.85 percent of men (Mbilinyi 1972, 64), although illiteracy was decreasing for younger men and women.

2. UWT was called Umoja wa Wanawake wa Tanganyika before the union of Tanganyika and Zanzibar into "Tanzania." For the sake of simplicity, I use Umoja wa Wanawake wa Tanzania throughout the text.

3. "Stop Licences to Bars that Allow Minis, say Dar TANU Elders," *Daily News*, Saturday, 10 June 1972, p. 5.

4. Her husband was Rashidi Kawawa, a close ally of President Nyerere. He served in numerous top leadership positions in Tanzania, including vice president of Tanzania (1962–1972), prime minister (1972–1977), and minister for defense and national service (1977–1985).

5. The Jipemoyo project was a collaborative research project between Tanzanian and Finnish researchers that sought to apply "participatory" principles to rural research in Western Bagamoyo District, focusing on "the role of culture in the restructuring process of rural Tanzania" (Swantz 1977).

6. JALA, like most other laws and acts of this period, was modified over the years but remains in force as of 2016.

7. The new court system was created by the Magistrates' Courts Acts of 1963 and retained by the Magistrates' Courts Act of 1984. For a concise historical overview of the development of the Tanzanian legal system until 1989, see Bierwagen and Peter 1989.

8. For detailed analyses and critiques of the LMA, see Calaguas, Drost, and Fluet 2007; Rwebangira 1996, 14–31; Rwezaura and Wanitzek 1988; Rwezaura 1991, 1998; Tenga and Peter 1996; Ivaska 2011, 166–205.

9. When the proposed draft of the LMA was discussed in Parliament in March 1970, only 7 of the 170 MPs were female (Ivaska 2011, 186).

10. *The Standard* (Dar es Salaam), 22 January 1971, cited in Mbilinyi 1972, 67.

11. Unsigned letter to *The Standard* (Dar es Salaam), 24 September 1969, cited in Ivaska 2011, 178. Some women demanded sarcastically that if polygamy was legalized, then polyandry should be legalized as well in the name of gender equality (Ivaska 2011, 181–182).

12. "'Humiliation' of Masai Tribe," *The Times* [London], 8 February 1968, 5.

13. "'Humiliation' of Masai Tribe," *The Times* [London], 8 February 1968, 5.

14. These interventions are detailed in Hodgson 2001a, especially chapters 4 and 5.

15. A 1975 survey found that more than 50 percent of Maasai homesteads surveyed engaged in some kind of at least small-scale cultivation (Hatfield 1976, 20).

16. In 1959, for example, the Masai Federal Council agreed on "quotas" for girls for the fourteen primary schools in Masai District, ranging from two to fourteen per school, for a total of seventy-eight girls. "Minutes of the First Meeting of the Executive Committee of the Masai Federal Council, Held at Monduli 19th–24th September 1958." TNA 471/L.5/1/4.

17. *Nationalist*, 6 April 1968. Cited in Schneider 2006, 115.

18. According to a survey conducted in 1971, two-thirds of urban women in Tanzania were rural-urban migrants (Johnson 1985, 245). Unfortunately, the survey concluded that "as a result of their concentration in activities that yield low incomes, the average earnings of self-employed women [were] 148 shillings per month, well below the male average of 543 shillings" (in 1971, seven shillings was approximately equal to $1) (Johnson 1985, 146). Women tended to work in cash crop agriculture (41.8 percent), crafts and manufacturing (11.5 percent), street trading (23.3 percent), house rental (9.3 percent), and the most profitable field for them, the bar, hotel, and restaurant businesses (4.9 percent) (Johnson 1985, 248). In contrast, men in the informal economy had more lucrative work in such fields as portage, transport, building construction, and fishing (Johnson 1985, 248). These marked gender differences in the type of work and income from the informal sector reflected enduring ideas about what kind of work was appropriate for men and women; their differential access to education, technology, training, and capital; and distinct expectations about their rights and responsibilities as wives and husbands, mothers and fathers (Johnson 1985). In fact, according to Johnson (1985, 252), "marriage, rather than providing additional access to capital through the husband's earnings or credit, seems to be a hindrance to the access to capital for women's investments in self-employment activities."

19. From fieldnotes, 6 April 1992.

20. From fieldnotes, 30 January 1992.

21. From fieldnotes, 6 April 1992; 8 April 1992; 18 April 1992.

22. From fieldnotes, 8 April 1992; 17 April 1992; 6 May 1992; 22 May 1992; 14 June 1992; 4 August 1992.

23. In her demographic survey of Maasai in northern Tanzania, Ernestina Coast (2001, 79) found three "daughters of the homestead" out of a survey sample of 1,545 household heads.

24. Since the case is public record in the primary court of Monduli, I will use the real names of all involved.

25. With the permission of the magistrate, I attended and recorded all the hearings for the case. I also obtained the official court documents. I am responsible for all the translations from Swahili and Maa to English. References to these primary materials are abbreviated in the text as follows:

D: the official court decision, Ladala Kisika v. Aluya Ladala. Case no. 100 of 1992 in Primary Court of Kisongo, Monduli District (five pages).

OCT: Official Court Transcript of the case, which consists of written summaries of the proceedings as recorded by the court reporter (ten pages).

TT: Transcription of my unofficial tape recording of the proceedings (seventy-five pages).

CHAPTER 3

Criminalizing Culture

Human Rights, NGOs, and the Politics of Anti-FGM Campaigns

"MWEDO URGED TO STEP UP fight against female genital mutilation," read the headline in an August 2006 issue of the *Arusha Times,* a weekly newspaper in northern Tanzania.[1] Since Tanzania made female genital mutilation (FGM) illegal in 1998, there have been constant articles in the English- and Swahili-language press outlining the dangers of FGM, announcing yet another campaign to stop it, praising the successful eradication efforts of local, national, and international women's organizations, and lamenting the stubborn persistence of the practice among certain ethnic groups, most notably Maasai.[2] So as one of the two main nongovernmental organizations (NGOs) working with Maasai women, it seemed only natural (to the national press and most Tanzanians) that MWEDO (Maasai Women Development Organization) would join the fight to eradicate FGM. But the fact that MWEDO was being "urged" suggests that the organization was somehow reluctant to get involved in the anti-FGM campaigns. And indeed it was. Most Maasai women leaders, including the leaders of MWEDO, have tried to resist demands to focus their efforts and resources on eradicating FGM, insisting instead on the need to address a different set of priorities: namely, economic and political empowerment.

But the newspaper article also reflects other changes that have taken place since the early 1990s in the social, political, economic, and legal landscapes snaping the lives of Maasai men and women. These changes include the controversial but successful globalization of liberal forms of feminism that prioritize individual rights, personal autonomy, and equality between men and women; the corresponding institutionalization and expansion of new legal regimes pertaining to "women's human rights" through international protocols and organizations; the rise of NGOs like MWEDO as the dominant form for "development," advocacy, and political action; and the implementation of neoliberal policies that have produced new political spaces for debate and dissent but have also exacerbated the undermining of pastoralist livelihoods.

There are also, however, continuities between the contemporary situation and those examined in the previous two chapters. "Culture," now in the form of "customary practice" and "tradition," is still reified and demonized, presumed to be only a source for the oppression of women, not their empowerment. Elite men and women still deign to know what is best for rural, illiterate women. And law is firmly embraced by these elites as a key tool for producing and enforcing social change, especially the eradication of these oppressive cultural practices. The reluctance of colonial officers to interfere with practices like female circumcision, despite pressure from the St. Joan's Alliance and other organizations, has been replaced with the fervent, missionary-like zeal of transnational and national feminists to make the criminalization and eradication of female genital mutilation one of their top political priorities.

How and why did female genital mutilation become a priority for international feminist groups and eventually national feminist organizations in Tanzania? Why were the leaders of MWEDO reluctant to join the "fight" against FGM? To answer these questions, this chapter explores, among other things, how the recent reframing of FGM from a health issue to a human rights issue has intensified the pressure on Maasai women activists to focus their energy and resources on its eradication. International donors, transnational activists, the Tanzanian state, and even Tanzanians feminists continue to condemn and even criminalize Maasai for one specific cultural practice—FGM—and use its presence or absence as a measure of Maasai progress and "modernity." In contrast, although many Maasai activists are concerned about FGM, they are far more alarmed by the increasing impoverishment and political marginalization of their communities, especially Maasai women, and have chosen to concentrate on the priorities of their constituencies: economic security and political empowerment. From their perspective, the conflict over FGM is not a "problem of culture" but a problem of power, of the continued assumption by many Euro-American donors and activists, and increasingly by African elites, that they can speak for (rather than listen to) rural, poorly educated women or even well-educated African women who are deemed culturally "other."

Thus the study of how and why FGM was criminalized in Tanzania, and the subsequent, state endorsed, NGO-led anti-FGM campaigns, provides a useful prism through which to analyze the political dynamics of national, and now international, efforts to criminalize certain cultural practices. I interrogate this history to try to document not only *how* FGM became a key focus of international feminist advocacy, but *why* the practice—instead of a broad array of other women's "rights" concerns—became such a site of international and, eventually, national attention and contention. Glimpses of the reasons can be gleaned from the record, especially when read against the historical backdrop provided in the previous chapters and the contemporary political-economic context, which has produced uncomfortable alignments among the agendas and assumptions of individual rights, liberal feminism, and neoliberal policies.[3]

I focus here on two key aspects of this situation: First, I examine the history of these contemporary initiatives to reframe specific practices as forms of violence against women, and thus violations of women's human rights, in order to analyze the shifting definitions of and relation between "law" and "culture." As I will discuss below, the implementation of the legal regime of "women's human rights" internationally, and eventually in Tanzania, drew on and differed from colonial and socialist imaginings and practices in significant ways. Moreover, the focus on "culture" as the primary "problem" of Maasai (and other rural women in the Global South) and "law" as the dominant mode for rectifying injustice has obscured other forms of oppression and injustice.

Second, I explore how social differences—not just gender and race but now, increasingly, class—have shaped these debates. I examine the politics of these dynamics and the imbrications of power in every aspect of the design, implementation, and experience of these new transnational legal regimes. These intertwined domains of power include elite representations of and assumptions about rural women in international protocols and national laws, the dismissal of the priorities of "grassroots" women by national feminist NGOs, and the consequences, or "perils and pitfalls" (Shell-Duncan

2008), of the international anti-FGM campaign and the larger "problem of culture" for the agendas and struggles of Maasai women, especially now that FGM has been reframed as a human rights issue.[4]

HUMAN RIGHTS, TRANSNATIONAL FEMINISM, AND THE DEMONIZATION OF CULTURE

The concept of universal human rights—that all human beings, regardless of gender, age, nationality, or other differences, share certain inalienable rights—has a long, much-debated history (see, for example, Cmiel 2004; Hunt 2007). Most scholars locate the emergence of the ideas behind universal human rights in the Enlightenment, an intellectual movement of the seventeenth and eighteenth century that drew on the work of such philosophers as René Descartes and John Locke to argue for the pre-eminence of reason, the individual, and science over tradition and religion. These ideas led, eventually, to the British ideas of "natural justice" and the "repugnancy clause" discussed in chapter 1. When the League of Nations was formed in the aftermath of World War I to provide a forum for nation-states to resolve their disputes through nonviolent means, its charter mandated that its member nations ensure such vaguely defined rights as "to secure and maintain fair conditions of labour for men, women and children" and "to secure just treatment of the native inhabitants of territories under their control" (Article 23).[5]

The atrocities of World War II, however, convinced these nation-states, reorganized since 1945 as the United Nations,[6] that they needed a much more specific delineation of the rights of individuals. After some debate, the General Assembly of the United Nations passed the Universal Declaration of Human Rights ("the Declaration") in 1948, which, together with several ensuing covenants and other international protocols, was eventually ratified by a majority of nation-states and became the backbone of international law and advocacy. The Declaration held that "the equal and inalienable rights of all members of the human family is the foundation of freedom, justice and peace in the world" and that "human rights should be protected by the rule of law" (Preamble). According to Article 2, "Everyone is entitled to all the rights and freedoms set forth in this Declaration without distinction of any kind, such as race, colour, sex, language, religion, political or other opinion, national or social origin, property, birth or other status." Among other provisions, the Declaration prohibited slavery (Article 4) and torture (Article 5) and asserted the rights of individuals to own property (Article 17), exercise freedom of religion (Article 18) and freedom of opinion and expression (Article 19), work (Article 23), receive equal pay for equal work (Article 23), receive an education (Article 26), and participate in the cultural life of the community (Article 27). Article 16 detailed several rights related to marriage, including that "men and women *of full age* without any limitation due to race, nationality or religion, have the right to marry and to found a family"; that both spouses enter into marriage "with free and full *consent*"; and that "*the family is the natural and fundamental group unit of society* and is entitled to protection by society and the State" (my emphases).

To ensure the promotion and protection of these "human rights and fundamental freedoms" (Preamble), the Declaration outlined several key legal philosophies and procedures, similar to those entailed by the "natural justice" of the British analyzed in chapter 1. Human beings were "endowed with reason and conscience and should act towards one another in a spirit of brotherhood" (Article 1). Every person had "the right to recognition everywhere as a person before the law" (Article 6), the right to an "effective remedy" by "the competent national tribunals" for violations of rights "granted him by the constitution or by law" (Article 8), and the right to a "fair and public hearing by an independent and impartial tribunal" (Article 10). Anyone charged with a penal offense had the right "to be presumed innocent until proven guilty according to law in a public trial at which he has had all the guarantees necessary for his defense" (Article 11).

As this brief overview suggests, the Declaration reflected an array of culturally specific ideas and assumptions. First and foremost, the Declaration promoted a particular notion of "personhood"; the "person" it defined and protected was presumed to be self-contained, free from the burdens of social affiliations, relations, and responsibilities. This social autonomy was mirrored in the economic and legal autonomy ascribed to each individual, regardless of that person's status, such as a person's right to own property ("private property" was itself a historical product) and to be recognized before the law. Second, the Declaration emphasized and expanded the power of the "rule of law" by creating a new transnational legal regime that reinforced state legal regimes and trumped other ways of expressing and seeking justice. Despite claims to "universality" and thus some kind of supra-cultural content, the specific form of justice conveyed in the Declaration—the formal justice of written laws, specific legal procedures, and individual (rather than, say, collective) rights—reflected a particular political-economic context in which private property, nation-states, and courts of law were now the dominant, "natural" norm. Moreover, this new transnational legal regime strengthened the power of states to regulate the behavior of its citizens, even in their most intimate encounters.

Over time, women's rights activists, predominantly from the Global North, voiced increasing concern with what they perceived as the androcentric frame and assumptions of the Declaration and related legal protocols. Although the UN adopted the Convention on the Elimination of all Forms of Discrimination against Women (the "Convention") in 1979,[7] which was ratified by almost one hundred states in 1989, the Convention and its monitoring organization, the Committee on the Elimination of Discrimination against Women (CEDAW), were seen as relatively weak legal instruments. As an international bill of rights for women, the Convention provided important legal mechanisms for women activists, who could pressure their governments to sign and implement its provisions and report regularly on their compliance to CEDAW. But the Convention was difficult to implement, impossible to enforce, and had no direct provision addressing violence against women (Bunch 1990, 495–96).

In a now famous 1990 article, Charlotte Bunch reviewed the long-standing exclusion of women's experiences and rights in international debates and statements on human rights. Although "sex" was listed as one of numerous "distinctions" that would not be tolerated as grounds for denying the rights set forth in the Declaration, questions of gender were rarely addressed in international discussions. As Bunch explained:

> When it is suggested that governments and human rights organizations should respond to women's rights as concerns that deserve attention, a number of excuses are offered for why this cannot be done. The responses tend to follow one or more of these lines: (1) sex discrimination is too trivial, or not as important, or will come after larger issues of survival that require more serious attention; (2) abuse of women, while regrettable, is a cultural, private, or individual issue and not a political matter requiring state action; (3) while appropriate for other action, women's rights are not human rights per se; or (4) when the abuse of women is recognized, it is considered inevitable or so pervasive that any consideration of it is futile or will overwhelm other human rights questions. (Bunch 1990, 488)

In particular, the narrow definition of human rights supported by many in the Global North as solely state violations of civil and political rights (so-called "first-generation rights") rather than economic and social rights such as food, water, health, and education ("second-generation rights") limited their applicability to women (cf. Butegwa 1995; Charlesworth 1995). As Riane Eisler argued, "The underlying problem for human rights theory, as for most fields of theory, is that the yardstick that has been developed for defining and measuring human rights has been based on the male as the norm" (1987, 297, quoted in Bunch 1990, 492). According to Bunch, Eisler, and others, dominant versions of human rights, by considering men as the norm, were unable to address some of the specific needs and problems confronted by women such as reproductive rights; adequate maternity care, benefits, and protection; legal recognition of rape, domestic violence, and sexual harassment as criminal offenses; and codification of the rights of men and women in so-called "family" matters. These issues could, however, be advanced using a human rights strategy that set *humans*, not *men*, as the standard.

In response, a global transnational feminist movement emerged in the 1990s to challenge these narrow, androcentric definitions of human rights by demonstrating "both how traditionally accepted human rights abuses are specifically affected by gender, and how many other violations against women have remained invisible within prevailing approaches to human rights" (Bunch, Frost, and Reilly 1998, 1; see also Fraser 2006). Building on the limited success of reframing women's "needs" into "rights" that could be legislated, monitored, and enforced, activists also began to increasingly adopt the language of violence to describe and advocate for women's rights.[8] The logic, explained Bunch, was straightforward: "Sex discrimination kills women daily" (1990, 489). According to Bunch and other feminists, the most egregious forms of violence against women included wife beating, incest, rape, dowry deaths, FGM, and sexual slavery. Other forms of sexual discrimination included women's subordination in marriage, child custody, inheritance, property ownership, access to credit, education, access to health services, and reproductive rights (cf. Bunch and Carrillo 1991). Some activists argued that all these forms of discrimination and violence against women were related, since women's economic, political, and social vulnerability made them especially susceptible to violent treatment and physical abuse. And since, they believed, many of these gender inequalities were codified in customary, religious, and even state laws, international pressure in the form of legal protocols and advocacy was needed to reform these laws to uphold the human rights of women.

Key moments in the campaign included the UN's Third World Conference on Women in 1985 in Nairobi, Kenya, where ideas of women's rights
as human rights were first debated among women in the NGO Forum and
where global networks of women's groups were crystallized; the second
UN World Conference on Human Rights in Vienna in 1993, where activist women and women's organizations from Africa and elsewhere successfully mobilized and lobbied for formal UN recognition of women's rights as
human rights; passage of the Declaration on the Elimination of Violence
against Women by the UN General Assembly in 1993; and the UN's Fourth
World Conference on Women in 1995 in Beijing, where the campaign gained
further visibility, momentum, and sophistication.[9]

Over the years, increasing numbers of African women reframed their
political struggles in the new terms provided by the expanding international
"women's rights as human rights" movement (Bunch 1990; Schuler 1995;
Hodgson 2003). But most of the African women who participated in the
1985 NGO Forum in Nairobi—and those who subsequently became active
in the international women's rights movement—were elite, educated urban women, often activists, lawyers, and academics from dominant ethnic
groups. They tended to share the modernist perspectives of their Euro-
American feminist counterparts: that rural, uneducated women like Maasai
lived as victims in patriarchal worlds shaped forcefully by the drudgery of
endless household labor, domestic violence, and primitive "cultural" practices like polygyny, arranged marriage, and FGM (e.g., Aina 1998). Rural
women, especially those who still maintained a distinct ethnic identity,
were associated with "culture" and "tradition," precisely the domains the
international women's movement was trying to challenge with its liberal
claims to universal human rights and values, premised on notions of individual agency and autonomy. Rural or grassroots women could be spoken
for and helped, but certainly had little to contribute to the struggle for wom-
en's advancement. Although similar to the recurring tensions between elite,
urban women and uneducated, rural grassroots women described by many
authors (e.g., Hodgson 2003), the marginalization of groups like Maasai was
heightened because of their seeming "excess" of culture.

These ideas about rural women and culture were directly expressed in
many of the international and regional legal protocols. The 1979 Convention
included a specific article (Article 14) about the plight of "rural women"
that detailed their "particular problems" and "significant roles" and man-

dated that states ensure that these women were able to "participate in and benefit from rural development." The developmentalist focus was reflected in the provisions about development planning, adequate health care, social security programs, literacy, loans, and more. When the Declaration on the Elimination of Violence against Women was adopted in 1993, the concerns about rural women were framed in a very different language that now invoked "culture" and "violence." The 1993 Declaration claimed that certain kinds of women, including "women belonging to minority groups, indigenous women, and women living in rural or remote communities" were "especially vulnerable to violence" (Preamble). Included in its description of forms of "violence against women" were "female genital mutilation and other traditional practices harmful to women" (Article 2). It urged states to "adopt all measures, especially in the field of education, to modify the social and cultural patterns of conduct of men and women and to eliminate prejudices, customary practices and all other practices based on the idea of the inferiority or superiority of either of the sexes and on stereotyped roles for men and women" (Article 4j). The 1993 Declaration thus depicted minority, indigenous, and rural women as somehow more vulnerable than others to violence, reframed FGM as a form of violence against women, warned about other such "traditional harmful practices," and presumed that men and women across the globe sought lives in which gender did not shape roles, rights, and responsibilities.

The support of many elite African women for these ideas was evident in "The Protocol to the African Charter on Human and Peoples' Rights on the Rights of Women in Africa" (the "Protocol") that was adopted by the African Union in 2003 and ratified in 2005.[10] Like the 1993 Declaration, the 2003 Protocol called for the elimination of "harmful cultural and traditional practices," specifically FGM and scarification (Articles 2 and 4), and decreed that the minimum age for marriage for women should be eighteen years old and that "monogamy is encouraged as the preferred form of marriage" (Article 6). In contrast to the Declaration, however, the Protocol recognized that "culture" could have positive aspects: Article 17 called for a woman's right to "live in a positive cultural context and to participate in the determination of cultural policies."[11] As these examples suggest, in general rural women were depicted by feminists from both the Global North and Global South as needing increased protections, in part because some of their customary practices, like early marriage, female initiation, and polygyny, were now characterized as "harmful cultural and traditional practices."

Reframing/Renaming Female Circumcision

Eventually, with the emergence and dominance of "women's human rights" as an activist platform, female genital cutting was renamed female genital "mutilation" and reframed from a health concern to a form of gender-based violence and thus a human-rights violation.[12] Together, these renamings and reframings mobilized international and national activists to focus on the eradication of FGM as a key priority. In 1979, the World Health Organization (WHO) organized the first international conference on female circumcision in Khartoum, Sudan (Hernlund and Shell-Duncan 2007, 13). At that time, most activists and policymakers still considered female circumcision to be primarily a health issue and thus a topic of debate for doctors, public health officials, and other medical practitioners and policymakers about the possible effects on a woman's health, including such immediate problems as excessive bleeding and infection and longer-term concerns like lack of sexual response and obstructed childbirth. As Ylva Hernlund and Bettina Shell-Duncan have argued, however, it was (and is) difficult to agree on the medical "facts" as to the real or potential health effects of different kinds of genital cutting because of incomplete, inaccurate, and inconsistent data (see, e.g., Shell-Duncan and Hernlund 2000; Shell-Duncan 2001; Hernlund and Shell-Duncan 2007). Part of the problem was that "extreme cases of infibulation are often used to generalize about health risks associated with all forms of FGC" (Hernlund and Shell-Duncan 2007, 15).[13]

But 1979 was also the year that Fran Hosken published her controversial report, "The Hosken Report: Genital and Sexual Mutilation of Females" (Hosken 1979), which helped launch the widespread, if uneven and controversial, renaming of female circumcision to female "genital mutilation." Although Hosken was not the first person to name the practice "mutilation," the extensive circulation of her report and her fierce advocacy gradually shifted the name of the practice. Calling the practice "mutilation" instead of "circumcision" or "cutting" not only galvanized international attention and activism on the issue, but it also enabled a reframing of the practice from a health issue to a legal one. In 1984, for example, following a seminar in Dakar, Senegal, the Inter-African Committee (IAC) was formed to coordinate national and international efforts to eliminate what is now referred to as FGM (Hernlund and Shell-Duncan 2007, 13). The anti-FGM campaigns were still primarily framed in health terms, as the IAC developed and implemented grassroots educational programs to try to convince people to stop or modify the practice because of its potentially negative health effects. But "culture" was now invoked: FGM was labeled as one of four "harmful traditional practices" that included "childhood marriage and early pregnancy, nutritional taboos, and certain childhood spacing and delivery practices" (Hernlund and Shell-Duncan 2007, 13). By the 1990s, many activists and policymakers had adopted the term, which also spread through the popularity of such books as *Warrior Marks: Female Genital Mutilation and the Sexual Blinding of Women* (Walker and Parmar 1993) by renowned African American author Alice Walker and British filmmaker Prathiba Parmar, and their related movie "Warrior Marks" (Parmar 1993). And in 1993, as discussed above, as part of the expanding logic and success of the "women's rights as human rights" movement, FGM was officially classified as a form of violence against women and thus a human rights violation at the Vienna World Conference on Human Rights (Hernlund and Shell-Duncan 2007, 28).

FEMINIST NGOs AND THE POLITICS OF ANTI-FGM CAMPAIGNS IN TANZANIA

Now that FGM was reframed as a human rights violation, activists could and did demand that states eradicate the practice through criminalization, not just through education and "awareness raising." Elite African women themselves began to mobilize national campaigns for criminalization and eradication. In Tanzania, "female genital mutilation" was prohibited in 1998 with the passage of the Sexual Offences Special Provisions Act (SOSPA), which amended the 1930 Penal Code. Section 21 of SOSPA criminalized FGM on anyone under the age of eighteen. Practitioners could be imprisoned for five to fifteen years, fined up to 300,000 shillings, or both. The law was the product of numerous pressures that are not easily classified as "internal" or "external," given the complex imbrication of the state, national and "local" NGOs, and other actors in activist regimes.

At the same time that the campaign for women's human rights and the concern with FGM was gaining international visibility and traction, Tanzania, like many other countries in the Global South, was undergoing significant economic and political restructuring or, to use the rhetoric of the time, "reforms." Under pressure from the International Monetary Fund

(IMF), international donors, and other global institutions, Tanzania signed a "Structural Adjustment Program" (SAP) in 1986 with the World Bank/IMF. President Nyerere retired in 1985, and the newly elected president, Ali Hassan Mwinyi, moved quickly to institute an array of economic "reforms" that transformed President Nyerere's socialist vision of Ujamaa, the collective good, into a capitalist paradise of foreign investment, individual profit, privatization, economic growth, and increased "efficiency" and "productivity." The reality of these interventions over the years was, of course, more complicated, but key changes included the sale of state-owned parastatals to private companies, often multinationals; the withdrawal of state support from social services like health and education; and the encouragement of individual and international investment in "profitable" industries such as mining, tourism, commercial agriculture, and production of export crops like flowers and seeds. As a result of both international and national pressure, these economic reforms were accompanied by political reforms, such as the introduction of multiple political parties, decentralization of decision making and resource control from the central government to local authorities, expansion of independent media, and the emergence of "civil society" organizations (CSOs) and nongovernmental organizations (NGOs).[14]

The consequences of these changes for Tanzania and Tanzanians were contradictory: intensified class stratification; immense impoverishment of many rural households; stark regional and class inequities in access to quality, affordable education and health services; rapid alienation of land once new laws introduced the possibility of individual (especially foreign) ownership; and the creation of new sites and institutions for political debate. For Maasai and other "second-class" citizens in Tanzania, the neoliberal economic and political reforms exacerbated their precarious economic situation. The state, elites, and now, increasingly, foreign companies took their land for more "productive" enterprises like commercial agriculture, mining, tourism, and hunting and wildlife reserves, further limiting Maasai's ability to find grazing and water to support their herds (Hodgson 2001a, 2011a). Maasai men and women continued to seek ways to diversify their sources of income, but the legacies of poor quality education, lack of infrastructure and access, and discrimination limited these possibilities. Maasai women, like many rural women, were especially impacted by these new economic "reforms." The gendered consequences included increased household labor demands (in the wake of increased male migration), intensified impoverishment, decline in school attendance, and increased maternal mortality and other female health problems with the withdrawal of support for health care (Government of Tanzania 1990; Tanzania Gender Networking Programme [TGNP] 1993a, 1994, 2007).

During this period of intense change, several national feminist organizations emerged in Tanzania that, in contrast to UWT (chapter 2), were independent from state and party control. Two of the most prominent NGOs were the Tanzanian Media Women's Association (TAMWA) and Tanzania Gender Networking Programme (TGNP), both based in Dar es Salaam. Both organizations were deeply involved in promoting "women's rights," but only TAMWA took on FGM as a priority; it advocated intensely in the late 1990s for the Tanzania government to criminalize the practice.[15] TAMWA was established in the wake of the 1985 UN NGO Forum by Fatma Alloo and other female journalists who were concerned with the discrimination they encountered in their industry and the biased representations of women in the media. Over the years, their program and mission expanded from publishing a newsletter and producing a radio program (there was no television in Tanzania until the late 1990s) to focus more broadly on using media advocacy to advance the legal and political rights of women and children (Sheikh 2004, Henry and Alloo 2005, TAMWA 2013). Their vision is "to see a peaceful Tanzanian society, which respects human rights with a gender perspective" and their mission is "advocating for women and children's rights by conducting awareness raising activities for cultural, policy and legal changes/transformation in society through the use of media" (TAMWA 2013).

TGNP developed in 1992 from a series of conversations and workshops among a group of Tanzanian women, many of whom had been involved in other organizations like the Women's Research and Documentation Project (WRDP) at the University of Dar es Salaam and had participated in the UN Decade Conference for Women in Nairobi in 1985 (TGNP 1993b; Meena and Mbilinyi 1991). TGNP focused on advocacy, lobbying, compiling and sharing information, and creating forums for dialogue and debate, all to inform and advance the empowerment of women. The organization, and some of its core members, produced numerous publications in Swahili and English to share information about the situation of women and men in Tanzania and strategies for change, including an occasional newsletter, *Ulingo wa Jinsia* ("Gender Platform"), pamphlets about pressing political or economic issues, and other works (see, for example, TGNP 1993a, 2007; Mascarenhas 2007). In 2013, TGNP described its mission as follows: "Tanzania Gender Networking Programme (TGNP) is fundamentally an activist organization, non-partisan, non-denominational and non-governmental civil society organisation committed to the goal of contributing to the building of a vibrant transformative feminist movement that challenges patriarchy and neo-liberalism at all levels, and advocates for gender equality/equity, women's empowerment, social justice and social transformation in Tanzania and beyond" (TGNP 2013). TGNP is now housed in a large building and grounds in Dar, with numerous offices, meetings rooms, and a library and resource center.

TGNP and TAMWA have both been led over the years by accomplished, well-educated urban women.[16] They have tried to "reach out" to rural, illiterate women, but have had limited success. In these efforts, both organizations have been confronted by the challenges of geography (Dar es Salaam is about a twelve-hour drive from Arusha), class differences in education and outlook, language differences (much of their work is conducted in Swahili and English, which many rural women do not speak), their lack of access to and comfort in rural areas (bad roads, long drives, lack of infrastructure), and of course the limits to their own time and resources. But perhaps even more daunting have been their attitudes and assumptions about the lives of these rural women, especially those like Maasai who still fiercely embrace their sense of ethnic identity. As one TGNP leader explained to me, "Some folks still have the attitude that 'we need to educate' rural women rather than listen and learn from them." The problem, according to several leaders of TGNP and TAMWA, was the "culture" of Maasai and other women, a culture deemed inherently patriarchal, static, and oppressive. As Fatma Alloo explained, "In the rural areas . . . a lot more work has to be done, as the strong cultural affiliations are much more difficult to penetrate than in the urban centres" (Henry and Alloo 2005).

TAMWA's concern for FGM as a violation of women's human rights and a form of gender-based violence seems to have emerged alongside international attention to and reframing of the practice. Early issues of their occasional publication, Sauti ya Siti (Voice of Women), from the late 1980s made no mention of FGM. Instead, they featured articles within the dominant "Women-in-Development" (WID) paradigm of the time about recognizing the value of housework, appropriate technology, concerns about environmental degradation, raising healthy children, and so forth.[17] By 1991, concern had broadened to include attention to "violence" against women and children. An article in the October–December 1991 issue, for example, described the formation of a new "Committee against Sexual Harassment, Discrimination and Violence against Women and Children," of which TAMWA was a member.[18] The purpose of the organization was "to enhance the struggle and safeguard the rights of women and children in matters such as rape, sexual harassment, family conflicts, discrimination in workplaces, custody and maintenance."[19] No mention was made of FGM anywhere in the article.

By the end of 1992, TAMWA had fully embraced the language and vision of "women's rights are human rights" and the argument that violence against women was a violation of human rights. With support from the Swedish International Development Agency (SIDA), they published a special issue of *Sauti ya Siti* in November 1992 titled "On Violence against Women." The long feature article by the editor, Leila Sheikh Hashim, reviewed the many facets of life in which women from "Southern Africa" were exploited and the ways these forms of violence against women violated the principles of both the 1948 UN Declaration and 1981 African Charter (Hashim 1992). Her nuanced discussion of gender relations, power, and female subordination explored both structural causes of female oppression, such as poverty and, specifically, structural adjustment policies, but also "cultural and traditional beliefs," which had helped turn women into "beasts of burden" (Hashim 1992, 3). "Female circumcision" was mentioned in the section on "Health" as one of several practices that could be "hazardous" for women, but not as a form of violence against women (Hashim 1992, 4). But the final article in the issue, titled "Another Form of Violence: The Maasai Female and Circumcision," did frame female circumcision as a form of violence against women, at least in the title. The article, supposedly written by a Maasai woman named Naserian, discussed the circumstances of her own cutting, a friend who got sick from the procedure, her understanding of the reasons for the practice, and concerns about the spread of HIV through cutting. Despite these concerns, Naserian argued that she would "have to circumcise" her daughters "or they will be outcasts and may not be able to get husbands," but she would at least ensure that the circumciser was not drunk and used a fresh blade and that her daughters would be given antibiotics after the procedure (Naserian 1992).

During this period, occasional articles on "female circumcision" appeared in the *Daily News*, the government-sponsored newspaper. Most of the articles framed the practice as a "harmful traditional practice" and called for its gradual eradication on health and medical grounds. According to one article, John Malecela, the prime minister and first vice president, "said he was personally against circumcision of girls. He, however, was afraid because to some people the practice was held in great reverence as there are tribes who view it as a demonstration of a 'real woman'. Ndugu Malecela said persuasive efforts should be made to dissuade the people against female circumcision and mutilation of genital organs by telling [*sic*] its physiological disadvantages and inherent dangers."[20]

Over time, TAMWA developed its concern with "sexual violence" in four specific areas: child abuse, sexual harassment, rape, and FGM (Sheikh 2004, 117). According to Leila Sheikh, one of TAMWA's founders, in 1997 they began a fierce, multipronged campaign to convince the government and the public that FGM (and the other forms of sexual violence) should be criminalized. These activities included commissioning a series of media stories, meetings with members of Parliament, and "legal literacy" workshops with lawyers, police officers, and community members (Sheikh 2004, 117–21). Much to their surprise, Parliament responded quickly, passing the Sexual Offences Special Provisions Act (SOSPA), which outlawed FGM, among other things. TAMWA took the lead in raising awareness about the new laws, especially the FGM provision, through publicity, training, and awareness raising.

Dissatisfied with their slow progress after a few years, in 2004 they organized a national coalition, the Network Against Female Genital Mutilation (NAFGEM), composed of groups of women lawyers, legal rights centers, and others to coordinate and intensify eradication campaigns.[21] In early 2006, TAMWA and NAFGEM launched an intensive media campaign, with almost daily articles in the various English- and Swahili-language newspapers, a rally to commemorate the UN's "International Day of Zero Tolerance of Female Genital Mutilation," and increased pressure on the government to enforce the anti-FGM law. According to one newspaper article, Ananilea Nkya, the executive director of TAMWA at the time, listed the various international protocols the Tanzanian government had signed, arguing that "with this commitment, Tanzania should be seen fighting the vice and more resources should be allocated towards eradication of this outdated practice."[22] Tanzanian activists claimed that a reported decline in the prevalence of FGM from 18 percent in 1996 to 15 percent in 2005 was due to their "awareness campaigns," rather than, perhaps, the increased secrecy of the practice.[23] Over the years, activists became increasingly forceful in demanding that "the government" and the police take action to implement and enforce the 1998 law. According to one 2006 report, "the law has not been effectively enforced since then; there have been some arrests under this legislation, but the prosecutions have been very slow to take place" (Legal and Human Rights Center 2006, 59). While some news stories proclaimed small victories in eradicating the practice ("Genital Mutilators Lay down Tools in Monduli; Maasai Morans Vow Not to Marry Circumcised Girls"), other articles were less triumphant ("Mass FGM Ceremonies Planned in Tanzania").[24]

While this history of TAMWA, NAFGEM, and other Tanzanian NGOs promoting the eradication of FGM through criminalization and awareness raising suggests that it was a "local" initiative, all these organizations received substantial resources from international advocacy and development organizations like Equality Now (based in the United States and the United Kingdom with, eventually, an office in Nairobi) and V-Day (based in the United States), as well as bilateral aid organizations from the United States, Sweden, Norway, and Germany. Equality Now, for example, was founded in 1992 "to work for the protection of the human rights of women and girls throughout the world" (Equality Now 1999). As part of what some now call "governance feminism," they advocated a legalistic approach, working with grassroots organizations like NAFGEM to implement laws criminalizing FGM.[25] FGM was one of four kinds of human rights violations they focused on, the other three being trafficking, legal discrimination, and sexual violence.[26] While Equality Now preferred to channel its funds and advice through NAFGEM and other grassroots organizations, its leaders were also willing to speak directly to the press. In a scathing article in 2010, for example, Faiza Jama Mohamed, the Nairobi office director of Equality Now, questioned the persistence of the practice in Tanzania: "What is the use of having a law against FGM if the government has no plans to implement it?" Moreover, she continued, "Despite being aware of the preparations undertaken by communities to conduct mass mutilations, the police in Tarime [a district in Tanzania] have failed to prevent the mutilations." There had also been "no known arrests of any perpetrators related to the cases of the girls who have already been subjected to FGM."[27]

In addition to the lure of donor resources, Tanzania and other African states faced direct pressure from the United States, Norway, the World Health Organization (WHO), and other international actors to eradicate the practice (Boyle and Preves 2000). As of 1997, for example, states like Tanzania had to provide evidence that they were combating FGM in order to receive certain kinds of international loans and aid from the United States (Hernlund and Shell-Duncan 2007, 39–40).[28] Similarly, a 1999 WHO review of anti-FGM programs declared that "protecting the rights of each and every citizen is the responsibility of national governments" and specifically recommended that "governments must enact and/or use anti-FGM laws to protect girls" (WHO 1999, 13–14, cited in Hernlund and Shell-Duncan 2007, 39). In 2003, the Norwegian government launched a multiyear International Action Plan for Combating Female Genital Mutilation, and anti-FGM campaigns subsequently became a key priority for Norwegian development funding in the name of "gender equality" and "women's rights" (Østebø 2013).

"These Are Not Our Priorities"

So what did this reframing of FGM from a health concern into a human rights violation and its emergence as a (if not *the*) key priority for advocacy and funding to improve "women's human rights" mean for Maasai NGOs like MWEDO and the everyday lives of Maasai men and women? Why was MWEDO so reluctant to participate in the anti-FGM campaigns? How did Maasai men and women respond to the campaigns and to the criminalization of FGM in 1998? How were these dynamics shaped by debates about culture, colonial legacies, class relations, and contemporary contexts of political and economic neoliberal "reforms"?

The Maasai Women Development Organization was registered as an NGO in 2000 "to work towards the empowerment of disadvantaged Maasai women economically, politically, culturally, and socially through implementing activities in capacity building, advocacy, and promotion of human rights within the Maasai community" (MWEDO 2005, 6). It was started, in part, in response to the marginalization of Maasai women in the leadership and work of the numerous local NGOs focused on Maasai, pastoralist, or "indigenous" issues that emerged in the 1990s. These NGOs, which grew rapidly from just two in 1991 to more than a hundred in 2000, were formed and run almost exclusively by educated Maasai men considered "junior elders" in the Maasai age system. Maasai women, with few exceptions, were relegated to the sidelines in the name of "culture" and "tradition" (Hodgson 2011a). One of the founders and the first executive director, Ndinini Kimesera ole Sikar, is an educated Maasai woman who was taken from her rural Maasai homestead as a small child to live with her uncle in the large city of Dar es Salaam for health reasons. She was educated and easily assimilated into the guiding norms of urban, elite, "Swahili" society, yet maintained strong ties with her rural base. After secondary school, she studied finance and then worked as a banker for several years before marrying an older Maasai man, moving to Arusha, and helping start MWEDO.

In 2006, MWEDO described its primary program areas as human rights and advocacy, household economic empowerment, public services development, and cultural citizenship. Work was conducted by a staff of five from a central office in the regional headquarters of Arusha through more than thirty-five village-based membership groups spread throughout four of the five so-called "pastoralist districts" (Monduli, Simanjiro, Kiteto, Ngorongoro, and Longido). MWEDO was so successful in attracting donor funds and members over the years that by 2011, the staff had expanded to fifteen, they claimed a membership of five thousand Maasai women, and they had moved to a large one-story office building on a gated compound with room for outdoor events and a showroom to display and sell fair trade handicrafts. Their headquarters in Arusha provides convenient access to other NGOs and for donor visits, but it is distant from the many communities they serve.

As evidenced by MWEDO's program in "cultural citizenship"[29] and use of the Maa language in workshops and meetings (despite government injunctions that only Swahili be used in such venues), the organization has tried to promote and protect Maasai culture and language in the face of radical social and economic changes. But their primary concern has been with the political and economic empowerment of women. According to MWEDO's 2005 five-year strategic plan, "MWEDO was initiated in 1999 by three Maasai women inspired by the government efforts towards achievement of the goal of sustainable and equitable human development. But the patriarchal relations, attitudes and practices between men and women and between elders and young in Maasailand prevent these efforts. The women realized the need for doing something to support the government's efforts in transforming and operationalising a qualitative shift in Maasailand and national development so that gender equality is recognized in Maasailand"

(MWEDO 2005, 4). As the cover of a MWEDO brochure stated, beneath a picture of a group of seated Maasai women, "women have equal rights within the society" (MWEDO n.d.).

To date, MWEDO has pursued three primary strategies to promote women's empowerment and equality in the context of their increasingly difficult lives. First and foremost, MWEDO has worked to strengthen the economic capacity, income, and autonomy of women through providing small start-up grants for group income-generating projects and training on how to keep accounts, run small businesses, and market their products. Many MWEDO groups, like those in Longido and Kimokowa, have used the money to start projects that produce beaded jewelry, ornaments, and other items for the tourist market. Others have purchased goats and even cattle to raise and sell for a profit. These projects are not without their problems (especially how to market beaded crafts to transient tourists in a flooded market), but Maasai women, as discussed below, have clamored to get involved.[30]

Secondly, MWEDO has promoted the education of pastoralist girls in secondary school and beyond through the provision of full financial support for tuition, room, board, and other needs, including a year of "pre-form I" training[31] where necessary. Their scholarships for girls to attend secondary school expanded from forty-five in 2005 to three hundred in 2013, and they recently started a secondary school for Maasai girls in Arusha and a health clinic in Kiteto, near Ndinini's home village. Funds have come from donors but also from Maasai community members; MWEDO met frequently with community members and leaders, both men and women, to convince them of the need to educate Maasai girls and encourage them to contribute to the Pastoralist Girls Education Fund.

Finally, MWEDO has conducted workshops and awareness-raising sessions on aspects of women's rights. In 2005, these included a large, USAID-sponsored workshop on human rights and democracy designed to educate women about their legal and political rights, including their right to vote (in preparation for the 2005 national presidential and parliamentary elections); a series of workshops about HIV/AIDS (which MWEDO framed as a women's right issue, as in their right to know how to protect their own bodies and decide who would be their sexual partners); and numerous training sessions with different member groups on land rights, livestock policies, legal rights (including marriage, divorce, and inheritance), and other relevant issues. Workshop participants were primarily uneducated Maasai women from rural areas, ranging from elderly grandmothers to young, nursing mothers. By 2011, however, Ndinini told me that she was "tired of endless workshops." As she explained, "What is the point of teaching people about their rights if they can't do anything?"

Focus group discussions, individual interviews, and informal conversations with MWEDO members in 2005 and 2006 suggested that they enthusiastically supported MWEDO's initiatives. One older woman explained to me, "Before we stayed home and waited for men, we were dependent on them for everything. But now we go out and support ourselves." "In the past," another woman interjected, "women had no cattle, but now we do." Older women were also avid supporters of providing secondary education to their daughters. "Papers have gotten heavy," noted a delegate to the 2006 MWEDO Annual General Meeting. "We can't understand them. Pastoralist women are far behind. We need education and MWEDO has helped." Or as another commented, "I really want girls to study. In the past they were married/sold off [kuozwa] and then some returned home because their husbands had no property. Then they became burdens to their fathers. But now they can support themselves." When one of the male delegates to the Annual General Meeting suggested that MWEDO also fund the education of Maasai boys, Nanyore, a younger female member of the MWEDO Board of Directors replied:

> MWEDO does not discriminate against boys. But because of the history of discrimination against girls, it has decided to help girls. We women are mothers of both girls and boys. But if a father has cattle, he uses it to educate boys. That is why Munka, Brown and others are here [referring to older Maasai men who were members of the Board of Directors]. Why are there no older educated women here? The money MWEDO is given is for educating Maasai girls. We would encourage men to start their own education fund—you have the money and ability, but we'll work with you.

Nanyore has herself benefited from MWEDO's education initiatives. As the fifth of six wives of an older man, mother of four, with only a primary school education, she decided several years ago that she was finished having children and wanted more education, including learning English, leadership, and computer skills so she could work with an NGO. Moreover, disgusted with the poor performance of local political leaders, she decided to compete in the election for ward councilor, and she won. She is now a respected politician and community leader who carefully navigates the

demands of her husband and family and her ambitions for economic security and personal advancement.

Nonetheless, although MWEDO supports women's empowerment with a
fairly typical agenda of political and economic initiatives in which cultural
issues are in the background, donors and mainstream feminist groups in
Tanzania foreground Maasai "culture" in their interactions and assessments
of MWEDO's work. Two examples suffice. The first involves MWEDO's relationship with one of their main international donors, which has an office
in Dar es Salaam. During my year of research with MWEDO in 2005–2006,
representatives from the donor group visited the MWEDO offices constantly,
usually with little notice and with official visitors in tow. MWEDO workers
were expected to suddenly drop their work to escort the donors and visitors
to one of their Maasai women's groups. Ndinini and other MWEDO staff
members made phone calls to group leaders, begged women like Nanyore
to ask group members to gather at the last minute to meet with the visitors,
purchased gifts for the women to give the visitors, organized transport and
food, and so forth. Inevitably, the same groups were visited every time, because they were only an hour from Arusha and easily accessible by a tarmac
road. During the visit, the women would dance and sing, give the visitors
gifts, and pose patiently for many, many pictures.

Although Ndinini was grateful for the substantial support MWEDO received from the donor, she confided that she sometimes wondered about
the "real" reasons for its support:

> I am not sure if we are just cultural tourism for them. I looked at their website
> the other day, and there is a big picture of one of their visits to Longido. I am
> worried that they are just interested in MWEDO because of the nice pictures of
> Maasai. But we want to get something out of them. We gave them a proposal
> for maternal health, but they were not interested. They asked us to prepare a
> proposal on family planning, but we weren't interested. They wanted to en-
> courage Maasai women to take birth control pills! Can you imagine!?! But
> what women need is food, health services, education and income—not pills!
> [The donor] is very heavy-handed!

My interviews with some of the donor staff members confirmed Ndinini's
suspicions. When asked why they worked with MWEDO, one senior expatri-
ate man quipped, "They make good photo ops!"

But it is not just white expatriates who romanticize and exoticize Maasai
women, treating them as photo ops to be seen and admired but not to be

listened to. Many Tanzanians do the same. In September 2005, Merry (a MWEDO staff person), Nanyore, and three other MWEDO group members traveled to Dar es Salaam to participate in the biannual Gender Festival organized by TGNP and FemAct (a feminist coalition that includes TGNP and TAMWA as members) on the topic of "Gender, Democracy and Development: Popular Struggles for an Alternative and Better World." For four days, more than two thousand women and men from grassroots organizations, civil society organizations, development groups, government, academia, and overseas participated in plenary sessions, workshops, and performances related to the theme. In addition, there was a large exhibition featuring booths of craft vendors, activist organizations, bookstores, and more. The MWEDO members ran a small booth on the fringes of the exhibition to sell beaded jewelry and crafts produced by member groups. An older *koko* (grandmother) and younger woman staffed the booth most of the time, in part because they barely spoke or understood Swahili (much less English), the dominant languages of the Gender Festival sessions. A third Maasai woman who had attended secondary school in Kenya and was fluent in Swahili and English also stayed with them. Nanyore and Merry, however, browsed the other exhibitions, attended some plenary and workshop sessions, and occasionally helped at the booth. Merry also presented a brief description of MWEDO's efforts to educate pastoralist girls at a workshop on "popular struggles over education." I spent the days sitting with the women in the booth, accompanying Merry and Nanyore to sessions and meals, and helping Merry prepare and type up her presentation.

From the first day, it was clear that the presence of the MWEDO women and booth created quite a stir among other Tanzanians. Many men and women tried on the jewelry, belts, and shirts to see how they looked, modeling to the exclamations and admiration of their friends (far fewer bought anything). By the last day, several neighboring vendors were visibly upset, complaining about why "the Maasai" received all the attention. "Why don't they take pictures of us?" Nanyore in particular was the focus of much attention, as she aggressively tried to sell the jewelry ("oh, you look terrific!") or proudly strode her slim, almost seven-foot frame through the crowds. On the days she dressed in Maasai clothes, she was thronged by men and women who wanted their picture taken with her, to the point where I suggested, only half-jokingly, that she start charging for the photos. "Are you really Maasai?" asked one woman. "Yes, original!" she responded. "See how

my ears are pierced?" (pointing to the holes on both the lower lobe and up-
per ear). At one of the plenary session, when she stood up to ask a question
about why there were not more female members of Parliament, ministers,
and government officials in attendance, she was mobbed by photographers
and participants taking pictures with their own cameras.

But the problem of culture was more than just a performance or display
of difference. On the third day, Nanyore wore an elegant dress and modest
gold jewelry, enjoying a respite from the constant attention of her admirers.
Together with Merry, we attended a workshop on "African Feminism: Theories and Discourses of Resistance." At one point in the discussion, a Tanzanian woman reminded everyone to "remember the problem of culture.
For example, among Maasai, where I have done research, women have no
rights, they are forced to marry instead of go to school, and are forced to un-
dergo female genital mutilation. Men can sleep around, while women can't."
Merry and Nanyore just rolled their eyes at me, but neither responded.
Afterward, I asked them if they agreed with the woman. "No," Nanyore
replied, "it is not that simple. And the problem is that it is always Maasai
who are given as the example of cultural oppression, but they never think
about their own cultural oppression." Perhaps more important, "challenging polygyny [which was also raised in the discussion as a sign of women's
oppression] and female cutting *are not our priorities.*" Instead, she listed land
rights, livestock, hunger, poverty, and education as the more important issues to be addressed.

These were the same priorities and urgent needs shared with me by Maasai men and women when I conducted interviews throughout Maasai areas
in 2005 and 2006: hunger, poverty, lack of clean and accessible water, and,
for many, lack of functioning and affordable health facilities. No one mentioned FGM, polygyny, or even arranged marriage as priorities for change.
The issue of "culture" was, however, raised at the 2006 MWEDO Annual
General Meeting in a fierce debate about cultural authenticity, exploitation, and protection. One woman described an incident in which a donor
group visited, took a lot of pictures, and claimed they would help, but never
followed through. Several women and men discussed the issue of Maasai
clothing and how people from other ethnic groups wore it at weddings and
other ceremonial occasions as symbols of their connection to an "authentic"
African past, or even to make claims to donors that they were Maasai. But
when, for example, Maasai men wore shirts and pants, they were accused

of no longer being Maasai. "I am wearing a T-shirt," proclaimed a younger man, "does that make me not Maasai?" Only one woman raised the issue of FGM: "What about the problem of circumcision [*kutahiri*]? It is part of our culture, but the government says don't do it. What do we do now?" No one responded, but many shook their heads and several muttered about the recent vehemence of government-sponsored anti-FGM campaigns.

THE POWER OF CULTURE AND THE POLITICS OF RIGHTS

So what does this story about FGM tell us about the role of culture and power in contemporary feminist activism and the possibilities and limitations of legal strategies for social change? Nanyore's comment, "[these] are not our priorities," gets to the crux of the problem. While she, Ndinini, and other Maasai activists may be concerned about FGM, polygyny, and other cultural practices, they are far more alarmed by the increasing impoverishment, lack of rights, and marginalization of Maasai women. What they find troubling is that the dominant society in Tanzania, including the main feminist organizations, do not seem to listen to, recognize, or support their priorities. Instead, these groups continue to condemn and even criminalize Maasai for one specific cultural practice—FGM—and use its presence or absence as a measure of Maasai progress and "modernity."[32]

Maanda, a Maasai activist who heads the Pastoralist Women's Council (PWC), the other large Maasai women's NGO in Tanzania that is discussed in more detail in chapter 4, told me a story about how the issue of FGM radically changed her relationship with TAMWA.[33] TAMWA supported Maanda when she fled her village as a young woman to pursue further education rather than marry against her will. She also worked for them for a few years in community outreach. But several years later, when TAMWA asked Maanda and PWC to collaborate in its national anti-FGM campaign, Maanda refused: "I told them it was not my priority, it would block my work." In response, "the woman in TAMWA just told me, 'you won't work against it because you are just an uneducated woman.'" Maanda even refused an offer of more than 200 million shillings (about $150,000) from a German donor "because I was not willing to work and campaign against the practice." Instead, "I believe that it should be dealt with indirectly, by educating girls so that they can make their own decisions." As members of Aang Serian, another community-based organization in northern Tanzania, explained in a letter to one of their donors: "If we were seen to be advocating for legal sanctions against offenders, and/or reporting them to authorities, Aang Serian would come to be regarded as an enemy—siding with the government and urban-based organizations to destroy the Maasai culture and identity" (Winterbottom, Koomen, and Burford 2009, 57).

Like Ndinini and most other educated Maasai women activists, Maanda argues that any effort should be toward seeking alternatives to the modification, which is only one small part of a long series of ceremonies and celebrations that ritually transform a Maasai girl into a Maasai woman (Hodgson 2001a, 2005; cf. Abusharaf 2001). According to Maanda, "it is about cultural survival. You can change the cutting, but you need to keep the ceremony, it is important." And in fact, in several Maasai communities the cutting of the clitoris is being replaced by a small, "ceremonial" cut on the inside of the thigh (see, for example, Hodgson 2001a, 241–49).

The fierce condemnation and criminalization of FGM has indeed produced an array of new problems for Maasai communities. First, the ceremony, which used to be a public celebration, has now become a secret event, often taking place separately from the other rituals that together were part of the multiday female initiation that transformed an older girl into a marriageable woman (see, for example, Hodgson 2001a, 241–49). Second, and more disturbing, many of my Maasai friends report that parents are having their girls "cut" at younger and younger ages to avoid possible disputes, arrest, and criminal prosecution and to ensure that their daughters can get married (see also Olekina 2005). Although the early initiation creates new problems about the status of these girl-women with regard to marriage, sex, and pregnancy, many parents see the marriage of girls as the only viable option to ensure their economic security in a time of increased economic vulnerability and insecurity (see also Archambault 2011).[34] As some Maasai women commented, "Parents don't subject girls to circumcision because they hate them but because they care about them and want them to be accepted and marry into good families" (Winterbottom, Koomen, and Burford 2009, 62–63). Finally, evidence suggests that, as in other times and places, there has been a politicization and resurgence of the practice in response to the new laws and anti-FGM campaigns (see, for example, Thomas 2003; Koomen 2013). Many Maasai, especially older women, perceive the fervent attacks on the practice as yet one more example of how they have been oppressed and dominated by mainstream society in Tanzania (see also Winterbottom, Koomen, and Burford 2009).

Even the "awareness" campaigns had little resonance with Maasai communities. Most of the campaigns echoed the rhetoric and assumptions of colonial and postcolonial development initiatives, with their emphasis on "educating" Maasai about their "backward" and "primitive" practices in an effort to develop and modernize them (Hodgson 2001a, 2001b). Moreover, the materials were often inappropriate or unintelligible to many Maasai women, as they were usually written in Swahili and the illustrations did not reflect the clothing, instruments, or context of Maasai ceremonies (Winterbottom, Koomen, and Burford 2009, 62). Some NGOs have developed curricular materials (like posters and skits) for schools to teach girls (and sometimes boys) about their rights and encourage them to refuse to be cut. But some schools have also become sites for the enforcement of the laws: girls have faced compulsory checks in school to determine whether they had been circumcised (Winterbottom, Koomen, and Burford 2009, 56).

Thus the stance of Maanda, Ndinini, and other educated Maasai activists on FGM is both pragmatic and political. It is pragmatic in the sense that they recognize that their constituents—rural, largely uneducated Maasai women—have more pressing priorities, such as ensuring the present and future survival and security of their families in increasingly difficult circumstances. Moreover, like the colonial officials discussed in chapter 2, they believe that the only way the practice will change is indirectly, through the education of girls (and boys). But their position is also political; it is intended to confront and challenge the structural power of TGNP, FemAct, TAMWA, and other Tanzanian and international women's groups who continue to "speak for" Maasai and other rural women, rather than listen to, learn from, and work with them.

Conflicting ideas of "culture," and the relationship of "culture" to "law," are central to these tensions. Most Tanzanians, especially Tanzanian feminists, have absorbed colonial and socialist ideas of "culture" as equivalent to "tradition," a predominantly negative set of static practices they believe have oppressed women and obstructed their progress toward equality and development. Their attacks on Maasai cultural practices echo repeated campaigns (like "Operation Dress Up" in the late 1960s) by colonial and postcolonial governments (and several religious denominations) to forcibly change other seemingly "primitive" aspects of Maasai culture, such as their attire, jewelry, and use of ochre on their skins (see chapters 1 and 2).

Yet their fascination with Maasai clothes, jewelry, and women suggests an acceptance, even an embrace, of culture as display and performance. Unfortunately for organizations like MWEDO and Maasai women like Nanyore, the result is that they figure more as photo ops than as protagonists struggling for political and economic empowerment.

In contrast, Maasai activists and their constituents view culture as dynamic and contested and often the site of female power and authority (see Hodgson 2005). They often disaggregate "culture" by applying a gender analysis to foreground "positive" practices (that is, those that are empowering for women, as discussed in the next chapter) and dispute "negative cultural practices" (which they see as disempowering) like domestic violence. Moreover, they make clear that the problems they face today are not inherent to their "cultures" and "traditions" but are the historical product of colonialism, missionary evangelization, capitalist industry, and the privatization of their land and natural resources. Even domestic violence and the "culture of patriarchy" are understood as historically produced, linked to national and international patriarchal regimes.

But the tensions also reveal different ideas about "gender" and "gender equality." Several Maasai women, in conversations with me, explained that while they wanted "equality" vis-à-vis Maasai men and all Tanzanians in terms of rights to control and inherit property and resources and access to health, education, and other social services, they were not necessarily seeking "equality" in terms of "women taking men's roles and men taking women's roles." Instead, as Mary Simat, a Kenyan Maasai activist, stated in 2004, "The key principle should be the *complementarity* of gender."[35] Many Maasai women, in other words, are seeking equality in terms of rights but not necessarily roles; most would be content to pursue their historical responsibilities of caring for young and sick animals, managing milk processing and distribution, trading, cooking, caring for children, and so on if the related rights and respect that used to accompany these roles were restored. But they also recognize that years of political and economic changes have undermined such possibilities and have imposed new regimes of cash, commodities, private property, and wage labor that require new ways of being and surviving.

Thus they confront the mainstream international women's movement with a more radical perspective on individual rights that recognizes how political-economic structures like capitalism, neoliberalism, or what some have called the "New World Order" produce structural obstacles to the free exercise of individual rights, so that the promotion of individual rights may at best mask and at worst perpetuate and aggravate these systemic inequalities and imperial relations. They also show how some of these seemingly universal, acultural rights are in fact inherently "culture-bound," with their naturalized assumptions about individual agency, liberal ideas of gender equality, and the inherent values and specific visions of modernity and progress (cf. Hodgson 2001b; Merry 2006, 228). Moreover, several examples in this chapter illustrate how the national and international women's movement itself, in its practices and policies toward Maasai women, has been complicit at times with imperialist "recolonization." If these organizations really cared about the health and well-being of Maasai women, why do they not support them in addressing the economic and political causes of disease, hunger, and insecurity? And if they really cared about the human rights of Maasai women, why do they not support the economic and political rights that Maasai women are seeking? Even if we acknowledge the interconnection of all rights, the question still remains as to *who decides which rights to pursue at any given time.* In the Maasai case, the convergence of the disparagement of rural women, the dismissal of "culture" as an obstacle to liberal ideas of gender "equality," and the reframing of the practice of FGM as a human rights violation have produced a political situation in which the priorities of Maasai and other rural women are dismissed by elites intent on implementing their own visions of women's rights, gender equality, and modern life.

CONCLUSION

As international campaigns to end the practice of FGM have shifted *the naming* of the practice from female circumcision to female genital mutilation and *the framing* of the practice from a health concern to a human rights violation in order to justify their interventions, they have broadened and intensified the pressure on grassroots organizations like MWEDO and PWC to join forces. These campaigns have downplayed the history and complicated cultural meanings of the practice for societies like Maasai, condemning FGM outright as a "traditional oppressive practice," a "harmful cultural practice," and now a form of gender-based violence. The differences between the agendas of Maasai activists and NGOs like MWEDO and those of the dominant Tanzanian society, including prominent national and transnational feminist NGOs, on the matter of FGM echo earlier debates in the colonial and postcolonial period and point to larger tensions over culture, power, and human rights (e.g., Pederson 1991; Thomas 2003; Nnaemeka 2005). As documented in this chapter, the expanding embrace of law at the transnational level through the emergence and spread of human rights frameworks has resulted in the categorization of almost every practice as either a right or a violation of a right. At the same time, the historical legacies of colonial efforts to produce customary law and reify culture as an obstacle to modernist progress has contributed to a situation in which certain practices are now framed as not just a barrier to progress but are condemned as a "harmful traditional practice," a form of violence against women and thus a human rights violation. The convergence in these new transnational legal regimes of the historically produced ideas of "law" as the dominant mode for seeking justice and "culture" as static and negative in colonial and later national legal regimes (chapters 1 and 2) has had real political effects on the daily lives of African peoples like Maasai.

The expansion and embrace of the human rights framework has strengthened the power of African elites to effect change through their control of the national legal apparatus, whose processes, procedures, and presumptions are themselves colonial products. Racialized assumptions about the inherent vulnerability and victimhood of rural, illiterate African women have now also become class assumptions, evident not just in the content of laws that criminalize certain cultural practices, but in the campaigns to enforce them. These laws and campaigns have, in turn, deflected attention and resources from the agendas and priorities of these rural men and women to strengthen their economic security and expand their political presence and power. Moreover, the assumptions in human rights protocols about the privileging of the individual, the demonization of culture, and the power of secular law often make it difficult to recognize and address the structural causes and contexts of gender injustice, such as the dismantling of health care, education, and other social services and the deepening impoverishment produced by neoliberal policies and practices. These neoliberal reforms did more than just change structures; they supported a distinct mode of personhood (often termed "homo economicus") premised on the logics of liberalism: self-contained, self-interested autonomous individuals striving for more wealth, productivity, and freedom from communal bonds. Given the mutual provenance of these economic and political changes and the philosophy behind human rights in the Enlightenment, it is not surprising that they share several common premises such as the privileging of individual rights and freedoms over the supposed tyranny of the collective, a preference for actions shaped by secular modes of reason and rationality instead of sacred connections and motivations, and a belief in the power of law as the fairest form of justice.

NOTES

1. *The Arusha Times*, Issue 00433, 19–26 August 2006.

2. The titles of recent headlines include "Communities Urged to Shun FGM," "Dangers of FGM in Childbirth," "The Crime That Is FGM," "Anti-FGM Rally to Mark Zero Tolerance Day," "How Secure Are Tanzanian Girls from FGM Today?"

3. My findings resonate with the more philosophical arguments of critical feminist scholars like Uma Narayan and Leti Volpp, who have examined why minority women / women of color / women from the Global South are positioned as suffering from "death by culture" (Narayan 1997) and more vulnerable to violence than majority women in the Global North (Volpp 2001).

4. Since I am interested in tracing how the language and framings of the practice have changed over time, I reproduce the terms used by authors and activists and in legal and other documents. In my own work, however, I choose to use the politically neutral term "modification" instead of "mutilation" or "cutting" (see also Kratz 2007). As a scholar seeking to understand how and why the practice occurs, its role within the social and ritual lives of men and women, and the meaning of the practice to all involved, I believe that the term "modification" enables understanding rather than immediate condemnation. Moreover, the phrase "female genital modification" complicates the too easy North-South divide by including consideration of such increasingly common cosmetic surgical procedures in the Global North as labiaplasty (reduction of "large" labias), vaginoplasty ("tightening" and "rejuvenating" of vaginas), and clitoral unhooding. For more information on these procedures, see, for example, Media Articles on Designer Vaginas (2001) and www.labiaplastysurgeon.com (accessed September 22, 2008).

5. The Covenant of the League of Nations was signed in June 1919 and took effect in January 1920. Several articles were amended in 1924.

6. The League of Nations was reorganized and renamed the United Nations in 1945 by the Charter of the United Nations.

7. Convention on the Elimination of All Forms of Discrimination against Women, General Assembly Resolution 34/180, United Nations Document A/Res/34/180 (1980).

8. See Hodgson 2003 for a more thorough discussion of the opportunities and limitations of the reframing of "needs" into "rights" as a strategy for women's rights activists, drawing on a case study of Women in Law and Development in Africa (WILDAF), a transnational African organization.

9. For detailed histories and background of the women's rights as human rights movement, see Bunch, Frost, and Reilly 1998; Cook 1994; Schuler 1995; Alfredson and Tomaševski 1995; Ackery 2008; Agosin 2001; Ferree and Tripp 2006; Lockwood 2006.

10. The Protocol to the African Charter on Human and Peoples' Rights on the Rights of Women was approved in July 2003, ratified by the minimum of fifteen countries by October 2005, and came into force in November 2005.

11. Joanna Bond argues that in contrast to the 1979 Convention, the Protocol's more nuanced understanding of "culture" and "customary" law "offers new hope for promoting gender equality on the continent" (2010, 512; see also Bond 2011).

12. Key works that explore the issues in a more analytical and less polemical fashion, and pay attention to how issues of cultural difference, politics, and context shape the practice and efforts to eradicate it, include Shell-Duncan and Hernlund 2000; Hernlund and Shell-Duncan 2007; Shell-Duncan 2008; Boyle 2002; Abusharaf 2006; and Gruenbaum 2001. I especially recommend the introduction to Hernlund and Shell-Duncan 2007 for a concise, thorough overview of how approaches to FGM have changed over time and the pros and cons of different naming and eradication strategies.

13. The phrase "FGM" describes different kinds of cutting, from small cuts on the clitoris, to "clitorectomy" (the excision of the clitoris), to forms of "infibulation" whereby the clitoris, labia minor, and substantial part of the labia major were cut out and then the outer lips were sewn together, leaving a small hole for urine to pass through.

14. For thoughtful analyses of these interventions and their gendered consequences, see Tripp 1989, 1994, 1997; Chachage and Mbilinyi 2003; Shivji 2006.

15. TGNP adopted the new language of FGM but never made it a priority issue for their advocacy. Thus for example, the 1993 Gender Profile only briefly mentioned "female circumcision" as a health issue (TGNP 1993a, 101), but presented a broad, nuanced structural analysis of the changing situation of men and women. By 2007, TGNP was using the phrase "female genital mutilation," arguing that it was one of several "traditions and customs," including bridewealth, early marriage, treatment of widows, and unequal division of labor, that needed to be changed (Mascarenhas 2007, 54–59).

16. My purpose here is not to disparage the important work of elite women working with these organizations, many of whom are my friends and colleagues. Like all of us, their attitudes have been shaped by their socialization, education, dominant media images, and other influences. Rather, I am trying to explore how these attitudes have shaped their relationships with Maasai women, both "elite" Maasai women like Ndinini and Maanda and their rural, illiterate counterparts.

17. Based on a review of the November 1988, December 1988, September 1989, and November 1989 issues in author's possession. The November 1988 issue did include a brief article about the legal rights of women in marriage.

18. The other members were listed as the Tanzania Women Legal Association (TAWLA), Medical Women Association of Tanzania (MEWATA), Department of Women Affairs of the Organisation of Tanzania Trade Unions (OTTU), Kikundi cha Waliomo katika Mapambano na Aids Tanzania (Organization to Fight Aids, WAMATA), and the Tanzania Welfare Counselling Mission (TAWECOMI). *Sauti ya Siti*, October–December 1991, 16–17.

19. "Committee against Sexual Harassment, Discrimination and Violence against Women and Children," *Sauti ya Siti*, October–December 1991, 16.

20. John Kulekana, "Seminar Denounces Female Circumcision," *Daily News*, 6 April 1993, 3.

21. As of 2006, members of NAFGEM included the Legal and Human Rights Centre, Dodoma InterAfrican Committee Tanzania, Women Wake Up, Tanzania Women Lawyers Association, Anti–Female Genital Mutilation Network, World Vision-Tanzania and TAMWA. Matilda Kasanga, "How Secure Are Tanzanian Girls from FGM Today?" *The Guardian*, 6 February 2006, 8.

22. Matilda Kasanga, "How Secure Are Tanzanian Girls from FGM Today?" *The Guardian*, 6 February 2006, 8.

23. "Tanzania: FGM on the Decline, Study Shows," 12 December 2006, IRINnews .org, citing data from Tanzania Demographic Health Survey, accessed December 12, 2006.

24. Valentine Marc Nkwame, "Genital Mutilators Lay Down Tools in Monduli; Maasai Morans Vow Not to Marry Circumcised Girls," *Arusha Times*, 30 March 2008; staff writer, "Mass FGM Ceremonies Planned in Tanzania," *afrol News*, 9 December 2010. Of course TAMWA and TGNP supported other programs and projects. For example, both were part of a successful coalition to demand changes in the late 1990s to a proposed new Land Act to recognize the rights of women to own, access, and inherit land (Mallya 2005).

25. "Governance feminism" refers to the spread of alliances between feminist activists and international and national legal regimes to pass laws to demand desired social changes (e.g., Halley et al. 2006).

26. www.equalitynow.org, accessed July 4, 2014. See also Equality Now 2011.

27. Staff writer, "Mass FGM Ceremonies Planned in Tanzania," *afrol News*, 9 December 2010.

28. As Hernlund and Shell-Duncan (2007, 39–40) report, "House Bill H.R. 3540 (the Foreign Operations, Export Financing, and Related Programs Appropriations Act of 1997) states that the 'Secretary of the Treasury shall instruct the United States Executive Director of each international institution to use the voice and vote of the United States to oppose any loan or other utilization of the funds of their respective institution, other than to address basic human needs for the government of any country which the Secretary of the Treasury determines' not to be in compliance with such demands."

29. In the brochure, "cultural citizenship" is described as follows: "The program presents overwhelming evidence, carefully documented and organized events of Maasai culture, and shows its potential validity and usefulness; example that of indigenous knowledge and its utility to human development. Likewise, the 'Arts' that is going beyond the Opera house or gallery. It is meant to encourage cultural mapping in development and provision of opportunities without hindering the good traditions and people of their culture" (MWEDO n.d.).

30. Although the potential of such micro-lending, petty trade, and small business projects to produce long-term structural improvements in women's economic security and autonomy is much debated by scholars, development practitioners, and even some Maasai women, most rural Maasai women have eagerly embraced these initiatives as at least short-term remedies to their increasingly dire situations. Moreover, MWEDO, like a number of organizations, has tried to counter the implicitly neoliberal "by-your-bootstraps" assumptions of these projects by requiring women to form groups to borrow, trade, and work, rather than receive loans and goods as individuals.

31. Pre-Form I training is a year of intensive remedial instruction in English, Swahili, math, and other subjects to prepare for the secondary school placement exams that determine which students can attend the much less expensive government secondary schools.

32. Among Euro-American feminists, of course, polygyny is also condemned, but such debates have little public space in a country like Tanzania, where Muslims constitute more than a third of the population.

33. For an overview of current TAMWA programs, see www.tamwa.org.

34. Similar dynamics seem to be happening in Kenya, according to Olekina (2005), Kipuri (2004), and other sources.

35. Mary Simat comments on behalf of Indigenous Peoples' of Africa Coordinating Committee, 11 May 2004. From author's notes.

CHAPTER 4

Demanding Justice

Collective Action, Moral Authority, and Female Forms of Power

ON APRIL 8, 2010, MORE than 1,500 Maasai women from many different villages converged on Loliondo, the headquarters of Ngorongoro District in Tanzania. The women had come together to return their membership cards to the longtime ruling political party, Chama Cha Mapinduzi (CCM). Many of them disobeyed stern police warnings that they would be shot if they walked to Loliondo; others were forcibly returned to their villages by trucks. Nonetheless, hundreds hid with their small children in the bushes overnight until the CCM office opened, then marched to the office and turned in 1,883 party membership cards. By renouncing their membership in CCM, the women explained that they were protesting the evictions of hundreds of Maasai from their area in July 2009, an action that included burning their homesteads and confiscating thousands of cattle. They were also protesting government plans to alienate even more village land by creating a buffer zone along the boundary of the Serengeti National Park.[1] As they left to walk the many miles back to their villages, they sang, "We are not for CCM, which sells our land." According to one report, one female leader "exhorted the authorities not to accuse or arrest any staff from CSOs [civil society organizations] in Loliondo or the women would return in the thousands. 'We have come to know our rights as women and as a community. This is our initiative.'"[2] The response of the government, the political party, and the mainstream media was shocked disbelief at the capacity for women, especially illiterate, rural Maasai women, to organize themselves; they instead accused various male CSO leaders of "instigating" the actions.[3]

This protest was just one of several recent actions staged by Maasai women in northern Tanzania over the past few years to demand justice—in their terms—from people and institutions, including CCM and the Tanzanian state, whom they perceive as fomenting injustice. The persistence of female collective action as a strategy for challenging injustice suggests possible limitations to, frustrations with, or even ignorance of the legalistic modes of action promoted by courts, states, and even national and transnational feminist organizations. Moreover, their demands for justice differ markedly from the obsession of feminist advocacy groups and donors with eradicating FGM or the continuing efforts by the state to impose preferred forms of marriage and family relations. How and why are Maasai women, like other African women, expressing their grievances through collective protests, despite colonial and postcolonial efforts to resolve disputes through legal channels and despite the recent dominance of human-rights-based frameworks? Why is collective protest the preferred form of seeking justice for these women? What are the underlying ideas of justice, personhood, agency, and power expressed by these actions?

In this chapter, I explore these collective actions by Maasai women against government corruption, land dispossession, and other concerns in order to examine their historical roots in customary forms of female collective protest and compare the ideas of justice, morality, and personhood that are deployed in those forms with those of human rights and other legal approaches. This chapter builds on the previous one to examine how the current emphasis on the liberal, rights-bearing "individual" as an autonomous male free agent obscures other modes of being, including a person's various connections and obligations to overlapping collectivities such as family, friends, and community.

PRECARIOUS LIVES, INSECURE LIVELIHOODS

The immediate events that precipitated the April 2010 protest were as follows: in July 2009, the Tanzanian government evicted hundreds of Maasai from eight villages near Loliondo to expand the hunting concession granted by the state to the Ortello Business Corporation (OBC), which is owned by a wealthy brigadier general from the United Arab Emirates.

Members of the Tanzanian police, Field Force Unit, and armed OBC guards burned Maasai homes, killed and confiscated their livestock, attacked men and women, and allegedly raped some women. Subsequently, rumors began circulating that the government was preparing to alienate an additional 1,500 square kilometers of village land to create a buffer zone and wildlife corridor around the Serengeti National Park.[4] These events were just the latest in a long history of efforts by the state to take away Maasai land for more "productive" and "profitable" endeavors throughout northern Tanzania, but especially in Ngorongoro District. As the site of both the Serengeti National Park (created in 1951 and comprising 14,763 square kilometers) and the Ngorongoro Conservation Authority (8,288 square kilometers), Ngorongoro District has long been at the center of conflicts between such different interests as community rights to land and livelihoods, big-game hunting, wildlife conservation, commercial agriculture, and tourism. Incidents of land grabbing by the state have intensified in recent decades in the wake of neoliberal economic reforms that have revised land laws and encouraged foreign investment, especially in the lucrative tourism and big-game hunting sectors. These incidents include an agreement by the state to override local arrangements and "lease" more than four thousand square kilometers of a game reserve to OBC in 1992 for hunting (usually in vehicles with machine guns), large-scale alienations of almost thirteen thousand acres of prime grazing land and permanent water sources to an American safari company in 2008, and illegal and quasi-legal alienations of smaller pieces of land to outsiders (including foreign investors) through corrupt village councils.[5]

As elsewhere in Tanzania, Maasai have become increasingly impoverished with the loss of their land and thus the foundation of their primary livelihood: herding cattle and smallstock. As one elderly Maasai woman I have known for years explained to me in 2005, "Life has become much more difficult since you left [I had last seen her in 2001], there is no rain, no water, and no wood, and people are sicker and hungrier. . . . It seems that people, especially children, are dying more often in these past years. . . . One problem is that people are selling their land to outsiders and others. Someone has problems, and then they sell their land for money, and then the land is gone. We [Maasai] are like an old ripped cloth, it keeps getting tattered and torn, and soon there will be nothing left." The evictions and alienation of their land have been accompanied (and enabled) by their continuing marginalization from political power, denigration of their social and cultural practices, and inequities in quality, accessible education and health care (Hodgson 2011a, 181–204; Sikar and Hodgson 2006). Not surprisingly, as I discussed in the previous chapter, Maasai men and women I interviewed in 2005 and 2006 were very aware of these injustices, describing their urgent needs as hunger, poverty, lack of clean water, and, for many, lack of functioning, affordable health facilities.

To survive, men and women have developed strategies to diversify their livelihoods (Homewood, Kristjanson, and Trench 2009). Most homesteads now cultivate small plots of maize and beans; others use tractors and hired labor to farm food crops and cash crops (such as flower seed or beer barley) on larger tracts of land (Hodgson 2011a). Many young men now leave home for months or years at a time to work in Dar es Salaam, Arusha, and other places as guards, laborers, or Tanzanite brokers (May and McCabe 2004; May and Ikayo 2007; Homewood, Kristjanson, and Trench 2009). Women's options are circumscribed by their primary responsibilities for child care, food provision and preparation, and household chores, and the increasing demand for their labor as herders and farmers in the wake of male migration and the increased enrollment of their children in schools. Nonetheless, many women have sought ways to make money through producing beadwork for sale to tourists, small livestock or dairy projects, brewing and selling alcoholic beverages, casual sex work, and other micro-enterprises. Although, as documented in earlier chapters, women have gradually lost much of their former political and economic power and rights since the onset of colonial rule, they are increasingly the de facto heads of households, responsible for paying school expenses for their children, medical fees, and more.

In response to these incursions into their lands and livelihoods, Maasai men and women have responded with the kinds of "everyday forms of resistance" described by James Scott (1987), most notably "trespassing" with their livestock to graze and water on prohibited lands. In addition, many of the male-dominated NGOs and CSOs that have emerged over the past few decades in the area have tried to challenge the evictions and other actions through court cases, policy debates, publicity campaigns, investigative reports, national and international advocacy, and more, mostly to no avail.[6] Although several prominent male Maasai activists have been trained as lawyers, they have become disheartened and embittered by the pervasive corruption of the Tanzanian legal system and the unwillingness of judges and magistrates to challenge the interests of dominant political elites. In contrast to these failed legal efforts, the various collective actions by Maasai women, including the April 2010 protest, have garnered substantial media attention and intensified the pressure on local and state officials to acknowledge Maasai rights and resolve the conflicts.

Maasai Women and Collective Protest

The 2010 protest in Loliondo was hardly an anomaly for Maasai women or African women more generally. African women have a long, documented history of collective protests, from precolonial Pokot "shaming parties" in Kenya (Edgerton and Conant 1964), to the infamous Igbo Women's War (Van Allen 1972; Matera, Bastian, and Kent 2011), to the recurrent protests by Nigerian women against Shell Oil (Ekine 2008). All these protests emphasize and express women's power, authority, and responsibilities as mothers. In contrast to dominant Euro-American ideas that the power of mothers is limited by their domestic and child care duties, most African women (and men) view these same duties as a central source of women's power within and beyond their households. While women as wives, daughters, and even sisters may now have to submit to the control of their fathers and husbands over their social relations and spatial mobility, as mothers they can challenge these men (and others) if their actions (or inactions) undermine women's capacity to care for their children.

For Maasai, as elsewhere, the protests are thus recognized by both men and women as legitimate expressions of women's moral authority to punish people who violate the social order, especially expectations of respect (*enkanyit*), and to demand justice on behalf of themselves and their families. In the past, as discussed in chapter 1, these violations usually involved serious affronts to women's responsibilities and rights as mothers, daughters, and wives. Recall the description provided by Hollis in 1910: "In the event of a man having intercourse with a pregnant woman, and thereby causing her to abort, he must submit to a punishment which is called ol-kishuroto. All the women of the neighborhood collect together and, having stripped, seize the guilty person and flog him, after which they slaughter as many of his cattle as they can, strangling and suffocating the animals with their garments" (480). Similarly, Maguire described how Kisongo Maasai women in the 1920s gathered to collectively beat women who purposefully aborted themselves or men who were blamed for the abortion. He reported that typically the women took an ox from the culprit, beat it to death with sticks, then ate the meat (Maguire 1928, 17).

Similar reports of *olkishoroto* continue to the present over such violations as a man who had sex with his real or classificatory daughter, or men who prevent their wives from participating in their regular collective fertility gatherings (*oloirishi*) (e.g., Spencer 1988). According to Aud Talle (2007, 356), among Maasai in Kenya:

> Fathers who sleep with their "daughters" are severely punished by women. Together the women organize a punitive delegation (olkishuroto) to his home-stead; there they undress him and bring him to the middle of the cattle corral for everybody to see. The man is mocked and abused by the women for his sexual propensity. "You can have mine," they say, exposing their genitals to show what they mean. One of the man's steers is slaughtered as a fine. Before the steer is put to death, the women will beat him with their belts. This act is a symbolic beating of the man.

Talle described how women also organized *olkishoroto* against other women in certain circumstances: "In the case of a stillbirth, women in the neighbor-hood take action and join a punitive delegation (*olkishuroto*) to the house of the woman. If she is found guilty of having had sex during pregnancy (by traces of remaining semen in the woman (*enkiriati enkiok*) or in the mouth or nose of the child), they abuse the woman and cut her along the nose, the ear-tip and the pubic bone with a razor blade (Talle 1988). Even the husband may be penalized if he admits that he has had sex with the woman during pregnancy" (2007, 366). Paul Spencer reported similar cases of what he called women's "mobbing" among Matapato Maasai in the late 1980s against both women and their husbands if the woman had a series of miscarriages, and against elder men accused of inappropriate sexual relations with their real or classificatory daughters. He described three such cases. In one case, a "habitual drunkard had started to show unbecoming familiarity with a 'daughter' of his age set, pawing at her arm or her body on several occa-sions." His male age mates warned him, but everyone believed that the women would soon "collect together for a mobbing, intent on slaughtering his cattle and beating the culprit himself if they could" (Spencer 1988, 206). In the second case, a man suspected of having seduced his own daughter fled when he heard that the women were gathering together. And in the third case, the man was "less prudent" and encountered the full force of the women's anger:

[Legena] was accused of raping a "daughter" of his age-set in the central corral of a village. Everyone in the locality was outraged, but his age mates argued that this was a matter to be settled by the women and took no action. The women gathered together in a mounting fury. When they appeared in Legena's village, other men fled, but Legena himself was determined to stop them killing his favorite ox and tried to hold them at bay. They seized him, hit his head, tore off his earrings severing his lobes, pounded his back, pulled his legs apart and stamped on his genitals. They then seized, slaughtered and cooked the ox themselves since no elder would venture near to undertake the task. Legena lived for another 30 years, but he was maimed for life. (Spencer 1988, 206)

"Lekton," a long-time Maasai friend of mine, recalled a similar incident among Maasai in Monduli Juu when he was a young man in the 1960s. A man had been secretly sleeping with his daughter and eventually impregnated her. The neighborhood women gathered together, beat the man, and cut off his penis. "That incident was always used as a reminder to me and other boys about appropriate behavior," Lekton explained. "We'd often warn each other, 'be careful, or you will end up like [the name of the man who was punished]!'" He recalled other incidents of *olkishoroto* from his youth that echoed the accounts recorded by Talle. For example, "If a child was born with lots of semen-like stuff around him, people believed that was a sign that the husband had kept sleeping with his pregnant wife. They believed that the semen slowed the development of the child. If the midwives saw this, they would call other women together to go to the man's house and beat him up. Sometimes they would turn the homestead gate (*oltim*) around to face inside out, which signaled that he had opened his homestead to enemies." When I asked if he had ever witnessed any instances of *olkishoroto*, Lekton replied, "I did witness a group of women looking for a man who had slept with one of his pregnant wives, but then I ran away too!" As he concluded, "Women really, really have power when they get together. They are controlled by older women, often the midwives, who galvanize the other women."[7]

These accounts of *olkishoroto*, like others, emphasize the collective nature of the women's "mobbing," their willingness to use violence against persons and property as punishment for illicit actions, and the recognition of all involved—both men and women—of the legitimacy of their actions. As Lekton suggests, the very threat of women's collective protest (and stories of past reprisals) generally served as an effective deterrent to potential misconduct.

Maanda, pwc, and the Mobilization of Women

The repeated collective protests in Loliondo, however, were not just contemporary manifestations of an enduring customary practice. The mobilizations were also enabled, in part, by the work of a Maasai women's NGO, Pastoral Women's Council (PWC), and the formidable leadership and example of PWC's founder, Maanda Ngoitiko. Like MWEDO, PWC was founded to respond to and represent the interests of Maasai women. In contrast to MWEDO, however, from the beginning PWC took a much more activist stance on economic and political matters and engaged with the local community in a more consistent, substantive manner.

Unlike Ndinini, Maanda faced considerable obstacles to pursuing her education. She was one of the only children from her extended family to attend the local primary school, which was several miles away, lacked textbooks and resources, and was staffed by a non-Maasai teacher who beat the Maasai children and yelled that they were "dirty, bad and backwards."[8] For years she was able to resist demands from her father to leave school and marry, but at fifteen she had to run away from home with the help of one of her uncles to escape an unwanted arranged marriage and pursue further education. After a brief stay in Loliondo, she spent the next few years in Dar es Salaam, where she worked for TAMWA by day and took secondary school courses at night. Once she completed her exams, she returned to work for KIPOC, a major Maasai NGO based in Loliondo, as their "women's and children's coordinator" and continued to study on her own, eventually reconciling with her father and family.[9] After a few years with KIPOC, the Irish embassy sponsored her for two years of study in Ireland to complete a diploma in Development Studies.

PWC started from the conjuncture of two processes: Maanda's frustration with the unwillingness of KIPOC to seriously address the concerns of Maasai women and the encouragement of hundreds of Maasai women attending the Annual General Meeting for KIPOC in 1997 to start an organization for them to meet and discuss issues. More than five thousand people from all over Ngorongoro District attended the meeting, half of them women. According to Maanda, "After the meeting, the women collected around me and said, 'Maanda, you have been with us a long time. Is it possible to start our own forum, to just meet and discuss issues?' Elaine Ward, who was a Canadian working with Ilaramatak [another Maasai NGO] at the time, happened to be at the meeting, so I asked her for help, and whether such a women's forum could happen. She said yes—absolutely—they had actually been thinking about such a thing. So that is how the Pastoralist Women's Council was born." For three months, Maanda met regularly with a group of ten women to discuss the structure and agendas of PWC. Initially, they decided to focus primarily on girls' education since, according to Maanda, "increasing numbers of girls in Loliondo were refusing to leave school and marry, [saying] 'we want to be like Maanda, we want to be educated.'" Several contacts, including prominent male Maasai activists, introduced Maanda to potential international donors, who provided funds to support the education of ten girls.

Over the next decade, PWC slowly built up its funding base and staff and expanded its programs and community involvement. By the time I visited their office in 2006, PWC was involved in an array of programs in northern Tanzania. In contrast to MWEDO's central location in the regional capital of Arusha, PWC was run out of a small building in the remote village of Soit Sambu, which made it accessible for community members but not convenient for donors, consultations with other NGOs, or national and international travel, given the long distances, bad roads, intermittent electricity, and minimal communications infrastructure. The small staff of five local people claimed to work with almost six thousand members, most of whom lived within walking distance in the surrounding areas of Ngorongoro District.[10] One of their major priorities continued to be the education of girls. In 2006, they provided scholarships for girls, managed a nearby secondary school for girls and boys, and focused on economic empowerment, raising legal awareness, and political advocacy projects. Like MWEDO, they encouraged women to form groups to earn money, but their projects were mostly livestock-related. One of their unique projects was the "Women's Solidarity Boma," which provided a haven for abused women who supported themselves caring for project livestock. Livestock were sold to subsidize children's school fees, and there was a revolving goat fund for women. To help ensure that Maasai girls even made it to secondary school, PWC also encouraged communities to start nursery schools for both boys and girls and carefully monitored the progress of girls in primary school. As Maanda explained, "We try to talk to their parents before they finish primary school. Sometimes we succeed, but sometimes there are problems. There are an increasing number of girls who are fleeing arranged marriages. One girl from Arash walked three days in the wild to Soit Sambu, avoiding the road in case she was caught!" Maanda, like many male and female Maasai activists and community members, believed that the education of girls was the key to their future empowerment, providing them both the practical and theoretical tools to determine their own paths. As one PWC member told me in 2006 during a group interview, "The PWC taught us the value of education, they emphasize the education of girls. Now we see the importance of girls' education. Now we can start. Many of our girls now go to school. They have learned to talk to men." When I asked why she thought it was important for girls to go to school, she responded, "A girl will help her parents; she won't forget her parents. But once a boy marries, he forgets his parents, saying 'I have my own kids!'" As the other women nodded vigorously in support her of statement, one interjected, "A girl loves her parents until the end!"

PWC's desire to be fully accountable to and representative of its members, most of whom were illiterate women, was best captured by the composition of its governing board: elected members from the community (the members of MWEDO's board, in contrast, were elite, educated men and women, mostly Maasai). In my interviews and conversations with PWC members throughout the area, they echoed their strong support of Maanda and the PWC. The PWC "brought light," explained one older woman, "before we were blind." "PWC opened our eyes," said another woman. "Now we demand our rights because of PWC's teaching." Members proudly described becoming less financially dependent on men, learning how to speak up at public meetings, and recognizing their rights to own their own property. After working with and studying numerous Maasai and pastoralist NGOs (Hodgson 2011a), I was especially struck by the pervasive sense of ownership of PWC by its members. "We are the leaders of the PWC," said one board member. "Those who run the PWC work for us. The PWC is my *enkang* (homestead)."

The key difference between MWEDO and PWC was their involvement in development, advocacy, and activism. MWEDO's work was primarily within a mainstream "women and development" (WID) paradigm: supporting education, adult literacy, income-generating projects, workshops, and so forth to raise women's awareness of their rights, provide them access to money of their own, and strengthen their autonomy. PWC's work was more radical, in part because of Maanda's more political and, at times, confrontational stance challenging corrupt state officials, illegal "land grabs," and male efforts (whether Maasai or not) to limit the involvement of women in their deliberations and decision making (Ngoitiko 2008). Maanda was fundamentally an advocate and activist concerned with gender equity, but she was also alarmed by the political and economic disenfranchisement of pastoralists more generally (see, for example, Ngoitiko et al. 2010). To these ends, she not only led PWC but also worked with her husband in another local organization, UCRT (Ujamaa Community Resource Team), "to empower marginalised people in the rangelands of northern Tanzania to secure rights to their natural resources and land in order to improve their livelihoods and ability to conserve their resources" (UCRT 2013). She was also elected to serve successive terms in one of the women's seats on the District Council, further extending her power and presence in local politics. Initially, Maanda experienced frequent harassment, expulsion from meetings, and even threats to her life by men alarmed by her example and the growing collective self-assertion of their wives and daughters. But according to Maanda, "things have changed. In the early days, men would slander us, especially me, or say that good things were only happening because of my father, not me. But now we have lots of support."

As a result, although some of PWC's work, like MWEDO's, was in the WID mode, PWC was also active in seeking not just economic and political empowerment but also using advocacy and activism to seek economic, political, and social *justice* within Maasai communities and between Maasai and the Tanzanian state. PWC's political engagement was partly a result of *how* they worked; their daily presence in the communities fostered close relationships and a deep understanding of and involvement in local politics. But it was also a product of *where* they worked: in Ngorongoro District, the epicenter of efforts by the Tanzanian state, capital, tourism firms, hunting firms, and others to take land away from residents.

Customary Forms, Contemporary Demands

The recent collective protests by Maasai women were thus a contemporary manifestation of *olkishoroto*, an enduring customary practice, and the engagement and involvement of PWC under the leadership of Maanda. While Maasai women in Tanzania and Kenya have continued to use *olkishoroto* to punish violations by men (and occasionally women) of women's rights, by the 1970s they had expanded the targets of *olkishoroto* to include elected officials, party members, and other Maasai and non-Maasai leaders whose actions, the women believed, were threatening their responsibility as mothers, which included not just ensuring the physical well-being of their children but their moral and cultural well-being as well.

In 1977, for example, a group of Maasai women mobilized in response to a government decree that Maasai men and women had to wear "modern" dress (shorts, shirts, skirts, or dresses) in order to ride buses to town: "At Kijungu where the ban [on dress] was proclaimed, a large group of women from all over the South got together to curse the Masai leader of the community. . . . Then they began collecting money for an en masse trip to Dar es Salaam to present their complaints to the president. The curse was eventually removed by a judicious slaughtering of a number of cattle and the women persuaded not to make the trip to Dar. In the North, the national parliamentarian was also cursed" (Hatfield 1977, 16). According to Colby Hatfield, the American sociologist who witnessed the incident, the women were upset because for them, "the skin skirt became . . . the symbol of their position in life" (Hatfield 1977, 16). As a result, the women mobilized to protest the inaction of most Maasai men in challenging the ban and the seeming complicity of other Maasai and non-Maasai men with the order: "a normally most apolitical segment of Masailand, the women, reacted in the best traditional manner when affronted unjustly by cursing those whom they felt should be responsible for pleading their cause, but were also determined to by-pass the entire political machine and make their grievances known to the Head of State" (Hatfield 1977, 16).

Similarly, in the early 2000s, Maasai women in Ngorongoro also protested what they perceived as another attack by the government on their cultural rights and moral authority: the criminalization of FGM. According to Lekton, when the police arrested some elders for allowing their daughters to be cut, a large group of women went to the police station and threatened to strip themselves naked unless the elders were released and the charges were dropped.

During this period, women from neighboring ethnic groups with histories of similar customary practices also began to mobilize against the Tanzanian state and its institutions. Katherine Snyder (1997, 2006) has documented how Iraqw women broadened the reach of their collective protests from demanding that (male) elders perform a key ritual (*masay*) in times of drought "to cleanse the community and enable the rains to fall" (Snyder 1997, 561), to marching in 1996 to meet with the district commissioner and then the prime minister of Tanzania to complain about male schoolteachers who were impregnating their daughters and, in 2000, to protest the sale of an illegal alcoholic beverage (*gongo*) that was causing male drunkenness and with it a host of social problems. Like Maasai women, the power of Iraqw women was premised on their strong spiritual relationship with their "benevolent female creator deity" Looaa, who, like the Maasai female deity Eng'ai, was responsible for caring for all living things, especially the "welfare of children and, by extension, the entire community" (Snyder 1997, 565). Therefore, according to Snyder, "when Iraqw women march, they are emphasizing their role as mothers of children, not as wives, and it is this role that carries power and authority" (2006, 93). Similarly, Barbaig women in Babati organized a series of protests in 1989 and 1990 condemning the inaction of male leaders over an array of social problems ("widespread alcoholism, violence, insecurity, foul language, and gang rape") that had arisen in their small trading community.[11]

Thus the 2010 CCM membership card protest has precedents within and beyond Maasai society. Indeed, the 2010 demonstration was not the first organized action by Maasai women against the Ortello Business Company (OBC) and its supporters in the state and CCM. In 2003, many Maasai families were angry at the OBC for encroaching on land beyond the boundaries of its lease to hunt, failing to provide promised community development support to surrounding villages, and hiring outsiders rather than residents for jobs in the compound. One day, a group of about five hundred women cut sticks, stripped themselves naked, and stood on the airstrip used by the OBC to land its large planes. The women stood fast as the plane circled and circled, unable to land. According to Timoth, a PWC staff member, the women wanted the "Arabs" (as they called the people who worked for OBC) to either return their land or fulfill the promises they had made when they took the land. Timoth later explained to me that the women were frustrated that their husbands and other Maasai men had not done more to challenge OBC; "the women told men off in the meetings: 'You are selling the land, let us lead the meeting!'"[12] Although there seems to have been no media reports on the action, news of the protest spread quickly throughout northern Tanzania.

Despite the short-term success by the women in 2003 of preventing the OBC planes from landing, OBC continued to occupy and hunt in the land granted to it by the Tanzanian state. The 2006 transfer of an additional twelve thousand acres of dry-season grazing land from the state-owned

Tanzania Breweries to Thomson Safaris, an American safari company, further upset the communities, who had long disputed the initial alienation of the land by the state and demanded its return (Gardner 2016). Conflicts between residents and representatives of OBC and Thomson escalated, including some violent encounters resulting in the death and maiming of several young Maasai men.[13] Maasai residents, both men and women, became increasingly resentful about the rapid erosion of the land on which their livelihood depended and what they viewed as the power of the state (and its legal apparatus) protecting outside investors like OBC and Thomson Safaris, rather than its own citizens. As one visitor to the area in 2010 reported, "Sandet [a male, Maasai elder] looked over the valley. He waved his staff across the expanse and said bitterly, 'It is very simple. A person is welcomed into a house and is entertained by the owner. Instead of just visiting, the person occupies all of the place and the owner becomes a refugee. . . . We have become squatters in our own home.'"[14] Sandet's last comment, "we have become squatters in our own home," expresses the sense of betrayal felt by many Maasai who have tried to comply with the ever-changing thicket of conflicting government laws and regulations, only to find that the rules have changed, yet again, in favor of others interested in obtaining Maasai land for big-game hunting, wildlife preservation, tourism, mining, and commercial farming. As one Maasai village government member complained to Benjamin Gardner: "They [Thomson Safaris] are owning the land through papers. That land is our traditional land. They have the right and protection of the government if they believe they own the land through papers. . . . Who to believe, paper or us? They have a legal paper from Dar es Salaam. What about the people in this area? This is our ancestors' land" (Gardner 2016, 119). His lament echoes that of many Maasai I spoke to, that the "papers" (laws and contracts) were used by the government to dispossess them from their land rather than to protect their rights to their land as citizens.

And so the April 2010 protest by the women was precipitated by both the longer processes of economic dispossession and political oppression as well as the more immediate manifestations of those processes: the evictions, burning of homesteads, physical assaults of men and women, confiscation of cattle, and news of plans for further alienation of village lands.

But there were important differences between the April 2010 protests and prior invocations of *olkishoroto* that demonstrate its persistence and adaptability to new issues, actors, and contexts.[15] First, the group of women who protested was much larger and more diverse than the delegations of neighborhood women who usually gathered to punish men (and sometimes women) who violated moral norms. In Loliondo, more than fifteen hundred women came together from many different villages, some more than twenty miles away. An additional four hundred women from Ololosokwan village tried to participate, but police forced them to return to their village after they ignored earlier police warnings that they would be shot if they tried to join the protest in Loliondo. But they had gathered more than a thousand party membership cards and were collecting more. According to their chairperson, Kooya Timan, "Unless CCM gives us everything to make up for 50 years of suffering, we will never go back." Another sixty women from Enguserosambu village were arrested and interrogated for hours. The dramatic size of the women's delegation reflected both the depth of their concerns over the evictions and land loss and that they were confronting an institution—CCM, the long-dominant political party—not an individual.

Second, in contrast to Maasai men like Lekton who knew to hide or otherwise try to avoid large delegations of women, in this case the women themselves had to hide in the surrounding bush to avoid the police, who were waiting on the elevated airstrip and in other areas to stop the women. Despite these threats and obstacles, "about 600 women made it through the harassment to the CCM office in the late morning today and surrendered 1,883 CCM cards."[16] As one commentator noted, "This is a very very remarkable achievement, after two days without food and an overnight drenching and police threats and harassment. I know these women, but I am stunned that they have been able to see this through."[17] The persistence of the women in the face of the sometimes violent efforts by police and others to block their protest speaks to their fierce sense of injustice. Although they did not physically attack the CCM staff or bare their bodies as described for past protests, turning in the CCM membership cards was itself a deeply meaningful act of symbolic violence, a deliberate disavowal of the long-term dominance of the party and, through the party, the state.

Third, leaders and allies of the women had notified journalists (both print and TV) about the protest in order to provide both publicity for the action and protection for the women. Access to these now widespread, relatively inexpensive media technologies conveyed the women's demands to national and even international audiences, thus magnifying the reach and reinforcing the validity of their protest and concerns. According to these reports, the women had three principal demands:

> 1) That the parliamentary committee's report into the evictions of July 2009, blocked by the CCM caucus in February, be tabled when Parliament opened the following week.
>
> 2) That the government disavow plans to cut village land by creating a buffer zone along the boundary of Serengeti Park.
>
> 3) That women be allowed to have a peaceful demonstration in Loliondo town, since previous request were turned down by the police.[18]

Although some CCM staff members initially dismissed the women, the CCM chair eventually arrived and tried to placate the women and consider their concerns. After long discussions with the him and his staff, the women left for their homes, promising to return in a week with five thousand cards if their demands were not met.[19]

The involvement of CSOs like PWC in organizing and supporting the protest was a topic of much debate by the government and media. As discussed above, the sustained involvement of PWC (among other CSOs) throughout communities surrounding Loliondo, and Maanda's fearless advocacy in protecting land rights, had developed and strengthened networks of women across villages through PWC's membership structure, thus enabling the large mobilization. But the CSOs were not directly involved in organizing the specific protest. Several prominent CSO leaders had in fact fled to Arusha several months earlier in fear of their own safety in the wake of the evictions and burnings in 2009 and harsh verbal attacks on NGOs and CSOs by government representatives. During the protest, the police "repeatedly asked 'Who helped organise you?'"[20] As news of the protest spread, the government started a "witch-hunt for perpetrators," accusing CSO leaders of "fomenting the protest" and threatening to close their programs.

Moral Authority and the Sacred Power of Mothers

Thus the April 2010 protest reflected the persistence of women's customary forms for expressing condemnation and demanding justice for themselves and their families, set within the drastically changed political and economic contexts of their lives. While the substance and scale of women's demands in Loliondo were perhaps relatively new—challenging evictions, land alienation, corrupt officials, and the resulting increase in the insecurity of their families—the form, collective protest, has a long history based, as elsewhere, in the moral authority and political power of women as mothers. According to several accounts, most of the women had small children with them, a clear statement that they were drawing on their status as mothers to protest those they saw as most responsible for undermining their ability to care for their children. These women, in other words, perceived the assault on their families—through the evictions, burnings, violence, dispossession of land, and more—as immoral; as violations of not just the social order, but the sacred order; and as an assault on their rights and responsibilities as mothers. Their power as mothers, as discussed in chapter 1, was predicated on their close relationship to their primarily female divinity, Eng'ai, with whom they shared material and metaphorical concerns with fertility, nurturance, and growth. Maasai women therefore saw themselves as "custodians of the moral order" (Spencer 1988, 207), responsible for challenging perceived violations to the social order, whether from incestuous men in the past or corrupt state and party officials in the present.

As a form of justice, *olkishoroto* differed in several important ways with the colonial, national, and international legal regimes described in earlier chapters. As discussed above, in contrast to rights-based regimes that claimed a separation of the secular and sacred, *olkishoroto* was predicated on a concept of morality in which the secular and sacred were deeply and irrevocably intertwined. The political efficacy and legitimacy of their protests was premised on their spiritual closeness to and sacred bonds with Eng'ai as women, especially as mothers.

Moreover, through their protests, Maasai women emphasized the need and power of challenging these perceived injustices *collectively* and not as individuals. As individuals they could do little to challenge the injustices they faced, even through the dominant legal regimes of lawyers, formal laws, individual rights, judges, and courtrooms that had been forged over the previous century. But together they were a force to be reckoned with, capable of sending Maasai men into hiding, overcoming the threats and violence of police, and directly confronting representatives of the state and political party. The collective nature of their actions expressed and reinforced the value of social connections and relationships rather than individual autonomy and rights. As mothers, women could never be completely independent individuals; they always had obligations and responsibilities to others, especially their children. Respect and power came from recognizing, affirming, and nurturing these social relationships with their children and with one another.

Finally, in contrast to the limited ability of human rights frameworks, with their focus on individual rights and legal remedies, to recognize and confront problems of economic inequality and collective disenfranchisement, the women's protests addressed the structural inequalities that have alienated them and their families from lands and livelihoods, and they directly challenged the involvement of the Tanzanian state in facilitating their subjugation and oppression. Indeed, while the national legal regimes that were predicated on colonial ideas of "natural justice" might have been used by the state and elites to try to protect Maasai women by regulating "harmful traditional practices," they were also used to protect the power of these same elites and their foreign allies by supporting the dispossession of Maasai men and women from their lands. As described in the previous chapter, the adoption and "vernacularization" (Merry 2006) of "women's human rights" by elite activists and policymakers in Tanzania has led them to focus their efforts on certain issues (like the criminalization of FGM) presumed to benefit rural women like Maasai, to the exclusion of others (like the protection of land holdings) that were in fact key priorities for Maasai.

LISTENING TO AND LEARNING FROM THE "GRASSROOTS"

The visibility of Maasai women's collective actions and their more radical demands for economic and political justice not only astounded the press and public, but they also challenged the attitudes of elite leaders and members of TGNP, TAMWA, and other national feminist organizations toward Maasai women. Several of these organizations mobilized to support the Maasai women and their communities in their struggles. FemAct (which includes TGNP and TAMWA in its membership), for example, sent a team to Loliondo to investigate the situation. They published a statement, signed by both TGNP and TAMWA,[21] protesting the evictions and circulated a video to publicize the dispute. In contrast to the anti-FGM campaigns described in chapter 3, in this case Maasai women welcomed the involvement of these national organizations, since they were mobilizing in support of (rather than against) the political priorities of Maasai women themselves.

A few months after the evictions, more than forty Maasai women from the area, many of them PWC members, attended the 2009 Gender Festival organized by TGNP in Dar (accompanied by ten men). In contrast to MWEDO members in 2005, who ran a booth to sell beadwork and handicrafts, made a presentation in a workshop on education, and attended other workshops and plenaries, the PWC members used the occasion to collectively demand economic and political justice. As Marjorie Mbilinyi, a founder of TGNP, described in a published interview, "On the occasion of the recent Gender Festival in Dar es Salaam last September 2009, for example, more than 50 women came from Loliondo (Ngorongoro District) to protest land grabbing: their homes were burnt down and they and their families were forcibly evicted from their land by our government, because of demands from a private hunting company! They marched into the Gender Festival singing and carrying their posters, read out their protest message, and later, went to carry out a sit-in demonstration at the office of the President, State House" (Anonymous 2010). As Kooya Timan, one of the Maasai participants, explained, "The government has successfully executed its operation, they have torched our houses so that OBC can hunt without any interference . . . are President (Jakaya) Kikwete's children sleeping outside like ours?" "Are we Tanzanians or refugees?" she asked. "We feel it was in the investor's interests that the government reacted."[22] Another participant, Pirias Maingo, echoed the complaint that Maasai were not being treated fairly as citizens by the government: "We are facing many problems in our own land, our children are disappearing, the women are being raped and the government is silent, we need to be told if we are Tanzanians or not." Like Kooya, she invoked President Kikwete's children: "We want to see President Kikwete, we want to ask him if his wife and children are also experiencing what our children are going through, we need him to witness the reality on the ground."[23]

At the meeting, the women presented a formal statement "prepared by 978 women" from seven villages that outlined their grievances and demands.[24] Like their protests, the statement began directly, with no polite preamble: "We women of Ngorongoro District are highly disappointed by the decision of the Government of the United Republic of Tanzania to burn down our homes and hand over our land to the hunting company from the United Arab Emirates, namely Otterlo [sic] Business Corporation (OBC)." They invoked their obligations as mothers to argue that the evictions had affected women and children the most, "especially because of *the huge responsibilities we have to care for our families* (emphasis mine)." Women complained about losing their homes, being forced to live in "drought stricken areas which lack water and pasture for our livestock" and having to walk more than fifty kilometers to fetch water. They provided a list of fourteen specific grievances and injustices: the burning of their homes without provision of alternative shelter; disappearance of one child; hunger; miscarriages by four women because of their "shock" due to the "violent manner" of the forced evictions; the rape of one woman by a Tanzanian Field Force officer; children dropping out of school because of the dislocations; death of livestock because of shortages of water and grazing land; lack of health services; the destruction of their furniture, food, money, livestock, and cooking utensils during the house burnings; and more. One item directly condemned the national legal apparatus as a source of injustice rather than justice: "Sixteen of our children have been framed with criminal cases, and jailed without following legal procedures for justice." But, they concluded, "greatest among all of these is that we have lost our land; we do not know where we will live; most of us were born here, and this is our permanent residence."

Given these many grievances, including "the lack of a space and place to speak openly after the Government rejected our request to carry out a peaceful march," they insisted that the government implement eleven demands. These included halting the ongoing evictions, providing emergency relief and social services, stopping the "unjust detention and framed court cases of our children," incorporating women "in all decision making processes regarding such actions and the future of our society," punishing all parties involved in the eviction, removing the hunting company and "ensuring the safety and security of their land," and paying compensation for all injuries and losses. Finally, they asked the government to "give permission to the women of Ngorongoro to hold a peaceful march and demonstration so that they can express their grievances to the people of Tanzania and the whole world."

As Marjorie told me later, "the Maasai women won over the rest of the Gender Festival" (about three thousand people attended in 2009) and helped them "negotiate the biases that non-pastoralist people have about pastoralists." "We learned," she said later, "from Maasai women at the 2009 Gender Festival about economic justice." As she explained in her 2010 interview, "In my experience working with pastoralist women in Ngorongoro, as well as grassroots women in many other places in Tanzania—you know the old saying from South Africa, 'when you touch a woman you touch a rock'—I have learned that there are many women who are prepared to stand up and denounce injustice completely, without fear, because they have nothing to lose. There are no benefits from the system they work and live in to discourage them from protesting. Moreover, they are driven by their commitment to their children and grand-children" (Anonymous 2010). Of course, Maasai women (and men), including Ndinini and Maanda and the members of MWEDO and PWC, have been seeking economic and political justice, in their own terms, for years. Fortunately, although their struggles to retain their land continue, at least some of the national feminist organizations like TGNP, TAMWA, and FemAct have begun to see beyond the stereotypes of rural women that still dominate transnational feminist discourse and listen to and learn from them, rather than preach to them.[25]

And so, by drawing on their long tradition of collective protest and modifying it to address current forms of injustice, Maasai women have emerged as a powerful political force to be reckoned with by the state and political party. As one Tanzanian reporter noted, when commenting on the 2010 Loliondo protests, "In the past, the Maasai were renowned for their warrior force, the morans. The age-sets still open and close to new spear carriers. But today the formidable army of the Maasai is their women."[26]

NOTES

1. "Ngorongoro Land Row: Government Forsakes Small Beleaguered Community for Revenue!" *The Guardian*, 15 April 2010. See also the YouTube video, "Loliondo Is Burning," http://www.youtube.com/watch?v=iqP2MRuJ4Ac.

2. "Loliondo, 8 April 2010" downloaded from http://xa.yimg.com/kq/groups /20674633/530364632/name/8+April+Loliondo+2.doc, 17 February 2011.

3. "Ngorongoro Land Row: Government Forsakes Small Beleaguered Community for Revenue!" *The Guardian*, 15 April 2010; Rose Mwalongo, "3 Held in Loliondo Over Women's Rally," *The Guardian*, 14 April 2010; Rose Mwalongo, "NGO Staff Held in Loliondo Released," *The Guardian*, 15 April 2010.

4. "Ngorongoro Land Row: Government Forsakes Small Beleaguered Community for Revenue!" *The Guardian*, 15 April 2010; Rose Mwalongo, "3 Held in Loliondo Over Women's Rally," *The Guardian*, 14 April 2010.

5. These and other incidents are documented in numerous scholarly works, investigative reports, advocacy campaigns, and newspaper articles with such titles as "Thirteen Years of Broken Promises in Loliondo" (*The Guardian*, 24 September 2005, 10) and "Ngorongoro Land Row: Government Forsakes Small Beleaguered Community for Revenue!" *The Guardian*, 15 April 2010. For overviews, see Ngoitiko et al. 2010; Feminist Activist Coalition (FemAct) 2009; Maasai Environmental Resource Coalition (MERC) 2002; Gardner 2016.

6. See, for example, the YouTube video "Loliondo Is Burning," http://www.youtube .com/watch?v=iqP2MRuJ4Ac.

7. Lekton, phone interview, 18 June 2011.

8. Maanda Ngoitiko, interview, 23 May 2006, Arusha, Tanzania. Translation from Swahili by author. This and all other quotations from Maanda are from this interview, unless otherwise noted.

9. For more information on KIPOC, see Hodgson 2011a.

10. In the past few years, PWC has started some new projects in an adjacent district (PWC 2012, 2013).

11. Yusuf Qwaray Lawi, "Thousands of Babati Women Rebel," *Business Times*, 11 May 1990, 1.

12. Notes from PINGOS Workshop on Advocacy Training, 19 September 2005; Timoth Yaile, interview, Ololosokwan, October 19, 2006.

13. Susanna Norlund, who first visited Tanzania as a tourist, began investigating these allegations and was quickly thrown out of the country as a *persona non grata*. She has done a heroic job of gathering information and describing these and other incidents on her blog, "View From the Termite Mound." On 8 August 2007, one man looking for lost sheep was run over by an OBC vehicle. On 28 September 2009, another man lost an eye when he was hit by a tear gas canister during a clash with police near the OBC compound. Susanna Norlund, "View From the Termite Mound," 11 July 2011, http://termitemoundview.blogspot.com.

14. Carl Soderberg, director of policy and communications for Minority Rights Group International, "We have become squatters in our own home," *Minorities in Focus: Personal Accounts from the Field*, 16 December 2010, http://minorityrights.wordpress.com/2010/12/16/part-2—"we-have-become-squatters-in-our-own-home-"/, accessed 17 January 2011.

15. The primary sources include reports from Susanna Norlund's blog, "View From the Termite Mound"; reports from *The Guardian* newspaper, which seems to be the only newspaper brave enough to publish accounts of the protest; and an anonymous eyewitness account published on the Internet. See, especially, Norlund's blog for 14 April 2010; "Loliondo Women Say Enough Is Enough"; "Ngorongoro Land Row: Government Forsakes Small Beleaguered Community for Revenue!" *The Guardian*, 15 April 2010; Rose Mwalongo, "3 Held in Loliondo Over Women's Rally," *The Guardian*, 14 April 2010; Rose Mwalongo, "NGO Staff Held in Loliondo Released," *The Guardian*, 15 April 2010; and the anonymous account titled "Loliondo, 8 April 2010," downloaded from http://xa.yimg.com/kq/groups/20674633/530364632/name/8+April+Loliondo+2.doc, 17 February 2011.

16. Post in Google Groups "Wanabidii," "Uregent [sic]–Ngorongoro," by Emmanuel Sulle reposting anonymous e-mails from an NGO worker on Loliondo, 12 April 2010.

17. Post in Google Groups "Wanabidii," "Uregent [sic]–Ngorongoro," by Emmanuel Sulle reposting anonymous e-mails from an NGO worker on Loliondo, 12 April 2010.

18. "Loliondo, 8 April 2010," downloaded from http://xa.yimg.com/kq/groups/20674633/530364632/name/8+April+Loliondo+2.doc, on 17 February 2011.

19. Post in Google Groups "Wanabidii," "Uregent [sic]–Ngorongoro," by Emmanuel Sulle reposting anonymous e-mails from an NGO worker on Loliondo, 12 April 2010.

20. "Ngorongoro Land Row: Government Forsakes Small Beleaguered Community for Revenue!" *The Guardian*, 15 April 2010.

21. The Feminist Activist Coalition, "Gross Violations of Human and Citizenship Rights in Tanzania," *Pambazuka News*, 27 August 2009, http://www.pambazuka.org/en/category/advocacy/58422, accessed 3 September 2009.

22. Florence Mugarula, "Loliondo Residents Criticize Government," *The Citizen*, 10 September 2009.

23. Florence Mugarula, "Loliondo Residents Criticize Government," *The Citizen*, 10 September 2009.

24. The statement was reprinted in TGNP's quarterly newsletter, *Ulingo wa Jinsia*, in Swahili and English. I draw my comments from the English translation. "Women of Ngorongoro District, Manyara Region on the Government Operation to Forcibly Evict Pastoralists in Support of Private Hunters in Loliondo," *Ulingo wa Jinsia* (TGNP) 27, no. 38 (July–September 2009), 8. The listed villages were Arash, Maaloni, Ololosokwan, Olipiri, Soitsambu, Olorien/Magaiduru, Piyaya, and Malambo.

25. Partly as a result of such insights, TGNP has recently developed the concept of "transformative feminism" to better recognize, reach out to, and work with (rather than for) "grassroots women," in part through the creation of regional networks, but neither MWEDO or PWC has become very involved (Kitunga and Mbilinyi 2009, TGNP 2013).

26. "Ngorongoro Land Row: Government Forsakes Small Beleaguered Community for Revenue!" *The Guardian*, 15 April 2010.

Conclusion

Gender Justice, Collective Action,
and the Limits of Legal Interventions

> We may want justice for women, but can we accept that
> there might be different ideas about justice and that different
> women might want, or choose, different futures from
> what we envision as best?
>
> —*Lila Abu-Lughod (2002, 787–88)*

ALTHOUGH I HAVE DRAWN ON historical and ethnographic material from Tanzania and self-identified Maasai communities to support my analysis, my arguments have a broader relevance to other situations in Africa and elsewhere in the Global South (and perhaps even colonized/marginalized communities in the Global North). By tracing some of the continuities and changes in different legal regimes—from indigenous legal regimes to colonial, national, and now transnational—the book has complicated claims that any given regime is natural, universal, or inherently (or morally) preferable. Law is not distinct from culture and does not exist outside of history. Each of the legal regimes I analyzed was a deeply cultural and historical product, premised on certain dominant assumptions, ideas, and practices, whether of elder Maasai men, British legal theorists, Tanzanian elites, or feminist activists. My intent is not to dismiss the value of any of these regimes; clearly for Aloya and others, some laws and legal procedures provided a space through which to challenge unwanted assertions of male control. Similarly, the struggle for and spread of "women's human rights" has supported the claims of women (and men) throughout the world for political recognition and certain legal protections. My point, instead, has been to document and foreground the centrality of *politics*, or, more broadly, *power* to these regimes: Who advocates for a certain legal regime and why? Why do certain legal regimes become normalized as "natural" and "universal"? How does the dominance of these regimes, especially the current national and international legal protocols based on individual rights, obscure other models of challenging injustice, such as the collective actions of Maasai women? What are the consequences for the everyday lives and aspirations of people like Maasai of these changing ideas of law and justice? The emergence of rights-based approaches to justice reverberates beyond the courtroom, shaping peoples' everyday experiences, relationships, and political struggles—what Lila Abu-Lughod (2011) has usefully called "the social life of rights."

A central term in all the debates discussed in the book has been "culture." Colonial officers struggled to distinguish between "law" and "custom" (a synonym for "culture") in their efforts to codify customary law. For Donald Cameron, Julius Lewin, and other key colonial actors described in chapter 1, indigenous legal regimes (like the Maasai elders council) were inherently "tribal" and thus "cultural," historically unique (and unchanging) approaches to resolving disputes. In contrast, British ideas of "natural justice," including the proper procedures for administering "justice," were considered not just historical developments, but, in their socioevolutionary schema, historical *improvements*; they were presumed to be morally superior, above culture, more encompassing and enduring.

At independence, the Tanzanian elites who took power adopted the British system with slight modifications, including formally recognizing colonial versions of customary law. But, under pressure from women's groups like UWT, they also passed new national laws like the Law of Marriage Act (LMA) to "modernize" and regulate the appropriate forms of marriage so as to overcome the assumed inequities of traditional marriages, especially of rural, illiterate, and poor women. The disparagement of "culture" as a negative feature of more "primitive" ethnic groups like Maasai, and thus an obstacle to the advancement of certain women, was now accepted wisdom. While the LMA and other laws provided opportunities for some women to challenge unwanted relationships, it also strengthened the presumed distinction between "law" and "culture," demonstrated the power of elites to use laws as a means to enforce their visions of proper gender roles and social relations, and further obscured the perspectives and priorities of groups like Maasai who generally lacked the language, education, and political connections to intercede in these debates. Moreover, the expanded reach of state law into the most intimate domains of life made indigenous modes of reconciling disputes and seeking justice (like the elders councils) seem increasingly outmoded.

By the time human rights, especially the transnational "women's rights as human rights" movement, emerged as a significant legal innovation in the 1980s and 1990s, these negative portrayals of cultural practices and the lives of rural women (and the presumed relation between the two), were encoded in key international protocols, such as the 1979 Convention on the Elimination of all Forms of Discrimination against Women, discussed in chapter 3. Rural women were depicted as inherently vulnerable to the predations of their male relatives and community members, helpless victims of their culture. As a result, certain cultural practices were not just condemned, but criminalized. The problem, as in earlier periods, was that while some community members were concerned about practices like FGM, most were far more troubled by their rapidly diminishing access to land and other resources on which their livelihoods depended. Gender relations among Maasai had indeed changed and even become more unequal, but these changes were the product of history, politics, and economics, not "culture." Laws—whether national or international—predicated on individual rights seemed inadequate to address the structural nature of these processes and collective sense of disenfranchisement. Not only were these laws promulgated by elites in their interests (such as the promotion of private property rights over collective/communal access), but they were implemented and enforced by the judicial structures of the state, the same state that was often the source of the land grabs and other injustices of most concern to Maasai and other second-class citizens.

Given this long history of the progressive demonization of "culture" and "custom" and representations of illiterate, rural women like Maasai as passive victims of their male-dominated cultures, the series of collective protests by Maasai women in Loliondo against the dominant political party (CCM), and thus the Tanzanian state, shocked these elites and shattered their stereotypes. The persistence of *olkishoroto*, a customary female practice for voicing grievances and challenging injustice, and its adaptation to new concerns and forms evinced both the power of women and existence of positive cultural practices. As a mechanism for demanding justice, *olkishoroto* contrasted markedly with the dominant legal regimes of rights, laws, and courts that had been introduced in the colonial era. *Olkishoroto* demonstrated the strength of collective action, evoked the sacred moral authority and responsibilities of women as mothers, and directly challenged the immoral actions of the state and political party.

Thus this book has shown the many ways in which the "problem of culture" is really a problem of power and of the enduring assumptions by colonial officers, Euro-American donors, activists, and now, increasingly, African elites that they can speak for (rather than listen to) rural, poorly educated women or even well-educated African women who are deemed culturally "other." The troubling contemporary portrayals of the culture of grassroots women like Maasai have long histories, rooted in the gendered, racialized struggles and legacies of colonial exploration, conquest, and rule. Blaming culture as the cause of current gender inequalities ignores this history and thus deflects attention from the political and economic causes and contexts of dispossession, marginalization, and oppression. The interventions into Maasai lives in the name of progress and productivity by colonial officers and state officials, and the more indirect changes produced by their engagement in socialist and capitalist economies, have reworked Maasai gender and generational relations, producing new ideas and practices of marriage, family, labor, wealth, politics, and more.

The problem, therefore, is not just that these assumptions are disparaging, essentialist, and ahistorical. They also justify paternalist interventions into the lives of Maasai and other peoples, often in the name of "saving" these seemingly vulnerable victims from their oppressive cultures. In this book, I have focused on interventions in the realm of law and justice, tracing how these racialized and class ideas about gender and culture shaped the development of formal law as the dominant mechanism of justice, through the implementation of native authorities, to state courts and laws, and to international women's human rights. These assumptions—and resulting interventions—promoted a vision of justice premised on "natural justice" and eventually "universal rights" that strengthened the authority of male elders, transformed indigenous legal regimes, and undermined peoples' ability to directly challenge the state. A historical analysis of gender relations and cultural practices shows the dynamism and contingency of discourses like "natural justice" and "universal rights" and the implications and imbrications of power in their formations and reformations.

By exploring the specific social histories, political struggles, and cultural assumptions that have produced certain gender justice regimes, the book demonstrates the theoretical and political importance of making gender a central point in understanding diverse visions and experiences of justice. "Gender justice" refers to the broad array of modes of defining and seeking justice between and among men and women, as well as the gendered assumptions and implications of different justice regimes. These regimes include human rights, international and national laws and protocols, customary and religious modes of dispute resolution, and collective action.

A gendered analysis moves beyond questions of whether women have rights, what rights they have, and whether they gained or lost rights and explores the centrality of gendered ideas and assumptions to ideas of justice (Stoeltje, Firmin-Sellers, and Ogwang 2002; Cornwall and Molyneux 2008; Merry 2006; Molyneux and Razavi 2003; Hodgson 2011b; Abu-Lughod 2002, 2013). Clearly the inclusion of women's rights as human rights has helped women throughout the world challenge oppression of various kinds. But, as the Maasai case has demonstrated, such rights-based approaches to justice often make it difficult to recognize and address the structural causes and context of gender injustice, such as the dismantling of health care, education, and other social services and the deepening impoverishment produced by neoliberal policies.

In contrast, the idea of justice pursued by Maasai women is predicated on distinct concepts of morality, collective responsibility, and oppression. Maasai women perceive themselves as having a moral obligation to challenge perceived violations to the social order, whether from incestuous men in the past or corrupt state and party officials in the present. Moreover, they emphasize the need to challenge these perceived injustices *collectively* and not as individuals. Unlike dominant human rights frameworks, which promote individual agency and liberal ideas of gender equality, the collective actions of Maasai women express the importance of social connections and relationships rather than individual autonomy and rights. They address the structural inequalities produced by colonialism, socialism, and capitalism, and they directly challenge the involvement of the Tanzanian state in facilitating their disenfranchisement and oppression. Attention to the ideas and experiences of illiterate, rural women, especially their customary forms of collective action, challenges the continued disparagement of their practices and recognizes their sometimes powerful ways of confronting and challenging injustice.

* * *

As I write this conclusion, the story of class interests, state land grabs, and Maasai demands for justice continues. Since 2010, the Tanzanian government has threatened several times to dispossess several Maasai villages of their legally obtained rights to the land in the interests of conservation, tourism, and big-game hunting.[1] Maasai men and women have responded to these continuing, sometimes violent intrusions in multiple ways. Male activists have sued Thomson Safaris (again) through the Tanzanian judicial system, but they have also brought suit against Thomson (an American company) in the United States to request documents and information about the alleged evictions and abuses to support their legal claims.[2] Maasai women, in turn, have maintained and expanded their tradition of *olkishoroto*, holding collective protests in Loliondo and Dar es Salaam to condemn CCM and the state for these actual and planned land grabs.[3] PWC has even begun to present the women's efforts to protect their land as the genesis of an emergent "grassroots social movement."[4] Meanwhile, the anti-FGM campaigns continue, and TGNP, TAMWA, and other Tanzanian feminists have launched new efforts to define and regulate their ideas of "appropriate" marital and sexual relations in the name of "women's human rights" through demands for revisions to the Constitution. But they have also lobbied for a constitutional provision to enforce the rights of women to own land.[5] And so the gendered struggles for justice continue, shaped by the legacies of the past, the politics of the present, and dreams for the future.

NOTES

1. See, for example, Jason Patinkin, "Tanzania's Maasai Battle Game Hunters for Grazing Land," *BBC News Africa*, 18 April 2013; Jason Patinkin, "Battle Over the Serengeti Pits Maasai against Dubai," *Christian Science Monitor*, 30 April 2013; Suzanna Nordlund, "Delayed Updates about the Attackers on Land Rights in Loliondo–Thomson Safaris, OBC, and the Government of Tanzania," Views from the Termite Mound, http://termitemoundview.blogspot.com, 18 May 2013; Charles Ole Ngereza, "Wardens Raze 114 Bomas; Thousands Stranded," *The Sunday Guardian/This Day*, 15 February 2015.

2. The federal court action was filed with the assistance of the NGO EarthRights International under 28 U.S.C. § 1782, a law that allows people to obtain documents and information from individuals or companies in the United States to support foreign

legal proceedings. Marissa Vahlsing and Lucy Claridge, "Maasai Villagers Turn to U.S. Courts for Information on Abusive Evictions by U.S. Safari Company." *EarthRights International*, 26 February 2014. See also Friedman-Rudovsky 2015; Mussa Juma, "Tanzania: Govt Taken to Court on Forced Eviction Issue," *The Citizen*, 3 December 2010; "Tanzanian Court to Hear Maasai Community Land Rights Case Involving US-Based Safari Company." *Minority Rights Group International*, 4 December 2014.

3. "Tanzania: Maasai Women Take Bold Steps to Defend their Rights in Loliondo Land Rift," *The Citizen*, 23 April 2013.

4. "Women's Rights and Leadership Forums: Advancing the Land Rights of Pastoralist Women in Tanzania," http://www.maliasili.org/fighting-for-land-learning-from-maasai-women-in-northern-tanzania/, accessed 23 June 2015.

5. Deogratias Mushi, "Tanzania: New Constitution Moves Tanzania Closer to Gender Parity," *Tanzania Daily News*, 1 October 2014.

Bibliography

Laws, Acts, Ordinances, and Decrees

Tanganyika/Tanzania

1920	Tanganyika Order in Council
1920	Native Courts Ordinance
1921	Marriage Ordinance
1929	Native Courts Amendment Ordinance
1951	Local Courts Ordinance
1961	The Judicature and Application of Laws Act
1963	Customary Law (Declaration) Order
1963	Magistrates' Courts Act
1971	Law of Marriage Act
1998	Sexual Offenses Special Provisions Act

Regional/Continental

1982	African Charter on Human and People's Rights
2003	Protocol to the African Charter on Human and Peoples' Rights on the Rights of Women in Africa

International

1919	Covenant of the League of Nations
1945	Charter of the United Nations
1948	The Universal Declaration of Human Rights
1979	Convention on the Elimination of All Forms of Discrimination against Women
1993	Declaration on the Elimination of Violence against Women

Archives Consulted

Tanzanian National Archives—Arusha (ATNA) (Arusha, Tanzania)
Tanzania National Archives—Dar es Salaam (TNA) (Dar es Salaam, Tanzania)

Rhodes House Library (RHL) (Oxford, England)
British National Archives (formerly Public Record Office) (Kew Gardens, United Kingdom)
Women's Library, London School of Economics (London, United Kingdom)
Schomburg Library, New York Public Library (New York, USA)

BOOKS AND ARTICLES

Abu-Lughod, Lila. 2002. "Do Muslim Women Really Need Saving? Anthropological Reflections on Cultural Relativism and Its Others." *American Anthropologist* 104, no. 3: 783–90.

———. 2011. "The Active Social Life of 'Muslim Women's Rights.'" In *Gender and Culture at the Limit of Rights*, edited by Dorothy L. Hodgson. Philadelphia: University of Pennsylvania Press.

———. 2013. *Do Muslim Women Need Saving?* Cambridge, Mass.: Harvard University Press.

Abusharaf, Rogaia Mustafa. 2001. "Virtuous Cuts: Female Genital Circumcision in an African Ontology." *Differences: A Journal of Feminist Cultural Studies* 12, no. 1: 112–40.

———, ed. 2006. *Female Circumcision: Multicultural Perspectives*. Philadelphia: University of Pennsylvania Press.

Ackerly, Brooke A. 2008. *Universal Human Rights in a World of Difference*. Cambridge: Cambridge University Press.

Agosín, Marjorie, ed. 2001. *Women, Gender and Human Rights: A Global Perspective*. New Brunswick, N.J.: Rutgers University Press.

Aina, Olabisi. 1998. "African Women at the Grassroots: The Silent Partners of the Women's Movement." In *Sisterhood: Feminisms & Power: From Africa to the Diaspora*, edited by Obioma Nnaemeka. Trenton, N.J.: Africa World Press.

Alfredson, Gudmundur, and Katarina Tomaševski, eds. 1995. *A Thematic Guide to the Documents on the Human Rights of Women*. The Hague: Martinus Nijhoff Publishers for the Raoul Wallenberg Institute for Human Rights.

Allman, Jean. 1996. "Rounding up Spinsters: Gender Chaos and Unmarried Women in Colonial Asante." *Journal of African History* 37, no. 2: 195–214.

An-Na'im, Abdullahi A., ed. 2002. *Cultural Transformation and Human Rights in Africa*. London: Zed Books.

Anonymous. 2010. "Models, Priorities, Pressures of Women Today in Africa: Interview with Marjorie Mbilinyi." http://www.sidint.net/node/4722. Accessed June 12, 2013.

Archambault, Caroline S. 2011. "Ethnographic Empathy and the Social Context of Rights: 'Rescuing' Maasai Girls from Early Marriage." *American Anthropologist* 113, no. 4: 632–43.

Benedek, Wolfgang, Esther M. Kisaayake, and Gerd Oberleitner, eds. 2002. *Human Rights of Women: International Instruments and African Experiences*. London: Zed Books.

Bernsten, John. 1980. "The Enemy Is Us: Eponymy in the Historiography of the Maasai." *History in Africa* 7: 1–21.

Bianco, Barbara. 2000. "Gender and Material Culture in West Pokot, Kenya." In *Rethinking Pastoralism in Africa: Gender, Culture and the Myth of the Patriarchal Pastoralist*, edited by Dorothy L. Hodgson. Oxford: James Currey.

Bierwagen, Rainer Michael, and Chris Maina Peter. 1989. "Administration of Justice in Tanzania and Zanzibar: A Comparison of Two Judicial Systems in One Country." *International and Comparative Law Quarterly* 38, no. 2: 395–412.

Blacking, John, and Noam J. Pines. 1968. "Professor Julius Lewin." *African Studies* 27, no. 1: 45–46.

Boddy, Janice. 2007. *Civilizing Women: British Crusades in Colonial Sudan*. Princeton, N.J.: Princeton University Press.

———. 2008. "Clash of Selves: Gender, Personhood, and Human Rights Discourse in Colonial Sudan." *Canadian Journal of African Studies* 41, no. 3: 402–26.

Bohannon, Paul. 1957. *Justice and Judgment among the Tiv*. Oxford: Oxford University Press.

Bond, Joanna E. 2010. "Gender, Discourse and Customary Law in Africa." *Southern California Law Review* 83: 509–74.

———. 2011. "Women's Rights, Customary Law, and the Promise of the Protocol on the Rights of Women in Africa." In *The Future of African Customary Law*, edited by Jeanmarie French, Paolo Galizzi, and Tracy E. Higgins. Cambridge: Cambridge University Press.

Boyle, Elizabeth Heger. 2002. *Female Genital Cutting: Cultural Conflict in the Global Community*. Baltimore: Johns Hopkins University Press.

Boyle, Elizabeth Heger, and Sharon E. Preves. 2000. "National Politics as International Process: The Case of Anti–Female Genital Cutting Laws." *Law and Society Review* 34, no. 3: 703–37.

Bunch, Charlotte. 1990. "Women's Rights as Human Rights: Toward a Re-Vision of Human Rights." *Human Rights Quarterly* 12: 486–98.

Bunch, Charlotte, and Roxanna Carrillo. 1991. *Gender Violence: A Development and Human Rights Issue*. New Brunswick, N.J.: Center for Women's Global Leadership.

Bunch, Charlotte, and Niamh Reilly. 1995. "The Global Campaign: Violence Against Women Violates Human Rights." In *From Basic Needs to Basic Rights: Women's Claim to Human Rights*, edited by Margaret Schuler. Washington, D.C.: Women, Law and Development International.

Bunch, Charlotte, Samantha Frost, and Niamh Reilly. 1998. "Making the Global Local: International Networking for Women's Human Rights." Unpublished manuscript.

Burton, Antoinette. 1994. *Burdens of History: British Feminism, Indian Women, and Imperial Culture, 1865–1915*. Chapel Hill: University of North Carolina Press.

Butegwa, Florence. 1995. "International Human Rights Law and Practice: Implications for Women." In *From Basic Needs to Basic Rights: Women's Claim to Human Rights*, edited by Margaret Schuler. Washington, D.C.: Women, Law and Development International.

Byfield, Judith. 2001. "Women, Marriage, Divorce and the Emerging Colonial State in Abeokuta (Nigeria) 1892–1904." In *"Wicked" Women and the Reconfiguration of Gender in Tanzania*, edited by Dorothy L. Hodgson and Sheryl A. McCurdy. Portsmouth, N.H.: Heinemann Social History of Africa Series.

Calaguas, Mark, Cristina M. Drost, and Edward R. Fluet. 2007. "Legal Pluralism and Women's Rights: A Study in Postcolonial Tanzania." *Columbia Journal of Gender and Law* 16, no. 2: 471–549.

Cameron, Donald. 1930. *Tanganyika Territory, Native Administration Memoranda No. II, Native Courts*, 2nd ed. Dar es Salaam: Government Printer.

————. 1937. "Native Administration in Tanganyika and Nigeria." *Journal of the Royal African Society* 36, no. 145: 3–29.

Caplan, Gerald M. 1964. "The Making of 'Natural Justice' in British Africa: An Exercise in Comparative Law." *Journal of Public Law* 13, no. 1: 120–34.

Chachage, Seithy L., and Marjorie Mbilinyi, eds. 2003. *Against Neoliberalism*. Dar es Salaam: TGNP & E&D Limited.

Chanock, Martin. 1985. *Law, Custom and Social Order: The Colonial Experience in Malawi and Zambia*. Cambridge: Cambridge University Press.

Charlesworth, Hilary. 1995. "Human Rights Are Men's Rights." In *Women's Rights, Human Rights: International Feminist Perspectives*, edited by Julie Peters and Andrea Wolper. New York: Routledge.

Clarke, Kamari Maxine, and Mark Goodale, eds. 2010. *Mirrors of Justice: Law and Power in the Post–Cold War Era*. Cambridge: Cambridge University Press.

Cmiel, Kenneth. 2004. "The Recent History of Human Rights." *The American Historical Review* 109, no. 10: 117–35.

Coast, Ernestina. 2001. "Maasai Demography." PhD dissertation, London School of Economics.

————. 2007. "Wasting Semen: Context and Condom Use among the Maasai." *Culture, Health & Sexuality* 9, no. 4: 387–401.

Comaroff, Jean, and John Comaroff. 2007. "Law and Disorder in the Postcolony." *Social Anthropology* 15, no. 2: 133–52.

Comaroff, John. 2001. "Colonialism, Culture and the Law: A Foreword." *Law and Social Inquiry* 26, no. 2: 101–10.

Cook, Rebecca J., ed. 1994. *Human Rights of Women: National and International Perspectives*. Philadelphia: University of Pennsylvania Press.

Cornwall, Andrea, and Maxine Molyneux, eds. 2008. *The Politics of Rights: Dilemmas for Feminist Praxis*. London: Routledge.

Cowan, Jane K., Marie-Bénédicte Dembour, and Richard A. Wilson, eds. 2001. *Culture and Rights: Anthropological Perspectives*. Cambridge: Cambridge University Press.

Edgerton, Robert B., and Francis P. Conant. 1964. "Kilipat: The 'Shaming Party' among the Pokot of East Africa." *Southwestern Journal of Anthropology* 20: 404–18.

Eisler, Riane. 1987. "Human Rights: Towards an Integrated Theory for Action." *Human Rights Quarterly* 9: 287–308.

Ekine, Sokari. 2008. "Women's Responses to State Violence in the Niger Delta." *Feminist Africa* 10: 67–83.

Equality Now. 1999. *Equality Now 1998–1999 Report*. http://www.equalitynow.org/sites/default/files/annualreport_98-99.pdf

————. 2011. *Protecting Girls from Undergoing Female Genital Mutilation: The Experience of Working with the Maasai Communities in Kenya and Tanzania*. New York: Equality Now.

Feminist Activist Coalition (FemAct). 2009. "Loliondo Findings." *Pambazuka News*, Issue 449, 23 September 2009.

Ferree, Myra Marx, and Aili Marie Tripp, eds. 2006. *Global Feminism: Transnational Women's Activism, Organizing and Human Rights*. New York: New York University Press.

Forde, Daryll. 1965. "Justice and Judgment among the Southern Ibo under Colonial Rule." In *African Law: Adaptation and Development*, edited by Hilda Kuper and Leo Kuper. Berkeley: University of California Press.

Fraser, Arvonne S. 2006. "Becoming Human: The Origins and Development of Women's Human Rights." In *Women's Rights: A Human Rights Quarterly Reader,* edited by Bert B. Lockwood. Baltimore: Johns Hopkins University Press.

Fraser, Nancy. 2009. *Scales of Justice: Reimagining Political Space in a Globalizing World.* New York: Columbia University Press.

Friedman-Rudovsky, Jeanne. 2015. "Casualties of Conservation: The Eco-Tourism Industry Is Saving Tanzania's Animals but Threatening its Indigenous Peoples." *Vice Magazine* 22, no. 5: 66–81.

Galaty, John. 1993. "Maasai Expansion and the New East African Pastoralism." In *Being Maasai,* edited by Thomas Spear and Richard Waller. London: James Currey.

Gardner, Benjamin. 2016. *Selling the Serengeti: The Cultural Politics of Safari Tourism.* Athens: University of Georgia Press.

Geiger, Susan. 1982. "Umoja wa Wanawake wa Tanzania and the Needs of the Rural Poor." *African Studies Review* 25, nos. 2 and 3: 45–65.

———. 1987. "Women in Nationalist Struggle: TANU Activists in Dar es Salaam." *International Journal of African Historical Studies* 20, no. 1: 1–26.

———. 1997. *TANU Women: Gender and Culture in the Making of Tanganyikan Nationalism, 1955–1965.* Portsmouth, N.H.: Heinemann.

Gluckman, Max. 1955. *The Judicial Process among the Barotse of Northern Rhodesia.* Manchester: Manchester University Press.

———. 1965. *The Ideas in Barotse Jurisprudence.* New Haven, Conn.: Yale University Press.

Goodale, Mark, and Sally Engle Merry, eds. 2003. *The Practice of Human Rights: Tracking Law Between the Global and the Local.* Cambridge: Cambridge University Press.

Government of Tanzania and United Nations Children's Fund. 1990. *Women and Children in Tanzania: A Situation Analysis.* Dar es Salaam: UNICEF.

Griffiths, Anne M. O. 1997. *In the Shadow of Marriage: Gender and Justice in an African Community.* Chicago: University of Chicago Press.

Gruenbaum, Ellen. 2001. *The Female Circumcision Controversy: An Anthropological Perspective.* Philadelphia: University of Pennsylvania Press.

Gulliver, Philip. 1963. *Social Control in an African Society: A Study of Arusha: Agricultural Masai of Northern Tanganyika.* Boston: Boston University Press.

Halley, Janet, Prabha Kotiswaran, Hila Shamir, and Chantal Thomas. 2006. "From the International to the Local in Feminist Legal Responses to Rape, Prostitution/Sex Work, and Sex Trafficking: Four Studies in Contemporary Governance Feminism." *Harvard Journal of Law & Gender* 29: 335–422.

Hashim, Leila Sheikh. 1992. "Violence Against Women Is a Violation of Human Rights." *Sauti ya Siti* (November): 3–10.

Hatfield, Colby. 1975. "End of Tour Report of C. R. Hatfield, Jr. Sociologist, Masai Range Development Project (1975–1977)." Prepared for USAID. In author's possession.

———. 1976. "Current Trends in Masai Development: A Baseline Survey." Masai Project Evaluation Paper No. 3. Report Prepared for MLRMP/USAID. In author's possession.

———. 1977. "The Impact of Social and Technical Change in Masailand and its Implications for Future Development." Report prepared for Food and Agriculture Officer, USAID, Dar es Salaam. In author's possession.

Hay, Margaret, and Marcia Wright, eds. 1982. *African Women and the Law: Historical Perspectives*. Boston: Boston University Papers on Africa VII.

Henry, Joanne, and Fatma Alloo. 2005. "Mobilising Tanzania's Women: Joanne Henry Interviews Fatma Alloo." *Feminist Africa 4*, www.feministafrica.org/index.php/mobilizing-tanzania.

Hernlund, Ylva, and Bettina Shell-Duncan, eds. 2007. *Transcultural Bodies: Female Genital Cutting in Global Context*. New Brunswick, N.J.: Rutgers University Press.

Hodgson, Dorothy L. 2000. "Taking Stock: State Control, Ethnic Identity, and Pastoralist Development in Tanganyika, 1940–1961." *Journal of African History* 41, no. 1: 55–78.

———. 2001a. *Once Intrepid Warriors: Gender, Ethnicity and the Cultural Politics of Maasai Development*. Bloomington: Indiana University Press.

———, ed. 2001b. *Gendered Modernities: Ethnographic Perspectives*. New York: Palgrave.

———. 2003. "Women's Rights as Human Rights: Women in Law and Development in Africa." *Africa Today* 49, no. 2: 1–26.

———. 2005. *The Church of Women: Gendered Encounters between Maasai and Missionaries*. Bloomington: Indiana University Press.

———. 2011a. *Being Maasai, Becoming Indigenous: Postcolonial Politics in a Neoliberal World*. Bloomington: Indiana University Press.

———, ed. 2011b. *Gender and Culture at the Limit of Rights*. Philadelphia: University of Pennsylvania Press.

———. 2011c. "The Politics of Naming: Ethical Dilemmas and Disciplinary Divides in Anthropology and History." In *Anthrohistory: Unsettling Knowledge, Questioning Discipline*, edited by Edward Murphy, David William Cohen, Chandra Bhimull, Fernando Coronil, Monica E. Patterson, and Julie Skurski. Ann Arbor: University of Michigan Press.

Hollis, Alfred C. 1905. *The Masai: Their Language and Folklore*. Freeport, N.Y.: Books for Libraries Press.

———. 1910. "A Note on the Masai System of Relationships and Other Matters Connected Therewith." *Journal of the Royal Anthropological Institute* 40, no. 21: 473–82.

Homewood, Katherine, Patti Kristjanson, and Pippa Chenevix Trench, eds. 2009. *Staying Maasai? Livelihoods, Conservation and Development in Eastern African Rangelands*. New York: Springer.

Hosken, Fran P. 1979. *The Hosken Report: Genital and Sexual Mutilation of Females*. New York: Women's International Network News.

Hunt, Lynn. 2007. *Inventing Human Rights: A History*. New York: W. W. Norton & Co.

Hyden, Goran. 1980. *Beyond Ujamaa in Tanzania: Underdevelopment and an Uncaptured Peasantry*. Berkeley: University of California Press.

———. 1999. "Top Down Democracy in Tanzania." *Journal of Democracy* 10, no. 4: 142–55.

Ibhawoh, Bonny, and J. I. Dibua. 2003. "Deconstructing Ujamaa: The Legacy of Julius Nyerere in the Quest for Social and Economic Development in Africa." *African Journal of Political Science* 8, no. 1: 59–83.

Iliffe, John. 1969. *Tanganyika Under German Rule 1905–1912*. Cambridge: Cambridge University Press.

———. 1979. *A Modern History of Tanganyika*. Cambridge: Cambridge University Press.

Ivaska, Andrew M. 2002. "Anti-Mini Militants Meet Modern Misses: Urban Style, Gender and the Politics of 'National Culture' in 1960s Dar es Salaam." *Gender and History* 14, no. 3: 584–607.

———. 2011. *Cultured States: Youth, Gender and Modern Style in 1960s Dar es Salaam.* Durham, N.C.: Duke University Press.

Jacobs, Alan. 1970. "Maasai Marriage and Bridewealth." *Mila* 1: 25–36. Institute of African Studies, University of Nairobi.

Jennings, Michael. 2008. *Surrogates of the State: NGOs, Development and Ujamaa in Tanzania.* Bloomfield, Conn.: Kumarian Press.

Johnson, Willene A. 1985. "Women and Self-Employment in Urban Tanzania." *Review of Black Political Economy* 14, nos. 2/3: 245–57.

Kabeer, Naila. 2011. "Between Affiliation and Autonomy: Navigating Pathways of Women's Empowerment and Gender Justice in Rural Bangladesh." *Development and Change* 42, no. 2: 499–528.

Kanogo, Tabitha. 2005. *African Womanhood in Colonial Kenya, 1900–1950.* Oxford: James Currey.

Khamasi, Jennifer Wanjiku, and Susan Nyamburu Maina-Chinkuyu. 2005. *Sexuality: An African Perspective: The Politics of Self and Cultural Beliefs.* Nairobi: Moi University Press.

"Kilusu." 1956–1957. "Masai and Their Finery." *East African Annual,* 1956–1957: 135–37.

Kipuri, Naomi. 2004. "Female Genital Mutilation." *Indigenous Affairs* 1–2: 22–27.

Kitunga, Demere, and Marjorie Mbilinyi. 2009. "Rooting Transformative Feminism Struggles in Tanzania at the Grassroots." *Review of African Political Economy* 36, no. 121: 433–41.

Koomen, Jonneke. 2013. "Global Governance and the Politics of Culture: Campaigns against Female Circumcision in East Africa." *Gender, Place & Culture* 21, no. 2: 244–61.

Krapf, J. Lewis. 1968 [1860]. *Travels, Researches and Missionary Labours During an Eighteen Years' Research in Eastern Africa.* 2nd ed. London: Frank Cass & Co.

Kratz, Corinne. 2007. "Seeing Asylum, Debating Values, and Setting Precedents in the 1990s: The Cases of Kassindja and Abanakwah in the United States." In *Transcultural Bodies: Female Genital Cutting in Global Context,* edited by Yliva Hernlund and Bettina Shell-Duncan. New Brunswick, N.J.: Rutgers University Press.

Kuhanga, Veneranda, and Wema Kalokola. 1990. "UWT Has Failed to Reach Rural Women, But Has Succeeded in Other Ways." *Sauti ya Siti,* October–December: 25–27.

Kuper, Hilda, and Leo Kuper, eds. 1965. *African Law: Adaptation and Development.* Berkeley: University of California Press.

Lal, Priya. 2010. "Militants, Mothers, and the National Family: Ujamaa, Gender, and Rural Development in Postcolonial Tanzania." *Journal of African History* 51, no. 1: 1–20.

———. 2015. *African Socialism in Postcolonial Tanzania: Between the Village and the World.* New York: Cambridge University Press.

Leakey, Louis S. B. 1930. "Some Notes on the Masai of Kenya Colony." *Journal of the Royal Anthropological Institute of Great Britain and Ireland* 60: 185–206.

Legal and Human Rights Center (LHRC). 2006. *Tanzania Human Rights Report 2006: Progress through Human Rights.* Dar es Salaam: LHRC.

Lewin, Julius. 1938. "The Recognition of Native Law and Custom in British Africa." *Journal of Comparative Legislation and International Law*, 3rd series, 20: 16–23.

Lockwood, Bert B., ed. 2006. *Women's Rights: A Human Rights Quarterly Reader*. Baltimore: Johns Hopkins University Press.

Lovett, Margot. 2001. "'She Thinks She's Like a Man': Marriage and (De)constructing Gender Identity in Colonial Buha, Western Tanzania, 1943–1960." In *"Wicked" Women and the Reconfiguration of Gender in Tanzania*, edited by Dorothy L. Hodgson and Sheryl A. McCurdy. Portsmouth, N.H.: Heinemann Social History of Africa Series.

Maasai Environmental Resource Coalition (MERC). 2002. *The Killing Fields of Loliondo: The Hunting Operations of the Ortello Business Company and their Impact on Maasai Rights, Wildlife and Environment*. Washington, D.C.: MERC.

Maasai Women Development Organization (MWEDO). n.d. *Programs and Activities*. In author's possession.

———. 2005. *Five Year Strategic Plan 2005–2009*. In author's possession.

Macdonald, J. R. L. 1899. "Notes on the Ethnology of Tribes Met with During Progress of the Juba Expedition of 1897–99." *Journal of the Royal Anthropological Institute of Great Britain and Ireland* 29, nos. 3/4: 226–47.

Madabida, H. R. 1974. "The Umoja wa Wanawake wa Tanganyika: Its Role in Tanzania." Class paper, University of Dar es Salaam. Schomburg Library Microfilm R-3629 no. 24.

Maguire, R. A. J. 1928. "The Masai Penal Code." *Journal of the African Society* 28, no. 109: 12–18.

Mallya, Ernest. 2005. "Women NGOs and the Policy Process in Tanzania: The Case of the Land Act of 1999." *African Study Monographs* 26, no. 4: 183–200.

Mann, Kristin. 1982. "Women's Rights in Law and Practice: Marriage and Dispute Settlement in Colonial Lagos." In *African Women and the Law: Historical Perspectives*, edited by Margaret Jean Hay and Marcia Wright. Boston: Boston University Papers on Africa VII.

Mann, Kristen, and Richard Roberts, eds. 1991. *Law in Colonial Africa*. Portsmouth, N.H.: Heinemann.

Mascarenhas, Ophelia. 2007. *Gender Profile of Tanzania: Enhancing Gender Equity*. Dar es Salaam: TGNP and SIDA.

Mascarenhas, Ophelia, and Marjorie Mbilinyi. 1983. *Women in Tanzania: An Analytical Bibliography*. Uppsala, Sweden: Scandinavian Institute of Development Studies.

Matera, Marc, Misty L. Bastian, and Susan Kingsley Kent. 2011. *The Women's War of 1929: Gender and Violence in Colonial Nigeria*. New York: Palgrave Macmillan.

May, Ann, and Frances Ndipapa Ole Ikayo. 2007. "Wearing Ilkarash: Narratives of Image, Identity and Change Among Maasai Labour Migrants in Tanzania." *Development and Change* 38, no. 2: 275–98.

May, Ann, and Terrence McCabe. 2004. "City Work in a Time of AIDS: Maasai Labor Migration in Tanzania." *Africa Today* 51, no. 2: 3–32.

Mbilinyi, Marjorie. 1972. "The 'New Woman' and Traditional Norms in Tanzania." *The Journal of Modern African Studies* 10, no. 1: 57–72.

———. 1988. "Runaway Wives: Forced Labour and Forced Marriage in Colonial Rungwe." *International Journal of the Sociology of Law* 16, no. 1: 1–29.

———. 1989. "'This Is Unforgettable Business': Colonial State Intervention in Urban Tanzania." In *Women and the State in Africa*, edited by Jane Parpart and Kathleen A. Staudt. Boulder, Colo.: Lynne Rienner.

Mbogoni, Lawrence E. Y. 2013. "The Trial of Oldus Elishira (1955): Murder, Politics and Justice in Late Colonial Tanganyika." In *Aspects of Colonial History*. Dar es Salaam: Mkuki na Nyota.

Media Articles on Designer Vaginas. 2001. "Genital Landscaping, Labia Remodelling and Vestal Vaginas: Female Genital Mutilation or Female Genital Cosmetic Surgery." *Jenda: A Journal of Culture and African Women's Studies* 1, no. 1: 1–24.

Meena, Ruth, and Marjorie Mbilinyi. 1991. "Women's Research and Documentation Project (Tanzania)." *Signs* 16, no. 4: 852–59.

Merker, Moritz. 1910 [1904]. *Die Masai. Ethnographische Monographie eines ostafrikanischen Semitenvolkes.* 2nd ed. Berlin: Dietrich Reimer.

Merry, Sally Engle. 1988. "Legal Pluralism." *Law and Society Review* 22, no. 5: 869–96.

———. 2006. *Human Rights and Gender Violence: Translating International Law into Local Justice.* Chicago: University of Chicago Press.

Mohanty, Chandra. 1991. "Under Western Eyes: Feminist Scholarship and Colonial Discourses." In *Third World Women and the Politics of Feminism*, edited by Chandra Mohanty, Anna Russo, and Lourdes Torres. Bloomington: Indiana University Press.

———. 2003. *Feminism without Borders: Decolonizing Theory, Practicing Solidarity.* Durham, N.C.: Duke University Press.

Mol, Frans. 1977. *Maa: A Dictionary of the Maasai Language and Folklore.* Nairobi: Maasai Centre Lemek.

———. 1996. *Maasai Language and Culture Dictionary.* Narok: Maasai Centre Lemek.

Molyneux, Maxine, and Shahra Razavi, eds. 2002. *Gender Justice, Development, and Rights.* Oxford: Oxford University Press.

Moore, Sally Falk. 1986. *Social Facts and Fabrications: "Customary" Law on Kilimanjaro, 1880–1980.* Cambridge: Cambridge University Press.

Morgan, Henry Louis. 1877. *Ancient Society.* London: MacMillan & Co.

Morris, H. F., and James S. Read. 1972. *Indirect Rule and the Search for Justice: Essays in East African Legal History.* Oxford: Clarendon Press.

Mulligan-Hansel, Kathleen Marie. 1999. "The Political Economy of Contemporary Women's Organizations in Tanzania: Socialism, Liberalization and Gendered Fields of Power." PhD dissertation, University of Wisconsin-Madison.

Murphy, Edward, David William Cohen, Chandra Bhimull, Fernando Coronil, Monica E. Patterson, and Julie Skurski, eds. 2011. *Anthrohistory: Unsettling Knowledge, Questioning Discipline.* Ann Arbor: University of Michigan Press.

Nader, Laura. 1991. *Harmony Ideology: Justice and Control in a Zapotec Mountain Village.* Stanford, Calif.: Stanford University Press.

Narayan, Uma. 1997. *Dislocating Cultures: Identities, Traditions and Third World Feminisms.* New York: Routledge.

Naserian. 1992. "Another Form of Violence: The Maasai Female and Circumcision." *Sauti ya Siti*, November 1992, 35.

Ndagala, Daniel. 1990. "Territory, Pastoralists and Livestock: Resource Control among Kisongo Maasai." PhD diss., Uppsala University.

Ngoitiko, Maanda. 2008. *The Pastoral Women's Council: Empowerment for Tanzania's Maasai*. Gatekeeper Series (International Institute for Environment and Development), 137e.

Ngoitiko, Maanda, Makko Sinandei, Partalala Meitaya, and Fred Nelson. 2010. "Pastoralist Activists: Negotiating Power Imbalance in the Tanzanian Serengeti." In *Community Rights, Conservation and Contested Land: The Politics of Natural Resource Governance in Africa*, edited by Fred Nelson. London: Earthscan.

Nnaemeka, Obioma. 2005. "African Women, Colonial Discourses, and Imperialist Interventions: Female Circumcision as Impetus." In *Female Circumcision and the Politics of Knowledge*, edited by Obioma Nnaemeka. Westport, Conn.: Praeger.

Nyerere, Julius. 1968. "The Arusha Declaration." In *Ujamaa: Essays on Socialism*. London: Oxford University Press.

Olekina, Ledama. 2005. "Maasai Women Speak Out. FGM. Why International Attempts to Stop Female Circumcision Are Putting Maasai Women at Even Greater Risk." *Cultural Survival Quarterly* (Winter): 21–23.

Østebø, Marit Tolo. 2013. "Translations of Gender Equality in International Aid: Perspectives from Norway and Ethiopia." PhD diss., University of Bergen.

Parmar, Pratibha. 1993. *Warrior Marks*. Film distributed by Women Make Movies.

Pastoralist Women's Council. 2012. "Organisational Strategy 2012–2016." http://www.pastoralwomenscouncil.org/uploads/1/0/7/1/10710001/pwc_strategic_plan_2012-2016_-_final.pdf. Accessed June 3, 2013.

———. 2013. Homepage. www.pastoralwomenscouncil.org. Accessed June 3, 2013.

Pederson, Susan. 1991. "National Bodies, Unspeakable Acts: The Sexual Politics of Colonial Policy-Making." *Journal of Modern History* 63, no. 4: 647–80.

Perham, Margery F. 1931. "The System of Native Administration in Tanganyika." *Africa* 4, no. 3: 302–13.

Peters, Julie, and Andrea Wolper, eds. 1995. *Women's Rights, Human Rights: International Feminist Perspectives*. New York: Routledge.

Pines, Noam J. 1985. "Professor Julius Lewin February 1907–September 1984." *African Studies* 44, no. 1: 97–100.

Rakstad, Jennifer L., Charlotte E. Kaiser, and Kris T. Pribadi. 2000. "The Progress of Tanzanian Women in the Law: Women in Legal Education, Legal Employment and Legal Reform." *Southern California Review of Law and Women's Studies* 10: 35–114.

Rwebangira, Magdalena K. 1996. *The Legal Status of Women and Poverty in Tanzania*. Uppsala, Sweden: Nordiska Afrikainstitutet.

Rwezaura, Barthazar A. 1991. "Tanzania: Family Law and the New Bill of Rights." *Journal of Family Law* 29, no. 2: 453–61.

———. 1998. "The Proposed Abolition of de facto Unions in Tanzania: A Case of Sailing Against the Social Current." In *The Changing Family: International Perspectives on the Family and Family Law*, edited by John Eekelaar and Thandabantu Nhlapo. Oxford: Hart Publishing.

Rwezaura, Barthazar A., and Ulrike Wanitzek. 1988. "Family Law Reform in Tanzania: A Socio-Legal Report." *International Journal of Law, Policy and the Family* 2, no. 1: 1–26.

Sankan, S.S. ole. 1971. *The Maasai*. Nairobi: Kenya Literature Bureau.

Schapera, Isaac. 1938. *A Handbook of Tswana Law and Custom*. Oxford: Oxford University Press.

Schmidt, Elizabeth. 1990. "Negotiated Spaces and Contested Terrain: Men, Women and the Law in Colonial Zimbabwe, 1890–1939." *Journal of Southern African Studies* 16, no. 4: 622–48.

Schneider, Leander. 2006. "The Maasai's New Clothes: A Developmentalist Modernity and its Exclusions. *Africa Today* 53, no. 1: 100–31.

Schuler, Margaret, ed. 1995. *From Basic Needs to Basic Rights: Women's Claim to Human Rights.* Washington, D.C.: Women, Law and Development International.

Scott, James. 1987. *Weapons of the Weak: Everyday Forms of Peasant Resistance.* New Haven, Conn.: Yale University Press.

Scully, Pamela. 2011. "Gender, History and Human Rights." In *Gender and Culture at the Limit of Rights,* edited by Dorothy L. Hodgson. Philadelphia: University of Pennsylvania Press.

Sen, Amartya. 2009. *The Idea of Justice.* Cambridge, Mass: Harvard University Press.

Shachar, Ayelet. 2001. *Multicultural Jurisdictions: Cultural Differences and Women's Rights.* Cambridge: Cambridge University Press.

Shadle, Brett. 1999. "'Changing Traditions to Meet Current Altering Conditions': Customary Law, African Courts and the Rejection of Codification in Kenya, 1930–60." *Journal of African History* 40, no. 3: 411–31.

———. 2006. *Girl Cases: Marriage and Colonialism in Gusiiland, Kenya, 1890–1970.* Portsmouth, N.H.: Heinemann.

Sheikh, Leila. 2004. "TAMWA: Levina's Song–Supporting Women in Tanzania." In *Composing a New Song: Stories of Empowerment from Africa,* edited by Hope Chigudu. London: The Commonwealth Foundation.

Shell-Duncan, Bettina. 2001. "The Medicalization of Female 'Circumcision': Harm Reduction or Promotion of a Dangerous Practice?" *Social Science and Medicine* 52: 1013–28.

———. 2008. "From Health to Human Rights: Female Genital Cutting and the Politics of Intervention." *American Anthropologist* 110, no. 2: 225–36.

Shell-Duncan, Bettina, and Ylva Hernlund, eds. 2000. *Female "Circumcision" in Africa: Culture, Controversy, and Change.* Boulder, CO: Lynn Rienner.

Shivji, Issa G. 2006. *Let the People Speak: Tanzania Down the Road to Neo-Liberalism.* Dakar, Senegal: CODESRIA.

Sikar, Ndinini Kimesera, and Dorothy L. Hodgson. 2006. "In the Shadow of the MDGs: Pastoralist Women and Children in Tanzania." Special issue of *Indigenous Affairs* on "Africa and the Millennium Development Goals," 1, no. 6: 30–37.

Snyder, Katherine A. 1997. "Elders' Authority and Women's Protest: The *Masay* Ritual and Social Change among the Iraqw of Tanzania." *Journal of the Royal Anthropological Institute* 3, no. 3: 561–76.

———. 2006. "Mothers on the March: Iraqw Women Negotiating the Public Sphere in Tanzania." *Africa Today* 53, no. 1: 79–100.

Spear, Thomas, and Richard Waller, eds. 1993. *Being Maasai: Ethnicity and Identity in East Africa.* Athens: Ohio University Press.

Spencer, Paul. 1988. *The Maasai of Matapato: A Study of Rituals of Rebellion.* Bloomington: Indiana University Press.

Spivak, Gayatri. 1988. "Can the Subaltern Speak?" In *Marxism and the Interpretation of Culture,* edited by Cary Nelson and Lawrence Grossberg. Champaign: University of Illinois Press.

St. Joan's Alliance. 1961. *A Venture in Faith: A History of St. Joan's Social and Political Alliance, formerly The Catholic Women's Suffrage Society, 1911–1961.* London: St. Joan's Alliance.

Steady, Filomena. 2006. *Women and Collective Action in Africa.* New York: Palgrave Macmillan.

Stoeltje, Beverly J., with Kathryn Firmin-Sellers and Okello Ogwang. 2002. "Introduction to Special Issue: Women, Language, and Law in Africa." *Africa Today* 49, no. 1: vii–xx.

Storrs-Fox, D. 1930. "Further Notes on the Masai of Kenya Colony." *Journal of the Royal Anthropological Institute of Great Britain and Ireland* 60: 447–65.

———. 1931. "Notes on Marriage Customs among the Masai." *The Journal of the East Africa and Uganda Natural History Society* 42/43: 183–92.

Sutton, John. 1993. "Becoming Masailand." In *Being Maasai*, edited by Thomas Spear and Richard Waller. London: James Currey.

Swantz, Marja-Liisa. 1977. "Bagamoyo Research Project 'Jipemoyo': Introduction to its General Aims and Approach." *Jipemoyo Development and Culture Research* 1: 10–22.

Talle, Aud. 1988. *Women at a Loss: Changes in Maasai Pastoralism and their Effects on Gender Relations.* Stockholm: Stockholm Studies in Social Anthropology.

———. 1995. "Desiring Difference: Risk Behavior among Young Maasai Men." In *Young People at Risk: Fighting AIDS in Northern Tanzania*, edited by K. I. Klepp, P. M. Biswalo, et al. Oslo: Scandinavian University Press.

———. 2007. "Serious Games: Licences and Prohibitions in Maasai Sexual Life." *Africa* 77, no. 3: 351–70.

Tanzania Gender Networking Programme (TGNP). 1993a. *Gender Profile of Tanzania.* Dar es Salaam: TGNP.

———. 1993b. *Our Histories: Women's Groups/NGOs and Official Programmes in Tanzania.* Dar es Salaam: TGNP.

———. 1994. "Structural Adjustment and Gender Empowerment or Disempowerment." Symposium Report, 26 February 1994.

———. 2007. *Gender Profile of Tanzania: Enhancing Gender Equity.* Dar es Salaam: TGNP.

———. 2013. "TGNP Mtandao." www.tgnp.org. Accessed June 6, 2013.

Tanzania Media Women's Association (TAMWA). 2013. Homepage. www.tamwa.org. Accessed June 6, 2013.

Tenga, Nakazael, and Chris Maina Peter. 1996. "The Right to Organise as Mother of All Rights: The Experience of Women in Tanzania." *The Journal of Modern African Studies* 34, no. 1: 143–62.

Thomas, Lynn M. 2003. *Politics of the Womb: Women, Reproduction and the State in Kenya.* Berkeley: University of California Press.

Thomson, Joseph. 1968 [1885]. *Through Masai Land.* London: Frank Cass.

Tripp, Aili Marie. 1989. "Women and the Changing Urban Household Economy in Tanzania." *Journal of Modern African Studies* 27, no. 4: 601–62.

———. 1994. "Gender, Political Participation and the Transformation of Associational Life in Uganda and Tanzania." *African Studies Review* 37, no. 1: 107–31.

———. 1997. *Changing the Rules: The Politics of Liberalization and the Urban Informal Economy in Tanzania.* Berkeley: University of California Press.

Ujamaa Community Resource Team (UCRT). 2013. Homepage. http://www.ujamaa-crt .org. Accessed June 10, 2013.

Van Allen, Judith. 1972. "'Sitting on a Man': Colonialism and the Lost Political Institutions of Igbo Women." *Canadian Journal of African Studies* 6, no. 2: 165–81.

Vansina, Jan. 1965. "A Traditional Legal System: The Kuba." In *African Law: Adaptation
and Development*, edited by Hilda Kuper and Leo Kuper. Berkeley: University of
California Press.

Volpp, Leti. 2001. "Feminism versus Multiculturalism." *Columbia Law Review* 101, no. 5:
1181–1218.

Von Freyhold, Michaela. 1979. *Ujamaa Villages in Tanzania: Analysis of a Social Experiment*. New York: Monthly Review Press.

Walker, Alice, and Pratibha Parmar. 1993. *Warrior Marks: Female Genital Mutilation and
the Sexual Blinding of Women*. New York: Harcourt Brace & Company.

Waller, Richard. 1988. "Emutai: Crisis and Response in Masailand 1883–1902." In *The
Ecology of Survival*, edited by Douglass Johnson and David Anderson. Boulder,
Colo.: Westview Press.

White, Luise. 1990. *The Comforts of Home: Prostitution in Colonial Nairobi*. Chicago:
University of Chicago Press.

White, Luise, Stephan F. Miescher, and David William Cohen, eds. 2001. *African Words,
African Voices: Critical Practices in Oral History*. Bloomington: Indiana University
Press.

Wilson, Richard A., ed. 1997. *Human Rights, Culture & Context: Anthropological Perspectives*. London: Pluto Press.

Winterbottom, Anna, Jonneke Koomen, and Gemma Burford. 2009. "Female Genital
Cutting: Cultural Rights and Rites of Defiance in Northern Tanzania." *African
Studies Review* 52, no. 1: 47–71.

World Health Organization (WHO). 1999. *Female Genital Mutilation: Programmes to
Date: What Works and What Doesn't. A Review*. Geneva: WHO.

Yeager, Rodger. 1989. *Tanzania. An African Experiment*. Boulder, Colo.: Westview Press.

Index

23–26, 31–33, 34, 41–42, 49–51, 61–62, 67–68, 80–82; on marriage, 38, 80–92; in native courts, 31, 38–39

civil society organizations (CSOs), 108–14, 136, 148. *See also under* CSO *name*

Clarke, J. C., 40–41

class: biases of, 66–67, 68, 126; ideology and interests of, 62, 64–65; stratification by, 108–109, 110

clitoridectomy. *See* female circumcision

collective protest/attack (*olkishoroto*): contemporary uses of, 143–50, 162; custom of, 25–26, 137–39, 148–50; as a form of justice, 133–34, 149–50, 161; lessons for elites from, 149–53; media technologies in, 147–48; power of, 159–61; in rights-based approaches, 3. *See also* activism/activists

colonial legal regime: in African historical context, 7–8; authority in, 32, 33, 49–51; civilized standards in, 27, 28–30; cultural change in, 123–24; customary law defined by, 33–34; custom codified in, 15–16, 19–20, 27, 39–42, 49, 50–51, 158; legacies of, 8, 49–52, 61–62, 126; Maasai justice under, 20–26; marriage in, 42–49; "natural" justice and "native" law in, 26–30; scope of, 33–39; social change in, 52; women's status in, 37–38, 52

Comaroff, Jean, 8

Comaroff, John, 7–8

commercial agriculture, 135, 146

Committee against Sexual Harassment, Discrimination, and Violence against Women, 111

Committee on the Elimination of Discrimination against Women (CEDAW), 102

complementarity of gender, 124

consent, 69–70, 85, 88–89, 92, 101

Convention on the Elimination of all Forms of Discrimination against Women, 102

courts: local, 54n11, 55n22; on marriage, 38, 80–90; in natural justice systems, 30; in the postcolonial legal regime, 67–68. *See also* native courts

cultural citizenship program (MWEDO), 115–16, 129n29

cultural practice: arbitration in, 39; in contemporary protests, 25–26, 137–39, 143–50; as oppression of women, 98–99

cultural/racial assumptions: in adjudication, 90–91; in anti-FGM campaigns, 98–100, 104, 110, 123, 125–26; in codified customary law, 8–9, 160; in colonial legal systems, 20, 30; in the postcolonial period, 62; in the problem of culture, 160–61; about rural women, 5, 70, 98–100, 104, 110, 123, 125–26, 159–60

culture: criminalization of, 1–2, 99; demonization of, 101–106, 158–59; Maasai as exemplars of, 10–13; in marginalization, 104; in oppression, 4, 30, 52, 60, 98, 110, 111, 120, 160; power of, 121–25; romanticization of, 118–20; in women's human rights, 4

customary law and justice: civil cases/ disputes in, 23–26, 31–33, 34, 41–42, 49–51, 61–62, 67–68, 80–82; codification of, 15–16, 27, 39–42, 49, 50–51, 158–59; in colonial rule, 28–30, 31–39, 158; defining, 28–29; divorce in, 31, 34; in the Judicature and Application of Laws Act, 67–68; in the LMA, 62, 80–90; Maasai idioms of, 20–26; marriage in, 42–49; in the national legal regime, 8–9, 61; as oppression, 4; in the postcolonial legal regime, 67–68; transgressions in, 23–24, 23–26

Customary Law Order, 68

customary practice: demonization of, 104–105; in family relations, 92; harmful practices in, 9, 107; in LMA debates, 69–70; marriage in, 42–49, 84–85, 158; in oppression, 123–24

Daily News, 112

daughters: in arranged marriage, 76–77, 80–90; disobedient, 38, 48, 49, 80–90; forced marriage of, 91–92; incest with, 23, 25, 138–39, 144–45; selling of, 48, 74, 91

rights campaign of, 103–105; on women's status, 36–38

fertility and fertility gatherings (*oloirishi*), 25–26, 138, 149

forced marriage, 35, 81–90, 88–89

free lover (*esindani*), 46–48, 58n65

Gardner, Benjamin, 146

gendered justice, 3, 20–26, 126, 161

gender equality: in the colonial legal regime, 36; in cultural context, 124–25; and feminist NGOS, 110, 114, 124–25; in marriage law, 70; in the national legal regime, 16, 61–62, 63–64; political-economic context of, 115–16, 124, 160

Gender Festival, 119–20, 150–53

gender inequalities: codification of, 103, 158–59; cultural assumptions in, 160; in human rights protocols, 126; political-economic context of, 115–16, 124, 160

gender injustice, causes of, 126, 161

gender relations: in colonial legal systems, 27, 49; *enkanyit* in, 22; political-economic context in, 160; in postcolonial marriage, 73–80; in socialist Tanzania, 63–64

generational relations, 73–80, 160

German colonialism in Tanganyika, 27

Germany, 113

girls: education for, 94n16, 116–17, 141–42; marriage of, 122; roles and responsibilities of, 12; selling of into marriage, 45–46; sexual relations for, 42–43. *See also* daughters

good life (*sinyati*), 22–23, 42, 93

grassroots organizations, 125–26

grassroots women, 66–67, 99, 150–53, 160. *See also* rural women

Hatfield, Colby, 71, 72–73, 144

health care, 73, 91, 120, 136, 161

heart and spirit (*oltau*), 22

Hernlund, Ylva, 106

historical anthropology, 13–15

historical context, 5–12, 24

Hollis, Alfred, 25, 137

homestead burnings, 133, 146, 148–49, 151–52

Hosken, Fran, 106

House of Commons (Britain), 34–35

human rights: abuses/violations, 103, 107, 125; frameworks for, 2–3, 126–27, 149, 161; universal, 100–103, 116–17. *See also* women's human rights

hunger, 120, 125, 136, 152

hunting, big game, 122, 134–35, 145–46, 151–52, 162

images of Maasai, 10–11, 20, 21, 73, 159–60. *See also* cultural/racial assumptions

incest, 23, 25, 138–39, 144–45, 149

income: in generational differences, 78; in the informal economy, 94n18; and neoliberal reforms, 108; projects for women, 65, 66, 116, 118, 136. *See also* livelihoods

indigenous legal regimes, 6–7, 20–26, 158

indirect rule, 27–28

individual rights, 3, 51, 100–102, 124–25, 127, 159

inequities: collective protest against, 150; in education, 108, 136; in health care, 91, 108, 136; in marriage, 91, 158

informal economy, 40, 94n18

infrastructure, 66, 108, 141

initiation ceremonies, 34–35, 40, 43, 104–105, 122. *See also* female circumcision; male circumcision

injustice: collective protests of, 134–36, 147–50, 152–53, 159–62; in legal regimes, 5, 51, 159; in rights-based frameworks, 3, 126–27, 158, 161–62

Inter-African Committee (IAC), 106–107

interdependence, social (*osotua*), 22–23, 42, 51, 91, 93. *See also* obligations, social

International Action Plan for Combating Female Genital Mutilation, 114

International Monetary Fund, 107–108

international women's movement. *See* feminism/feminist organizations

Iraqw women, 144–45

Islamic law, 61, 67–68

Jipemoyo Project, 93n5
Judicature and Application of Laws Act (JALA), 67
judicial authority, 33, 34
junior men, 33, 40, 49–51, 64, 74, 114. See also men; warriors (ilmurran)

Kawawa, Rashidi, 93n4
Kawawa, Sofia, 64, 65
Kikwete, Jakaya, 151
KIPOC, 140
Kisongo Maasai, 25, 137–38

labor: burdens in marriage, 74, 79–80, 108–109; division of household, 12
Laibon (diviner and prophet), 32–33, 50
Laibon Parit, 32, 34, 55n26
laigwenani lo mila (chairman of tradition/customs), 82, 92
Lal, Priya, 64
land: alienation of, 72, 108, 133–34, 135–36, 145–46, 148–49; rights to, 116, 120, 148
language: in anti-FGM campaigns, 110; barriers in adjudication, 83, 90–91; of justice idioms, 20–26; in marginalization, 70; in MWEDO programs, 115; in women's rights campaigns, 103. See also Maa language; Swahili language
Law of Marriage Act (LMA) of 1971, 62, 65, 68–70, 80–91, 158–59
League of Nations, 36, 100
legal authority, 7, 49–51, 61
legal consciousness, 21–22
legal pluralism, 8–9, 67–70
legal regimes: and FGM, 97–98; gendered justice in, 161; as historical context, 6–10; indigenous, 6–7, 158; law and culture in, 157; legacy of colonial, 49–52; power in, 7–8, 49–51, 61, 99, 126–27, 158–59; and protest/attack (olkishoroto), 159–60; secular, 26–27; of women's rights, 99. See also colonial legal regime; national legal regime; postcolonial legal regime; transnational legal regimes
Lewin, Julius, 28, 29, 54n10–11

livelihoods, 12–13, 71–72, 134–37. See also income
livestock management, 39–40, 71–72, 120, 141
Local Courts Ordinance (1951), 54n11
Loliondo protests, 133–34, 140, 144–48, 150–53, 159–60, 162

Maa language, 20–26, 70, 115
Maasai: as cultural exemplars, 10–13; evictions of, 134–36; justice idioms of, 20–26; relocation of in socialist Tanzania, 63, 71, 93; as supra-ethnic group, 53n1
Maasai dress, 64, 71, 73, 93, 119–21, 144
"Maasailand," 31–33
Maasai NGOS, 114–21
Maa-speaking peoples, 11, 20–21
MacMichael, Harold, 35
Maguire, R. A. J., 25, 34, 137–38
Maingo, Pirias, 151
Malecela, John, 112
male circumcision, 40
Mann, Kristin, 7
marginalization of Maasai: culture in, 104; economic, 70–73, 79–80, 143; political, 62, 79–80, 98–99, 135–36, 143; as punishment, 92
marriage: arranged, 50, 73–77, 80–91; authority in, 78, 80–90; Christian, 75–77, 79; companionate, 48, 75, 78; in court, 38, 80–92; customary forms of, 42–49, 74–75, 84–85, 158; disputes concerning, 24, 51, 80–92; gender and generational relations in, 73–80; of girls, 122; legislating of, 40–41, 67–70; subordination in, 103; in the Universal Declaration, 101
Masai Council. See Olkiama
Masai Development Project (MDP), 39–40
Masai Native Authority, 33
"The Masai Penal Code" (Maguire), 34
Masai Range Project (USAID), 71–72
Matapato Maasai, 138
Mbilinyi, Marjorie, 70, 151, 152–53
men: as activists, 162; age-set leaders, 32; roles and responsibilities of, 12;

paternalism, 68, 74, 79–80, 160
Perham, Margery, 27–28
personhood, 101–102, 126
political-economic context: in Aloya v. Aladala, 91–92; of arranged marriage, 77, 91; and FGM, 98–99, 122; of gender inequality, 115–16, 124, 160; individual rights in, 124–25; in legal regimes, 6; in the postcolonial period, 16; in social relations, 93; in women's rights, 52
political empowerment, 115–18
political justice, 151
politics: disenfranchisement in, 70, 72–73; in legal regimes, 158; Maasai structure in, 32–33; marginalization in, 62, 79–80, 98–99, 135–36, 143; participation in, 65, 72; reform in, 107–108; rights in, 102–103; in social change, 5
polygamy, 69, 70
polygyny, 48–49, 120
postcolonial legal regime: change in, 90–93; culture and law in, 123–24; gender and culture in, 63–67; law in, 8–9, 61–62; marginalization in, 70–73; marriage legislation in, 67–70, 73–79, 80–90. *See also* national legal regime
poverty, 11, 98–99, 108–109, 120, 135–36, 161
power: codification of, 19–20; of elites, 61, 126–27, 158–59; female, 25–26, 49–51, 124, 137, 148–50, 159–60; and FGM, 98–99; in historical anthropology, 13–14; in legal regimes, 7–8, 49–51, 61, 99, 126–27, 158–59; and the problem of culture, 160–61; in social change, 4
precolonial gendered justice, 20–26
priorities: in collective protests, 150; education as, 37–38, 120, 123; FGM as, 2, 114, 123; healthcare as, 120; hunger as, 120, 125, 136, 152; political marginalization as, 96–99; of rural men, 126
procreative power, 25–26
property, 9, 46, 69–70, 142
prostitute or free lover (*esindani*), 46–48, 58n65
protests, collective, 3, 25–26, 133–34, 137–39, 143–53, 159–62. *See also* activism/activists

"Protocol to the African Charter on Human and Peoples' Rights on the Rights of Women in Africa," 105–106

Rathbone, Eleanor, 35–38, 52
reciprocity (*osotua*), 22–23, 42, 51, 91, 93
repugnancy clause, 28–29, 52, 54n11, 100
respect, mutual (*enkanyit*): in individual rights, 93; in Maasai regulation, 32; in Maasai values, 22–24, 32, 42, 51, 75–76, 137; and marriage, 42, 75–76; social relationships in, 149–50
responsibility, 12, 137, 148–50, 161
restorative justice, 24
Revington, T. M., 40
rights-based frameworks, 2–3, 126–27, 149, 161
Roberts, Richard, 7
Rowe, Eric, 39
rural-urban migrants, 88, 94n18
rural women: assumptions about, 5, 70, 98–100, 104, 110, 123, 125–26, 159–60; class bias against, 66–67, 68; depiction of by feminists, 105–106; disenfranchisement of, 143, 161–62; economic opportunities for, 40, 94n18, 116, 129n30, 136; illiteracy of, 93n1; priorities of, 114, 120, 123, 125, 126, 136, 150, 152; in PWC, 142; rights workshops for, 116–17; romanticizing of, 118–19; and urban women's groups, 66–67; vulnerability of, 105. *See also* grassroots women

Sauti ya Siti (Voice of Women), 110–11
schools, 72–73, 94n16, 123, 141
Scott, James, 136
secular crimes in colonial legal regimes, 51
secular law, 26–27, 126–27, 149
Serengeti National Park, 133, 135
sex discrimination, 103
sex relations, 42–43
Sexual Offences Special Provisions Act (SOSPA), 107, 112
Sheikh, Leila Hashim, 111, 112
Shell-Duncan, Bettina, 106
Sikar, Ndinini Kimesera ole, 115–18

burden of, 74, 79–80, 108–9; in native courts, 31, 33; power of, 49–51, 124, 137, 148–50, 159–60; in socialist Tanzania, 63–67; status of, 34–38; in tropes of vulnerability and oppression, 5; urban, 64, 74, 94n18, 104, 110. *See also* elite women; mothers/motherhood; rural women; wives

"Women-in-Development" paradigm (WID), 110–11, 142–43

women's human rights: colonial presumptions on, 52; conferences on, 104; culture in, 4; FGM as violation of, 99, 105, 107, 125; legal regimes in, 9, 49, 97–98; MWEDO workshops on, 116–17; politics of, 121–25; in rights-based frameworks, 2; in the Universal Declaration, 102–3

Women's Research and Documentation Project (WRDP), 65–66

"women's rights as human rights" movement, 104, 107, 111, 159, 161

Women's Section of TANU, 64–65

"Women's Solidarity Boma," 141

World Health Organization, 106

World War II, 100

DOROTHY L. HODGSON
is Professor of Anthropology and Senior Associate Dean for Academic Affairs (Graduate School—New Brunswick) at Rutgers University and past President of the African Studies Association. As a historical anthropologist, she has worked in Tanzania, East Africa, for almost thirty years on such topics as gender, ethnicity, cultural politics, colonialism, nationalism, modernity, the missionary encounter, transnational organizing, and the indigenous rights movement. Her work has been supported by awards from the Rockefeller Foundation's Bellagio Center, National Endowment for the Humanities, the John Simon Guggenheim Memorial Foundation, Fulbright-Hays, American Council for Learned Societies, National Science Foundation, American Philosophical Society, Wenner-Gren Foundation, Social Science Research Council, and Center for Advanced Study in the Behavioral Sciences.

CPSIA information can be obtained
at www.ICGtesting.com
Printed in the USA
BVHW03s1201270718
522815BV00012B/21/P

9 780253 025355